# Wittgenstein and the Problem of Metaphysics

# Wittgenstein and the Problem of Metaphysics

## Aesthetics, Ethics and Subjectivity

Michael R. Smith, Jr

BLOOMSBURY ACADEMIC

LONDON · NEW YORK · OXFORD · NEW DELHI · SYDNEY

BLOOMSBURY ACADEMIC
Bloomsbury Publishing Plc
50 Bedford Square, London, WC1B 3DP, UK
1385 Broadway, New York, NY 10018, USA
29 Earlsfort Terrace, Dublin 2, Ireland

BLOOMSBURY, BLOOMSBURY ACADEMIC and the Diana logo are trademarks
of Bloomsbury Publishing Plc

First published in Great Britain 2022
This paperback edition published 2023

Copyright © Michael Smith, 2022

Michael Smith has asserted his right under the Copyright, Designs and Patents Act,
1988, to be identified as Author of this work.

For legal purposes the Acknowledgments on p. viii constitute an extension
of this copyright page.

Cover design by Charlotte Daniels
Cover image: Portrait of the Austrian philosopher Ludwig Josef Johann Wittgenstein
(1889–1951) by Moritz Nähr, 1930. (© IanDagnall Computing / Alamy Stock Photo)

All rights reserved. No part of this publication may be reproduced or transmitted
in any form or by any means, electronic or mechanical, including photocopying,
recording, or any information storage or retrieval system, without prior
permission in writing from the publishers.

Bloomsbury Publishing Plc does not have any control over, or responsibility for, any
third-party websites referred to or in this book. All internet addresses given in
this book were correct at the time of going to press. The author and publisher
regret any inconvenience caused if addresses have changed or sites have
ceased to exist, but can accept no responsibility for any such changes.

A catalogue record for this book is available from the British Library.

A catalog record for this book is available from the Library of Congress.

| ISBN: | HB: | 978-1-3501-8342-1 |
| | PB: | 978-1-3501-8873-0 |
| | ePDF: | 978-1-3501-8343-8 |
| | eBook: | 978-1-3501-8344-5 |

Typeset by RefineCatch Limited, Bungay, Suffolk

To find out more about our authors and books visit www.bloomsbury.com
and sign up for our newsletters.

*To Richard and Arthur,*
*for whatever the future may hold*

# Contents

| | |
|---|---|
| Acknowledgments | viii |
| Introduction: To Begin at the Beginning | 1 |
| 1   Everything Can Be Otherwise Than It Is | 19 |
| 2   The Rest Is Silence | 49 |
| 3   The Humble Origin of Words | 83 |
| 4   At the Foundation of Well-Founded Belief | 119 |
| 5   To Tell a Riddle | 149 |
| 6   Always an Elsewhere | 177 |
| Bibliography | 211 |
| Index | 221 |

# Acknowledgments

What follows is the result of some ten years of labor, and along the way, innumerable people have lent their assistance in its creation. I am all too aware that it is far from a perfect document, but as Bertrand Russell once told Wittgenstein, one must learn "to write imperfect things." My only hope is that the readily apparent flaws do not reflect too poorly on those whom, without which, this book would have been impossible.

To my friends, mentors, and colleagues at the Institute for Doctoral Studies in the Visual Arts, I owe the bulk of my thanks. I am particularly grateful to Christopher Lonegan, George Smith, Simonetta Moro, and Amy Curtis, each of whom, in his or her own way, has been instrumental to the stimulus of my thought and my development as a scholar and a person. I also owe a debt of gratitude to Sara Christensen Blair for her design assistance and Andrew Ranallo for editing a previous version of the text.

It goes without saying—but must be said nonetheless—that nothing accomplished herein could have been done without the patience, love, and support of my wife Laura and the rest of my family. I know no thanks is required, but you have it all the same.

# Introduction

## To Begin at the Beginning

"To begin at the beginning," Jessie Weston tells us, "Was the old story-telling formula, and it was a very sound one, if 'the beginning' could only be definitely ascertained!"[1] Indeed, one wonders if it is possible to divine a more definite and unshakable principle as this: Begin the story from the beginning. But which beginning?[2] And what of the moment that preceded it? Does that lay no claim to primacy, and if not, why not? As Weston herself quite rightly suggests, the problem to which we must own up to here involves the difficulty in devising a methodology that would allow us to discover a beginning befitting of the beginning—the 'originary' original as we might say. What shall be our criterion for delineating a true beginning from one that would merely pretend to be a beginning? And even more worrisome yet, what criterion shall we enlist to distinguish between the correct one and the false one? How are we to determine where the story ought to begin from or, rather, where it *must* have begun from—that singular wellspring from whence it had no choice but to arise? But this problem, which does, to be sure, confront anyone who would trace a narrative thread back from its mouth to its head waters, is one that inevitably presents itself to the philosopher as well. And right from the beginning, we have here what are, in short, the two overarching propositions on which this text will proceed: namely that philosophy, like story-telling, must begin by discerning its beginning, and that because of this imperative, it must also end up positing the very origin it would seek to discover. Philosophy, in other words, like every form of narration—and indeed every form of art—involves an act of creativity, a *sui generis*, an irreducible aesthetic gesture, one that is at the same time both groundless and the ground on which the very possibility of doing philosophy at all rests.

It is in this general vein that I propose to treat the work of Ludwig Wittgenstein, one of the twentieth century's most brilliant philosophers, and perhaps one of its most controversial as well. The basic idea to be developed in this text can be summed up as follows: We fail to understand the import and implication of Wittgenstein's philosophy if we fail to see it, first and foremost, as an aesthetic expression, one that belongs to what Barnett Newman has so aptly called the first "poetic outcry" of "awe and anger" let loose by our distant ancestors in the face of their own "self-awareness" and "helplessness before the void."[3] If, therefore, a work of philosophy is as much a work of art as it is an exercise in thought, it is because both are a response to the very same subjective vulnerability experienced when confronted with the meaninglessness of existence. Foucault once remarked that the "work of art opens a void, a moment of silence, a question without an answer, [provoking] a breach without reconciliation where the world is forced to question itself,"[4] and I would go so far as to say that the same applies to the work of philosophy as well. Both are a means of grappling with and interrogating the world, and in the process, remaking it. The job of the artist-philosopher is not so much one of discovery as it is of invention. The world is not something to be found out, it is something to be made; it is "always yet to be painted," as Merleau-Ponty puts it, "And even if it lasts millions of years . . . it will end without having been conquered in painting."[5] Similarly, for philosophy, the world is always something yet to be conquered in thought. Even if it were to go on for an eternity, philosophy would be incapable of totalizing the world under one rubric, despite its many attempts to do just that. The lesson that philosophy learns from art, therefore, is decidedly simple yet extraordinarily important: The world is an artifice, a thing to be created. *Everything* becomes a world.[6]

Where Wittgenstein is concerned, then, we have a philosopher whose work is cast in an entirely new mold when viewed as belonging to a tradition in philosophy that embraces the poetic instead of disparaging it. This does not mean that Wittgenstein's relationship to the aesthetic dimension of philosophy is without its difficulties. Like Boethius—who was both an accomplished poet in his own right and a sometimes critic of poetry[7]—Wittgenstein is often stylistically brilliant but notoriously silent where aesthetics problems are concerned. Besides a scant few comments made in the breathtakingly beautiful *Tractatus Logico-Philosophicus*—the only philosophical book he published in his lifetime—Wittgenstein had very little to say publicly about the topic. Research into his *Nachlass* since his death has revealed that he thought and wrote a good deal about various issues concerning art, music, aesthetics, and so on. The picture that these musings reveal to us is of a philosopher whose deep artistic bent framed and permeated every aspect of his philosophical project.

This is especially the case, as this book hopes to make clear, where metaphysics is concerned, which if possible was an even more problematic subject for

Wittgenstein than aesthetics was. Scornful remarks concerning the follies of abstruse metaphysical speculation are peppered throughout his corpus, and one must tread carefully when attempting to navigate the minefield of misgivings Wittgenstein harbored over the traditional questions perennially raised by first philosophy. While it is undoubtedly true that the source of these misgivings are numerous and complex, they can, I believe, all be traced back to a more general and overarching attitude on Wittgenstein's part, one that Nietzsche had already expressed before him: "Art is the highest human task, the true metaphysical activity."[8] In effect, this means that philosophy—and specifically metaphysics— was for Wittgenstein an essentially artistic activity. Properly speaking, of course, both belong to the realm of the nonsensical, and to undertake either endeavor is to engage, in a certain sense, in the obfuscation of thought. Although it is clear that the propositions of metaphysics (like works of art) "cannot be put into words," they do nevertheless "*make themselves manifest. They are what is mystical.*"[9] So despite the negative tenor towards philosophy that permeates the whole of the *Tractatus* (and indeed the whole of Wittgenstein's work, both early and late), there is still an important sense in which the pursuit of metaphysics is a task worth undertaking, precisely because it reaches out towards what Wittgenstein calls "the sense of the world."[10] Painters, Merleau-Ponty says, have always known this fact. In a painting we do not find a 'representation' of some fact about the world. "Ultimately, the painting relates to nothing at all among experienced things."[11] Rather, they show us how "things become things, how the world becomes world."[12] In this sense, art and metaphysics are akin: Neither tells us how things actually stand or do not stand in the world, but each gives us some sense of how it is possible for a world to be at all.

In saying that art and metaphysics are intimately related to one another, I do not mean that they amount to the same thing. Not all works of art are metaphysical, and not all metaphysics is artistic. What I do mean, however, is that both are caught up in the very same attempt to say the unsayable, a task with which Wittgenstein was all too familiar. His vehement attacks against speculative philosophy often run afoul of the very same linguistic misuses that he would seek to do away with. Indeed there can be little doubt that Wittgenstein was as much a practitioner of metaphysics as he was a critic of it.

Those familiar with the legacy of Wittgenstein's work will also be familiar with some of the heated disagreements concerning just how much he did or did not have to say about the subject of metaphysics. From the very first, many interpreters—most notably the Logical Positivists—have been wont to see in Wittgenstein a philosopher whose staunch anti-metaphysical stance was of near Humean proportions. In his beautifully crystalline *Tractatus*

*Logico-Philosophicus*, so the reasoning went, we have a book that, for whatever its flaws, demonstrated with convincing rigor what was already apparent to anyone with any modicum of common sense: Metaphysics is nonsense of the worst kind. Not only is it obviously false, but it gets in the way of the 'real' business of philosophy, which, when properly understood, consists only of the 'clarification' of the logical structures of language.

While it is true that most overtly positivistic breeds of interpreting Wittgenstein have largely waned over the years, there has been a renewed tendency in much of the secondary literature to recoup the idea of Wittgenstein as the quintessential anti-metaphysician.[13] From resolute readings, to therapeutic methods, to elucidations and clarifications of nonsense,[14] much of the writing on Wittgenstein over the past three decades has operated under the assumption that there is no positive metaphysical doctrine—whether implicit or otherwise—to be derived from Wittgenstein's work. Of course, just what kind of anti-metaphysical sentiment it embodies is a matter of some debate. James Conant, for instance, expresses the view that a resolute reading of the *Tractatus* "does not communicate anything, but it is not purely negative for all that. Its value consists precisely in the insights it affords in the ways in which language functions."[15] What insights it does offer, he writes elsewhere, are limited to *"letting language show itself,"*[16] which, if positive, is only marginally so. Other Wittgenstein interpreters have found more reason to be optimistic about the prospects of gleaning something other than a purely negative account of language. Marie McGinn—while generally sympathetic to the resolute reading—detracts from it in attempting to show that the project of clarification that Wittgenstein undertakes in both his early and later philosophy can "be understood as having a positive, as well as a negative, purpose."[17] Clarification in the former sense "does not necessarily involve a doomed attempt to take up a perspective on language from a point outside"[18] but rather allows the "reader to see clearly what the use of language makes clear."[19]

The differences here, though small, have important ramifications for how we make sense of what Wittgenstein has to tell us. For Conant and other resolute readers, the purpose of clarification is to purge the nonsense from language that disrupts its lucidity, whereas McGinn prefers to emphasize the ways in which nonsense can be a useful tool for revealing what the structure of language already makes evident to those who care to look closely enough. On one point, however, there seems to be a fairly widespread agreement. Alice Crary sums it up nicely in her introduction to *The New Wittgenstein* when she writes, "These papers have in common an understanding of Wittgenstein as aspiring, not to advance metaphysical theories, but rather to help us work ourselves out of confusions we become entangled in when philosophizing."[20] While there is no clear agreement in the contemporary field of Wittgensteinian studies as to what a method of this kind would look like, there is a general consensus where at least one fundamental question is concerned: How can positive or negative elucidations of language be advanced *without* simultaneously advancing metaphysical theories?

Much has been made over the years about the seemingly jarring differences between Wittgenstein's early and late work. But for those amenable to the reading of Wittgenstein outlined above, it is tempting to suggest that it is precisely this anti-metaphysical temperament that ties the disparate halves of his thought together. Indeed, many have done just this, Warren Goldfarb among them. In both the early and late Wittgenstein, he suggests, there is a similar attempt "to undermine metaphysics by showing the incoherence of the language in which one attempted to express it."[21] The overarching narrative of Wittgenstein's philosophical development that we thus glean from this suggestion would have us believe that, while the later Wittgenstein was a self-proclaimed detractor of the early Wittgenstein, they both fundamentally agreed on at least one issue: Philosophy concerns itself primarily with the clarification of language. The only real point of divergence between the two is in how they treat the problems of meaning. It is not surprising, then, that the method of clarification Wittgenstein used would subsequently alter in the later work according to the hypothesis that the meaning of a word was irrevocably tied up with its use. Nevertheless, this fact only belies Wittgenstein's deeper antagonism towards metaphysics in general. For Wittgenstein, metaphysical rumination is always to the detriment of our ability to get a clear view of language. Thus, the only real problem of import with which philosophy has to struggle is, as he puts it in §109 of the *Philosophical Investigations*, "The bewitchment of our understanding by the resources of our language."[22]

It is worth noting that there is plenty of textual evidence to support the sketch of the secondary literature outlined above. There are numerous instances in which we can read Wittgenstein as unabashedly lambasting the entire enterprise of metaphysical speculation. This, however, is not the point that I would like to contest in this book. To do so would require that we selectively ignore a great deal that Wittgenstein wrote concerning the ills of metaphysics. In saying this, I am not, I should stress, assenting to the resolute reading's insistence that we take the penultimate remark of the *Tractatus* literally and "throw away the ladder."[23] It is not my intention, in other words, to align myself with the idea—expressed by Cora Diamond—that there are no "ineffable truths" or "features of reality" to which the nonsense of the *Tractatus* corresponds.[24] Nor am I conversely endorsing the more orthodox view propounded by P.M.S. Hacker that the *Tractatus* contains "illuminating nonsense"[25] that shines light on "the ineffability of mystical insight into the essence of the world."[26] In fact, what I am suggesting is that each is in some sense partly correct. That is to say, in other words, that where Wittgenstein is concerned, we have a philosopher for whom metaphysics was something deeply problematic. He both loathed it for its pretenses to profundity and found in it something deeply revelatory, and any interpretation of his work that emphasizes one at the expense of the other is only telling half the story. To read Wittgenstein resolutely would therefore require us to not only take *one* remark seriously in isolation from the others that exist throughout the corpus of his work, but rather to see it as comprising only one part of a broader whole.[27]

If I were, however, to offer a resolute reading of but a singular remark from Wittgenstein's diverse output, it would be one that was quite likely never intended for publication, but which nevertheless sheds far more light on the whole of his work than does 6.54 of the *Tractatus*: "I think I summed up my attitude to philosophy when I said: philosophy ought really to be written only as a *poetic composition*."[28] In typical fashion, Wittgenstein concludes this line of thinking by admonishing himself for being unable to do "what he would like to be able to do,"[29] but for anyone who has taken even a cursory glance at the *Tractatus* it is clear that a serious aesthetic sensibility permeates its entire structure and content. What remains less clear is whether a similar preoccupation is equally prevalent in the *Investigations* and other of the late writings. If there is, it is certainly of a different variety than in the early ones, but part of what I aim to show in this text is just how much a profound concern with the poetic abides in nearly every phase of Wittgenstein's philosophical development, and just how much we miss if we forget this fact.

The point I am driving at here, one that I believe Wittgenstein was very much attuned to, is that the generative philosophical act—the first move in the game on which all the others depend—is a creative one. Before philosophy can properly be said to be philosophical, it must first become an undertaking whose primary impetus is artistic in nature. If one is, therefore, to be a philosopher and to do philosophy, one can only do so by first becoming an artist and making art. For many a 'hard-nosed' philosopher this is undoubtedly as disdainful an idea as could be conceived,[30] and those who might be inclined towards such an attitude are surely complicit in perpetuating Plato's condemnation of the poets and all "other imitators" who would "maim the thought of those who hear them."[31] This is despite the fact, as John Hartland-Swann points out, that Plato was assuredly a poet "in *some* sense," even though "dramatic artist" is probably a more befitting

*Introduction: To Begin at the Beginning* 7

descriptor for the author of the Dialogues.[32] And to be sure, there is no clear-cut answer to the question of what kind of artist Plato was (as is the case with most artists, whatever their medium), but whether he was a poet, dramatist, or something namelessly in between, there can be no doubt that Plato was, first and foremost, an artist, and a very good one at that. What, then, can we infer from this supposition if we were to take Whitehead's famous pronouncement at its face value?[33] Could we not say: Every philosopher who has followed in the path blazed by Plato has been—in *some* sense—an artist, and that the measure of one's skill as a philosopher and one's skill as an artist were interdependent? Would we not be compelled to conclude that for all his capability as a 'pure' philosopher that Plato was made even greater by his no-less impressive artistic accomplishment?

At the very foundations of Western thought, then, we find a notion that has long been left to languish in relative obscurity: the artist-philosopher, the fullest expression of which was already to be found in Plato. In carrying on his example, however, philosophers soon forgot just how much artistic ability was required of them. Although we can identify occasional resurfacings of the artist-philosopher throughout history—Lucretius, Montaigne, and Nietzsche being but a few examples—philosophy, in no small measure, has tended to shy away from the example set by Plato. This is not to say that in so doing we must become Platonists in the process. Rather, what we must do is hold Plato up as an exemplar of how philosophy ought to be done while at the same time distancing ourselves from the conclusions he reached in the course of his philosophizing. This means, in other words, placing more emphasis on the idea of Plato as artist-philosopher than on Plato as philosopher-king. What we require is not philosophers who can "rule as kings" or even kings who can "adequately philosophize;"[34] what we require is a philosopher who can think like an artist and write like a poet.

What follows in this text represents an attempt at reconstructing our understanding of Wittgenstein in the fashion outlined above. What I am arguing for, then, is a way of interpreting Wittgenstein that aligns with what Nietzsche once termed the "*artist*-philosopher";[35] that is, as someone for whom, to quote from Heidegger's Nietzsche lectures, "The artistic constitutes metaphysical activity pure and simple."[36] When I speak, therefore, of a 'problem of metaphysics' in Wittgenstein's thinking, I have in mind something more than just his self-conflicted attitude towards that particular branch of philosophy; I also have in mind his disposition towards treating such problems artistically. More than anything else, it is this artistic-metaphysical penchant that I take to be the single most defining characteristic of the philosophical work Wittgenstein did, both early and late.

In this regard, I find myself in agreement with the resolute reading and its variations. In general, the differences between the phases of Wittgenstein's philosophical life have been overstated. While there can be no doubt that it does develop and change, there are many aspects of it that remain constant throughout, one of which is exemplified by the desire to purge philosophy of metaphysics. That said, I do not think this fact about Wittgenstein's writings constitutes a skeleton key that unlocks all its doors. Far from comprising the ultimate bedrock of his entire philosophical landscape, we can see just as many examples where Wittgenstein is unambiguously engaging in metaphysics simply by attempting to delineate sense from nonsense. Whether we are talking about the picture theory of the *Tractatus* or the language-games of the *Investigations*, both depend on the implicit metaphysical claim that the ways in which language can be meaningful are tied up with and constrained by the conditions of reality in which it finds itself. Be it the logic of the world, or the form of life, both are presupposing something that comes prior to their being a language at all. In each case, however, the question is whether those systems of meaning making are even capable of stepping outside of themselves in order to adequately describe what they already take as a given.

One point, however, should not escape our attention here. In order to devise a criterion of meaning, Wittgenstein could not avoid the sort of Cartesian quest for certainty that has characterized so much of the Western metaphysical tradition. It is not enough, after all, to predicate a theory of meaning on a merely provisional supposition about the nature of reality. If the goal of philosophy is clarification via the elimination of metaphysics, then that clarification must involve recourse to some first principle beyond any conceivable doubt. This creates a problem for Wittgenstein, however. For on the one hand, he repeatedly rebuked the very possibility of metaphysics, and on the other hand, he needed to emulate one of its most well-worn tropes in order to overcome it. In fact, I would like to make the case that Wittgenstein only begins to come to something of a solution to this difficulty during the last years of his life, when he wrote the notes that now comprise the text of *On Certainty*. When interpreted through the lens of the problem of metaphysics, this last of Wittgenstein's three major works becomes central to understanding him, so much so that there may be good reason to treat it on par with the *Tractatus* and the *Investigations*. By disavowing ultimate certainty as the metaphysical prerequisite of meaningful language, while maintaining the necessity of fixed propositions as the basis of the language-game, we will see how *On Certainty* resolves, at least in part, the problem of metaphysics in Wittgenstein's philosophy.

As we have seen above, the secondary literature devoted to Wittgenstein's work is abundant and long-standing. This presents its challenges and benefits. On the one hand, it can be difficult to find a novel problematic on which to approach his work. After all, much of what *can* be written on Wittgenstein probably *has*. On the other hand, when it is the case that a philosophical discourse reaches the level of received orthodoxy, as much of Wittgenstein's has, there is an inherent danger that the codification of that discourse may become calcified and resistant to alternate and potentially fruitful modes of interpretation (which is precisely the assumption that the resolute reading operates under). Besides this, there are several fields of interest that may be further specified within the broader context of Wittgenstein's philosophy. These include the relationship between his early and his late philosophy, the relationship of his philosophical method to the Analytic and Continental traditions, and the implications of his work for metaphysics, all of which we will touch on to a greater or lesser extent.

The problems that stem from Wittgenstein's philosophy are in part due to the fact that so few philosophers resist categorization more staunchly than he does, and there are still fewer who are claimed by more competing philosophical camps than he is. It is a most telling fact that his influence is seen both in the Analytic and Continental traditions alike (less so in the latter, but not negligibly so), which is odd when one considers the gulf between the two, and even stranger that any one philosopher could be placed so comfortably on both sides of that intellectual divide. He has, for example, influenced thinkers as diverse as A. J. Ayer and Jean-François Lyotard. One of the reasons which might account for the wide net that Wittgenstein has cast in the corpus of Western philosophy might be a result of the litany of divergent thinkers that influenced him, such as Kierkegaard, Schopenhauer, Tolstoy, Russell and Frege, to name but a few. Wittgenstein's varied interests are thus all too evident in the equally varied subjects that he treats, such as logic, language, meaning, epistemology, ontology, mathematics, psychology, aesthetics, and ethics.

These topics, amongst others, will occupy us, in one form or another, for the remainder of this text. Chapter 1 will endeavor to offer a broader picture of the problem of metaphysics and the aesthetics of choice beyond the scope of Wittgenstein's work. Chapters 2 through 4 will concentrate specifically on Wittgenstein's most important philosophical texts with the intent of reading them for their metaphysical and aesthetic implications. The topic of Chapter 2 will be Wittgenstein's early philosophy, from 1911, when he first arrived at Cambridge, to 1918, when he completed the *Tractatus*. Chapter 3 will be devoted to the work Wittgenstein did upon his return to Cambridge and philosophy in

1929 up until 1947 when he resigned his professorship there, with particular attention being paid to the *Investigations*. Chapter 4 will consist of a reading of his work during the last years of his life, especially the notes that would later be published as *On Certainty*. The main contention in these three chapters will be that the problem of metaphysics and Wittgenstein's aesthetic response to it is a dominant force throughout the body of his philosophical work.

Not only does Wittgenstein's engagement with the problem of metaphysics go a long way towards suggesting a basic continuity in all of his work, one gets the sense that the question, 'What use is philosophy?' is constantly on his mind. Having believed himself to have solved the problems of philosophy, he states in the preface of the *Tractatus*, that the "thing in which the value of this work consists is that it shows how little is achieved when these problems are solved."[37] In the *Investigations* he asks, "What is your aim in philosophy? – To show the fly the way out of the fly-bottle."[38] From such remarks and others, Wittgenstein makes it abundantly clear that whatever intrinsic value philosophy has is limited to clearing up our confusions about language and its relation to the world, which is, in the end, a rather trivial task to set for philosophy. There is also, however, an ethical and aesthetic component to Wittgenstein's call for clarity. For him, the nature of reality is intimately linked to what can be said in language or, more precisely, what can be said meaningfully. When we misunderstand language, we misunderstand existence and our place therein. If there is a key to understanding what Wittgenstein means by ethics and aesthetics, it is this: What cannot be said is what is mystical. While the mysticism of the *Tractatus* is well known, it could be argued that there is an implicit mysticism in Wittgenstein's later work as well, and that this mysticism is intimately tied to the problem of metaphysics and the yearning for the metaphysical that so characterizes much of the Western tradition, and especially Wittgenstein's philosophy, which is a microcosm of this characterization.

Chapter 5 will focus primarily on the relationship between ethics and aesthetics—important subjects for Wittgenstein—and the problem of metaphysics. The aim of this chapter will be to show that there is a metaphysical component to the ethical and the aesthetic in Wittgenstein's work, and vice versa. The overarching aim of this chapter will be to present a theory of ethics and aesthetics (making use of Wittgenstein's work as its launching pad) that will address the problem of self-referential incoherence in metaphysics. The theory will not be outlined in detail here but, in brief, it depends on three basic concepts: the groundlessness of all metaphysical claims, the necessity to choose amongst groundless metaphysical claims, and the aesthetic preference that such choices inevitably create.

*Introduction: To Begin at the Beginning*

This brings up a tangential but not inconsequential point. If we are going to do justice to the breadth of Wittgenstein's philosophy we cannot ignore the great importance that he placed on art. His tastes are known to have been very rigidly oriented towards the classical, especially in his love for music, which is due in part, no doubt, to his upbringing in one of Vienna's most fabulously wealthy families. His aesthetic sensibilities also leaned heavily towards the minimalistic. As noted by Ray Monk in his biography of Wittgenstein,

> To understand the strength of Wittgenstein's feeling against superfluous ornamentation – to appreciate the *ethical* importance it had for him – one would have to be Viennese.... One would have to have felt ... that the once noble culture of Vienna ... since the latter half of the nineteenth century, atrophied into, in Paul Engelmann's words, an "arrogated base culture – a culture turned into its opposite, misused as an ornamental mask."[39]

Wittgenstein's distaste for ornament is seen not only in his philosophy, but also— and just as evidently—in the work he did in designing (along with Paul Engelmann) a starkly sparse and modern house for his sister Margret. There has been much fruitful scholarship that has attempted to examine the relation of the Stonborough House (as it has come to be known) with Wittgenstein's philosophy, especially that of the *Tractatus*. One of the more successful recent attempts at examining the philosophical implications of the Stonborough House has been written by Nana Last in her book *Wittgenstein's House: Language, Space, and Architecture*. In brief, Last suggests that Wittgenstein's notion of logical space in the *Tractatus* is intimately connected to how he treated architectural space. A central implication of her book is, as she states, "that spatial and visual practices and constructs are involved in the very process of concept formation in language, subjectivity, aesthetics, ethics, and throughout philosophy."[40] Visual practice and, more specifically, thinking *spatially* seem to have played a crucial role in forming Wittgenstein's thought, as is all but obvious where the picture theory of language is concerned. Last suggests that there are also "different spatialities at work"[41] in both the *Tractatus* and the *Investigations*, which "accords with the widely held view that Wittgenstein's late philosophy of language marks a decisive break from his early work."[42]

Though Wittgenstein's short stint as an architect gives us a concrete example of how he applied his aesthetic values in a particular case, his approach to architecture and philosophy was equally rigid, and in both pursuits, aesthetics was of the utmost importance to him. We therefore have from Wittgenstein a broader and more copiously rich body of art: his philosophy. If there is a connection between his architecture and his philosophy, it ought to be recognized that it lies in the fact that his architectural and philosophical practices were not so much separate fields of interest as they were different modes of expressing a larger system of aesthetics. The importance of aesthetics for Wittgenstein has been an oft-neglected and underappreciated point. It is a shame that the beauty of Wittgenstein's writing has not been given the attention by scholars that it is due. One of the points that this text will endeavor to make is that one cannot read Wittgenstein and understand him if one does not recognize the great artistic achievement of his writing. When admonished by Russell that "he ought not to *state* what he thinks true, but to give arguments for it," Wittgenstein paid it little heed, replying that "arguments spoilt its beauty, and that he would feel as if he was dirtying a flower with muddy hands." Indeed, Russell much admired Wittgenstein's aesthetic sensitivity, remarking how "the artist in intellect is so very rare,"[43] a quality that more than aptly describes Wittgenstein's own intellect, but one which, it is safe to say, is somewhat lacking in Russell's.[44] To say that Wittgenstein treated his philosophy as a work of art should seem obvious to anyone who has paid the least bit of attention to his writing and the laborious care that he put into crafting it.

Finally, Chapter 6 will examine the metaphysical relationship between subjectivity and the work of art, especially regarding the subjective universality of the Kantian judgment of taste. Specifically, the argument will be made that the axioms of metaphysics function in much the same way as do these judgments. That is to say, in other words, that when we advance an axiom of metaphysics as true, we are making a claim, based on our individual pleasure, which supposes universal validity for everyone else as well. To postulate an axiom is to give it the form of finality required for it to substantiate a truth. Thus truth, when it is understood as an aesthetic function manifested in the judgment of taste, is simply a product of our willingness to believe in it or, rather, our inability to imagine it otherwise. This does not, however, constitute a proof that any particular axiom of metaphysics is indubitably true. Truth, when it is understood as a manifestation of the judgment of taste, can only be a measure of the aesthetic preference produced by universalizable pleasure.

The second argument of this chapter concerns Kant's oft-maligned disinterested subject, a reiteration of which we can see in Wittgenstein's metaphysical subject, which was for the latter the 'limit of the world,' and thus the 'limit of thought.' This limit, I will suggest, is exhibited in the finality of form indicative of the judgment of taste, which is required if the metaphysical subject is to substantiate any axiom of metaphysics. The metaphysical subject and the judgments it postulates are thus not only the basis for the possibility of thought,

*Introduction: To Begin at the Beginning* 13

they are also the boundary beyond which thought cannot pass. It is a 'Being-for-itself,' to use Jean-Paul Sartre's term: a kind of suspended nothingness which provides us a profound aesthetic license and responsibility for the act of self-creation. Although Sartre was certainly critical of Kant's concept of a universal human nature, we cannot ignore the fact that the aesthetic act of self-creation is a redressed expression of the judgment of taste. This, of course, implies the very same finality of human nature implicit in Kant. Not only is the nothingness of Being a finality of form in its own right—it is the absolute condition of freedom—the act of self-creation produces the very same finality as does the judgment of taste. Sartre, like Kant and Wittgenstein, puts a subjective limitation on the world, which necessitates the concept of 'universal' subjectivity. Hence, it is quite correct to say that the disinterested subject does not exist. It is the limit of existence and is therefore not concomitant with it.

Although the disinterested, metaphysical subject is not an object in the world, it is nevertheless a basic requirement of a cognizable world. If nature is to be intelligible, it can only be as the aesthetic expression of the metaphysical subject. The fact cannot be overlooked, however, that this produces a dualism of Kant's sort between phenomenon and noumenon, a distinction which is echoed in Wittgenstein's separation of thought from non-thought. The result of this separation is that the metaphysical subject must, in principle, be unthinkable. Thought can only get a hold of what is within the world. Thus, we must be careful to distinguish, as Wittgenstein does, between the 'philosophical I' and the 'I of the natural sciences,' i.e., the human body. The latter is thinkable, whereas the former is not. The basic definitional framework postulated by the metaphysical subject is the scaffolding under which nature becomes thinkable. To put the matter differently, the 'I of the natural sciences' can be metaphysically defined according to a set of established axioms. The 'philosophical I,' however, cannot be structured according to such dictates because it is the basis for dictating definitions in the first place.

This brings us to an analogous problem regarding the work of art. On the one hand, there is a sense in which art is a perfectly explicable concept. This is undoubtedly the case, for example, where the formal, ideological, and historical components of art are concerned. These aspects of the work of art all exist within a metaphysical framework from which they derive their intelligibility. On the other hand, the framework itself can be given no such intelligibility. Art, in this sense, does not exist because there is no definition that serves to delimit its boundaries. This is not to say that we can simply dismiss the physical manifestation of the work of art as inconsequential. Even though the work of art in the metaphysical sense does not exist within the world, it is immanent in it. It exhibits the limit of the world from within the world, thus making it possible for us to cognize it. This is to say, in other words, that it gestures towards the other side of the limit without revealing it. What we thus encounter at the horizon of all possible thought is not the limit of thought per se (one does not 'encounter' a limit), but rather the inability to meaningfully represent the limit. As I will go on to suggest, this is one of the chief reasons why Wittgenstein believed that the work of art gestured out towards the mystical. Art does not so much represent what is on the other side of the limit so much as it leaves it unsaid and, in so doing, manages to say something that language cannot.

Finally, we will conclude this chapter by addressing Alain Badiou's reading of the *Tractatus* and the mysticism that permeates its final passages. According to Badiou, Wittgenstein's mysticism is the inevitable outcome of the correlation that he establishes between thought and states of affairs. What can be actualized in such a state can also be cognizable. This strict definition of sense, however, produces what Badiou sees as an unacceptably large extension of non-thought (including most of philosophy). Indeed, it is precisely this distinction that leads to what Badiou calls Wittgenstein's 'two regimes of sense.' The first is inter-worldly and can be framed in terms of the proposition; the second is extra-worldly and cannot. Thus, a proposition has a sense if it accurately describes a state of affairs. No such state of affairs, however, can stand in a representational relationship to the whole of existence. Consequently, there can be no such thing as a propositional account of value in the world. This would require that the proposition transcend existence, which it cannot do because it is concomitant with existence. The implication that Badiou draws from this division of sense is that truth can have no value, and value no truth—a prospect which does not, at least on the surface, seem to sit very well with Badiou's concept of generic procedures, a central component of his philosophical repertoire.

Despite Badiou's dislike of the division that Wittgenstein makes between truth and value, Badiou is careful to make a distinction of his own that is not dissimilar to Wittgenstein's. For Badiou, we must differentiate between truth (events which are based on the absolutely pure choice of the subject) and knowledge (events that are calculable according to an already established situation). Accordingly, a truth is not something that can be derived from knowledge. Truth stands only on the substrate of the metaphysical subject and is thus outside knowledge insofar as the subject is outside of existence. Knowledge is a derivative of truth and is hence of 'lesser value.' There is nothing novel about knowledge; truth is the only mechanism for Badiou that allows for the possibility of encountering the new. Such a possibility, however, requires that the metaphysical subject fix an undecidable event in place. It must be willing to make a wager, take a leap of faith or assert a universal without cause to do so. The metaphysical subject must, in other words, be willing to demand the agreement of everyone. Every decree of truth is always a judgment of taste that imparts it the form of finality. This decision on the part of the metaphysical subject can be given no justification. In the end, all axioms, all truth, and all knowledge can be traced to the archiaesthetic act of choice. We must first believe before we can know, and the only constituent of belief is the aesthetic propensity to choose one thing and not another.

# Notes

1 Jessie L. Weston, *From Ritual to Romance* (Mineola, NY: Dover Publications, Inc., 1997), 23.

2 "It is *so difficult* to find the beginning. Or, better: it is *difficult to begin* at the beginning. And not try to go further back." Ludwig Wittgenstein, *Culture and Value* (Chicago: University of Chicago Press, 1984), 24e.

3 Barnett Newman, "The First Man Was an Artist," in *Barnett Newman: Selected Writings and Interviews* (Berkeley, CA: University of California Press, 1992), 158.

4 Michel Foucault, *Madness and Civilization: A History of Insanity in the Age of Reason* (New York: Vintage Books, 1988), 288.

5 Maurice Merleau-Ponty, "Eye and Mind," in *The Primacy of Perception: And Other Essays on Phenomenological Psychology, the Philosophy of Art, History and Politics* (Evanston, IL: Northwestern University Press, 1964), 189.

6 Around the hero everything becomes a tragedy; around the demigod everything becomes a satyr-play; and around God everything becomes—what? perhaps a 'world'? Friedrich Nietzsche, *Beyond Good and Evil* (Lexington KY: SoHo Books, 2010), sec. 150.

7 Boethius famously begins the *Consolation of Philosophy* with a scene in which Lady Philosophy denounces the Muses of Poetry as "hysterical sluts" who "slay the rich and fruitful harvest of Reason with the barren thorns of Passion." See *The Consolation of Philosophy, trans. Victor Watts (London: Penguin Classics, 1999), 4.* This damnation, of course, is not without its irony, seeing as how Boethius weaves poetic passages in and out of his most celebrated text.

8 Friedrich Nietzsche, "The Birth of Tragedy from the Spirit of Music," in *The Birth of Tragedy & The Genealogy of Morals* (New York: Anchor Books, 1990), 17.

9 Ludwig Wittgenstein, *Tractatus Logico-Philosophicus*, trans. D. F. Pears and B. F. McGuinness (London: Routledge, 2001), sec. 6.522.

10 Ibid., sec. 6.41.

11 Merleau-Ponty, "Eye and Mind," 181.

12 Ibid.

13 This is despite the fact, as Silver Bronzo notes, that one of the primary targets of the resolute reading of Wittgenstein is the neo-positivist interpretations of the *Tractatus* dating from the 1920s, 1930s, and 1940s that we find in Carnap and others. See "The Resolute Reading and Its Critics: An Introduction to the Literature," *Wittgenstein-Studien* 3, no. 1 (March 2012): 45–80. When I say 'positivistic,' however, I do not have this specific sense of the word in mind. Rather, what I mean to connote by the use of it is a disdain for metaphysics in general and the belief that it can and should be purged from philosophy. When defined thusly, the resolute reading can be understood as 'positivistic' (although in a form that is 'playing possum').

14 See, e.g., Cora Diamond, *The Realistic Spirit: Wittgenstein, Philosophy, and the Mind* (Cambridge, MA: MIT Press, 1991); Alice Crary and Rupert Read, eds., *The New Wittgenstein* (London: Routledge, 2000); Marie McGinn, *Elucidating the Tractatus: Wittgenstein's Early Philosophy of Logic and Language* (Oxford: Oxford University Press, 2006); Rupert Read and Matthew A. Lavery, eds., *Beyond The Tractatus Wars: The New Wittgenstein Debate* (New York: Routledge, 2011).

15 James Conant and Ed Dain, "Throwing the Baby Out: A Reply to Roger White," in *Beyond The Tractatus Wars: The New Wittgenstein Debate*, ed. Rupert Read and Matthew A. Lavery (New York: Routledge, 2011), 81.

16 James Conant, "The Method of the Tractatus," in *From Frege to Wittgenstein: Perspectives on Early Analytic Philosophy*, ed. Erich H. Reck (Oxford: Oxford University Press, 2001), 424.

17 McGinn, *Elucidating the Tractatus*, 12.

18 Ibid., 252.

19 Ibid., 253.

20 Crary and Read, eds., *The New Wittgenstein*, 1.

21 Warren Goldfarb, "Das Überwinden: Anti-Metaphysical Readings of the Tractatus," in *Beyond The Tractatus Wars: The New Wittgenstein Debate*, ed. Rupert Read and Matthew A. Lavery (New York: Routledge, 2011), 14.

22 Ludwig Wittgenstein, *Philosophical Investigations*, 4th ed. (Oxford: Wiley-Blackwell, 2009), sec. 109.

23 Wittgenstein, *Tractatus Logico-Philosophicus*, 2001, sec. 6.54.

24 Cora Diamond, "Throwing Away the Ladder: How to Read the Tractatus," in *The Realistic Spirit: Wittgenstein, Philosophy, and the Mind* (Cambridge, MA: MIT Press, 1991), 181.

25 P. M. S. Hacker, "Was He Trying to Whistle It?," in *The New Wittgenstein*, ed. Alice Crary and Rupert Read (London: Routledge, 2000), 365.

26 Ibid., 381.

27 This is, in short, basically a reiteration of the critique that Hacker levels at the resolute reading. See "Was He Trying to Whistle It?"

28 Ludwig Wittgenstein, *Culture and Value* (Chicago: University of Chicago Press, 1984), 24.

29 Ibid.

30 Such disdain can readily be ascertained, for instance, in Bertrand Russell's deeply biased reading of Nietzsche in *A History of Western Philosophy*. Although this grotesque caricature likely ranks among the most frightfully inaccurate depictions of Nietzsche's work ever contrived, its introductory paragraph does contain at least one enlightening remark: "Nietzsche, though a professor, was a literary rather than an academic philosopher"(New York: Simon & Schuster, 1972), 760. While this passing comment may come across as seemingly off-hand and inconsequential, in reality it contains the whole of Russell's problematic critique of Nietzsche, so much so that one need not bother with the rest of the misleading text. What we are to understand by this statement can be summed up as follows: Nietzsche was an artistic philosopher, meaning not a 'serious' philosopher, from which we are to infer that he is not worthy of serious consideration. The remainder of Russell's interpretation consists merely of further elaboration on this basic premise.

31 Plato, *The Republic of Plato*, trans. Allan Bloom (New York: Basic Books, 1991), 595b.

32 John Hartland-Swann, "Plato as Poet: A Critical Interpretation," *Philosophy* 26, no. 96 (January 1951): 7.

33 Alfred North Whitehead, *Process and Reality*, 2nd edition (New York: Free Press, 1979), 39.

34 Plato, *The Republic of Plato*, 473d.

35 Friedrich Nietzsche, *The Will to Power*, Vintage Books Edition (New York: Random House, Inc., 1968), sec. 795.

36 Martin Heidegger, *Nietzsche*, trans. David Farrrell Krell, vol. 1 and 2 (San Francisco, CA: HarperCollins, 1991), 73.

37 *Philosophical Investigations*, 4.

38 Sec. 309.

39 *Ludwig Wittgenstein: The Duty of Genius* (New York: Penguin Books, 1991), 56.

40 Ray Monk, *Wittgenstein's House: Language, Space, and Architecture* (New York: Fordham University Press, 2008), 8.

41 Ibid., 9.

42 Ibid.

43 Quoted in Brian McGuinness, *Wittgenstein: A Life: Young Ludwig 1889–1921* (Berkeley, CA: University of California Press, 1988), 104.

44 Which is not to say that Russell was a poor writer or that his style lacked elegance, but it does lack something of the fiery poetic zeal that so characterizes Wittgenstein's work.

1

# Everything Can Be Otherwise Than It Is

The question of certainty and how to attain it is not a novelty in the history of philosophy. Just this kind of preoccupation was, from the outset, an implicit and fundamental aspect of the Socratic Method. When, for instance, Socrates asks his interlocutors in the first book of the *Republic* to produce a definition of justice, the foregone conclusion embedded within this query is that in fact, they do not know, but rather only think they do. The purpose, therefore, of this particular mode of inquiry is to demonstrate what Socrates already knew with certainty: "I know nothing"[1]—precisely the one thing his interlocutors *did not* know.

While this chapter is not itself an examination of how conceptions of certainty have changed and evolved over time, it does seek to shed light on the relationship between certainty and metaphysics, especially as it concerns aesthetics. As I discussed in the Introduction, the problem of metaphysics in Wittgenstein's work is typified by his dual attraction to and repulsion from this most speculative branch of philosophy. This produces, Marie McGinn reminds us, something of a tension between "the idea that Wittgenstein is putting forward metaphysical doctrines whilst also claiming that philosophical propositions are 'nonsensical', and insisting that anyone who understands him will recognize that the propositions of *TLP* fall into this class."[2] One way in which Wittgenstein attempted to circumvent this conflict was by delineating between what can only be shown (e.g., ineffable truths about the nature of reality) and what can be meaningfully said (e.g., the propositions of natural science). Even if this solution is accepted, however, most would be willing to admit—McGinn included—that the distinction between saying and showing does not "fully discharge this tension"[3] in Wittgenstein's seemingly incoherent stance on metaphysics. Just because this solution may be "an unpalatable one" does not mean, McGinn acknowledges, "That Wittgenstein was not attracted by it."[4] Indeed, we can only fully understand the *Tractatus*, she goes on, if we assume that it accepts the idea "that there are ineffable truths about reality which are mirrored in language"[5] while simultaneously accepting the claim that these very same "propositions are 'nonsensical' and to be 'thrown away.'"[6]

McGinn suggests that a "more judicious response" to the feud between the therapeutic and the metaphysical reading would be "to look for a third interpretation, one which combines the advantages of both and has the disadvantages of neither."[7] On the first point, I find myself in complete agreement. A third interpretation of Wittgenstein's work that splits the difference between the two others would surely be prudent, but I would like to take a moment to set out how my understanding of this task differs from the one put forward by her. McGinn's method—which she terms as the "*elucidatory*, or *clarificatory*, interpretation"[8]—assents to a therapeutic understanding of Wittgenstein's first book, but does not insist that such a reading shows the propositions of the *Tractatus* to be nonsensical. Rather, McGinn prefers to emphasize the way in which these remarks reveal a "certain order in the reader's perception of ... language."[9] Through elucidation, she contends, "Wittgenstein dissolves our sense of obligation to provide a philosophical foundation for logic" while simultaneously dispelling our need to establish a link between our "forms of description" and the "world as it really is."[10]

It is difficult to fault the rationale behind the development of McGinn's interpretation. Wittgenstein does indeed place some amount of emphasis on the idea that the propositions of the *Tractatus* are meant to serve as elucidations. Where I find myself in disagreement with her, however, is in the initial assumption that spurred her search for a third way of reading the early Wittgenstein. We do not, in fact, require an interpretation that 'gets rid' of the disadvantages and difficulties that dog the incessant conflicts between Tractarian disavowals of metaphysics on the one hand and the apparently inescapable metaphysical implications those cryptic remarks seem to advance. As I have already suggested, the way to read Wittgenstein (whether early or late) is to willingly accept this contradiction as an inseparable component of his thinking. This means, among other things, not jettisoning "the philosophical problems concerning the justification of logic and the relation between language and the world."[11] The question of justification is, I contend, exactly what is at issue where the problem of metaphysics in Wittgenstein's philosophy is concerned. More precisely, it is the inevitable impossibility of producing a justification without making use of a metaphysical doctrine that is the source of the self-referentially incoherent stance on metaphysics Wittgenstein adopts throughout the various phases of his intellectual life.

Many of these issues will be revisited in Chapter 4 when *On Certainty* is submitted to a more rigorous examination, but for the time being, I would like to

*Everything Can Be Otherwise Than It Is* 21

briefly consider a passage from that text—specifically §246—which I deem to be of particular importance for understanding the relationship between certitude and aesthetics in Wittgenstein's thought: "'Here I have arrived at a foundation of all my beliefs.' 'This position I will *hold*!' But isn't that, precisely, only because I am completely convinced of it?—What is 'being completely convinced' like?" As is often the case in much of his later work, Wittgenstein is much more likely to pose questions to his reader than answer them, and this is no exception. Although we can see Wittgenstein approaching several possible answers throughout the text, in true Socratic Method he never ultimately settles on a satisfactory one. The issue at stake is an important one, precisely because the answer to it reveals just how it is that Wittgenstein could legitimately hold two very opposing points of view on metaphysics. So while he never explicitly tells us what it is like to feel completely convinced of something, I propose that there is a profoundly aesthetic dimension to this sensation, one that does not shy away in the face of contradiction. More specifically, as we will see, a feeling of unshakable conviction has an element of the subjective universality that Kant attributed to judgments of taste, thus effecting a consolidating of the metaphysical and epistemological through the aesthetic. This strategy has the added benefit of aligning Wittgenstein's aesthetic proclivity with much of his other writing and shows just how much of an affinity the problem of metaphysics has for what Nietzsche called the 'metaphysics of art' in *The Birth of Tragedy*. Addressing these interrelated topics will, however, necessitate that we set Wittgenstein to one side for now and focus on explicating the problem of metaphysics and its relationship to aesthetics in a broader sense.

In many respects, the problem of metaphysics is related to the 'problem of the criterion' in epistemology, but instead of contending with questions such as 'What do we know?' and 'How do we know it?' the problem of metaphysics deals with the separate but related questions, 'What is the fundamental nature of reality?' and 'How do we devise a method for uncovering it?' Philosophers throughout history have often been tempted to answer these questions by appealing to a first principle deemed self-evidently true and indisputable. These principles, of course, vary considerably, but whether we are discussing the Aristotelean unmoved mover or the Cartesian *cogito*, in every case, their function is to provide a point of origin, a grounding upon which an edifice of thought may be built without exposing it to the risk of infinite regress. The difficulty, however, with all such 'self-evident' metaphysical principles is that they resist the kind of universal agreement that seem to be required of them. This, then, is one aspect of the problem of metaphysics: the inability to give indubitable and universally agreed upon first principles coupled with the desire to avoid regress.

It should also be stressed that this problem is fundamentally inseparable from the problem of the criterion. Every principle of metaphysics is always subject to epistemological consideration.

The problem of metaphysics—unlike the problem of the criterion—is not a phrase widely employed in philosophical parlance. One of the few instances of its use can be found in Hartley Burr Alexander's 1902 dissertation *The Problem of Metaphysics and the Meaning of Metaphysical Explanation: An Essay in Definitions*.[12] The "problem of metaphysics," as he sees it,

> May be variously stated: it may be a quest for the essence of things, or for a reality within things themselves, or for their truth. But in every case the real object of the inquiry is the discovery of a ground or *raison d'être which shall seem to us a sufficient reason why reality is what it is*. Such a ground . . . can only be satisfying when it embodies a motive or a purpose intelligible to us in terms of our motives and our purposes. It is only as revealing design that we consider any action to be reasonable. . . . The problem of metaphysics is thus *par excellence* the problem of teleology.[13]

While I am content with Alexander's summation of the problem of metaphysics as the inquiry into why reality is what it is, I will differ from him by insisting that metaphysics can in no way be intelligible to us in terms of our motives or purposes. In fact, I will go so far as to suggest that metaphysics is what makes intelligibility possible and, as such, cannot be intelligible itself. Thus, instead of characterizing the problem of metaphysics as 'the problem of teleology' *par excellence*, I will prefer to designate it as 'the problem of aesthetics.'

The term 'aesthetics,' as it is here being used, has a very specific and somewhat untraditional meaning. It is, first and foremost, used as the designation for the activity of selection without sufficient reason. As such, it is distinct from all conceptions of aesthetics that might pre-determinedly fix its meaning in place. It is a term that is here employed as a stand-in for undecidability; i.e., the utter and absolute freedom to change any precept without the encumbrance of justification. In this respect, it bears some resemblance to the judgment of taste because, as Kant maintains, "There can be no objective rule of taste that would determine what is beautiful through concepts."[14] This lack of an objective rule is called aesthetic by Kant because its "determining ground cannot be other than subjective."[15] My own use of the word 'aesthetic' will preserve this essential subjective feature.

This is key because, as I will maintain, the problem of metaphysics is typified by the maxim: Everything can be otherwise than it is.[16] That is to say, in other words, that there can be no such thing as a self-evidently true or certain principle of metaphysics that can be determined according to an objectively universal rule. This metaphysical maxim is, thus formulated, distinctly non-Kantian, and to a large extent, runs contrary to the majority of the Western metaphysical tradition that has valued—by and large—truth, certainty, and objectivity above all else. This characterization of metaphysics also distinguishes itself by being primarily axiomatic. That is to say, it is concerned with the business of defining terms. It thus follows that the one thing metaphysics cannot itself be about is 'the Truth' because it is the criterion by which we determine what counts as truth in any given situation. Definitions cannot be analyzed according to a truth function, nor can they be substantiated simply by making an appeal to self-evidence. The only ground on which a definition can be placed is our willingness to believe in it without reservation. This 'belief without reservation' I will term 'aesthetic' because it is subjective and cannot be determined in accordance with an objective rule.

My central claim can thus be summed up as follows: Every metaphysical proposition is fundamentally definitional and as such is aesthetic because there is no *a priori* mandate that requires our belief in the truth of any one definition as opposed to another. Consequently, the problem of metaphysics—which seeks to discover the *raison d'être* for why things are as they are—can only ever postulate its own contingency. In every 'reason for being,' there is an equal and opposite 'reason for not being.' Whenever we make a judgment as to why things are as they are, we always beg the question, "What would it be like if it were otherwise?"[17] When all is said and done, there is no reason to treat this definition as fundamental rather than any of the infinitely many we might choose. In the very attempt to determine why it is that things are this way instead of that way, we have already betrayed the aesthetic and subjective condition under which all axiomatic determinations, in general, are made. Since there is no metaphysical principle that commands our obedience, we are thrust into a position of limitless freedom, on the one hand, and inescapable responsibility, on the other. This freedom is the subjective freedom to choose amongst innumerable metaphysical axioms coupled with the responsibility for selecting amongst them. One could call this responsibility the impossibility of the non-choice. Collectively, I will assign the name of 'aesthetic choice,' or, alternatively, 'aesthetic preference,' to this 'imperative of freedom.'

First and foremost, the aesthetics of choice does not posit any axiom of metaphysics as necessarily and universally true. This is because judgments of taste, as Kant has frequently reminded us, are only subjectively universal and not objectively so. There is, consequently, no such thing as a self-evident axiom of metaphysics. The only substantiation such axioms can be granted is that of aesthetic preference. Thus, a theory of metaphysics that predicates itself on aesthetics implicitly leaves the door open to every possibility. Like any judgment of taste, it has the form of a universal call to assent but cannot mandate it. We can either choose to accept or reject any axiom of metaphysics as we see fit, and no proof can be leveraged for this choice save for the willingness to hold it up as a given truth that we then expect others to acknowledge or otherwise face the condemnations of 'bad taste.' According to this conception, aesthetic choice is—to borrow William James's phrase—the 'will to believe' in any supposition that, both in principle and practice, cannot be proven either true or false, but can only be accepted or rejected. It is, to state the matter in James's words, a "justification *of* faith, a defense of our right to adopt a believing attitude in religious matters, in spite of the fact that our merely logical intellect may not have been coerced."[18] Such a lack of coercion is, in fact, the very thing I deny to metaphysics, and consequently, we are obliged to offer a similar defense of the necessity to adopt a believing attitude in metaphysical matters as well.

After the fashion of James, we could call our 'aesthetics of choice' a kind of 'radical empiricism,' in as much as it regards "its most assured conclusions concerning matters of fact as hypotheses liable to modification in the course of future experience."[19] This aesthetics of choice regards no principle "as something with which all experience has got to square."[20] Instead, it regards every dogmatism as a denial of freedom and treats every alternative as concomitant with "one's general vision of the probable."[21] Given that each of us has a generally divergent vision of what is probable and what is not, it would be presumptuous to assume that any one viewpoint may be established that could simultaneously account for every possible one. It is even more presumptuous to assume that there is some onus on us to do so. We must, in other words, leave all 'matters of fact' open to the possibility of revision in the due course of new experiences. Doing so serves to demonstrate the extent to which past and present experiences are open to continual interpretation. As such, the aesthetics of choice specifically denies us the ability, *a priori*, to demarcate what is true objectively from what is true subjectively. In the end, all that we can admit is that truth is truth only insofar as it is true for someone at some particular point in time, at some particular place in the world, according to some predetermined set of criteria.

While a metaphysics predicated on an aesthetics of choice is implicitly pluralistic, it cannot, without violating its own principles, deny the possibility of

*Everything Can Be Otherwise Than It Is*          25

monism. A thoroughly pluralistic view of the universe, which admits to the viability of a multitude of various conceptions of existence, must also admit that monism is a concept of as much verisimilitude as any other, given that we are willing to ascribe to its tenets. In any given case, it is this willingness to believe that enables us to distinguish the true from the false, and thus belief can be a self-fulfilling prophecy. Belief makes truth possible, and without it truth would be a nonexistent concept. The truths of metaphysics, insofar as they are anything, are in each respect only something in relation to someone, hence their fundamentally aesthetic nature. The will to believe—which is simply the acknowledgment that all justification is ultimately predicated on a baseless supposition—can hang existence upon any thread it so chooses, and in so doing it creates 'existence' for us in the process. Whatever metaphysical truths may be, they are not divined but contrived by us. Whatever our convictions may be, the act of believing itself can fulfill the truth conditions that our convictions demand. Philosophy cannot be an inquiry into essences or truths or ideals, and, for that matter, philosophy is only an 'inquiry' if we understand by that term the 'invention' that inquiry breeds, which is in all instances a form of creative invention. Philosophy creates truth, and this happens, as Nietzsche notes (and here he prefigures James), "As soon as ever a philosophy begins to believe in itself. It always creates the world in its own image; it cannot do otherwise; philosophy is this tyrannical impulse itself, the most spiritual Will to Power, the will to 'creation of the world,' the will to causa prima."[22]

In every sense of the term, the aesthetics of choice is the expression of the will to *causa prima*. It is, in other words, the embodiment of 'master morality,' the morality of the 'noble man,' who "regards HIMSELF as a determiner of values; . . . he knows that it is he himself only who confers honour on things; he is a CREATOR OF VALUES. He honours whatever he recognizes in himself: such morality equals self-glorification."[23] Above all else, the morality of the master expresses the axiom: 'honor thyself as creator and arbiter of values.' It is the 'master' that values, as an end in itself, the freedom to discharge the will to power, which I will regard as fundamentally interrelated to the concept of aesthetic choice, insofar as it is subjective and not constricted by any outside dictates. The will to power is, I might add, an inherently creative activity that regards invention as the first undertaking of metaphysics. "It is the powerful who KNOW how to honour, it is their art, their domain for invention."[24] This art "is the highest human task, the true metaphysical activity,"[25] which does not seek to become "an imitation of nature but its metaphysical supplement, raised up beside it in order to overcome it."[26]

It is the formulation of such a 'metaphysics of art' that I will take to be the primary end of the aesthetics of choice, without which we would be incapable of conceiving truth and falsity. Our metaphysics of art must also recognize that there can be no ultimate certitude at the foundation of our knowledge that would compel the universal belief of everyone. The only 'mandate' that dictates our aesthetic choice is that of freedom: You are free to choose but choose you must. This injunction of choice entreats us to the realization that no *a priori* justification can be given except one that is predicated on the whim of our aesthetic fancy. It is in this sense that metaphysics is not so much a 'philosophy' or a 'science' as it is an 'art.' In all matters metaphysical, let us be artists, for each one of us will no doubt accept or reject any axiom of metaphysics according to our own aesthetic sensibilities. Yes, we could call the aesthetics of choice a kind of 'faith,' but not faith in what is given, but rather a faith in what might be. In James's words, "There are, then, cases where a fact cannot come at all unless a preliminary faith exists in its coming."[27]

While the aesthetics of choice and the metaphysics of art are indeed central topics of this chapter, I would like to stop here for a moment and dwell on a question that was, as we know, of considerable importance for Wittgenstein: To what extent—if at all—is it possible to extract metaphysics from philosophy? One of the problems that immediately presents itself when we pose this question harkens back to the seemingly self-contradictory utterances of the *Tractatus*. The proposition 'Metaphysical hypotheses are devoid of significance' is one that seems to make a significant claim about the nature of reality: There are no such things as significant metaphysical propositions. Beyond this initial difficulty, however, we are faced with the rather thorny issue of metaphysical inquiry more broadly speaking. If an investigation into the impossibility of metaphysics is not itself a form of metaphysics, then it is difficult to see how even the most egregious examples of metaphysical excogitation could make the grade. It would seem, then, that even the denial of metaphysics is itself metaphysics, and as such that metaphysics is an inescapable component of all philosophical activity precisely because every system of philosophy is predicated on any number of axiomatic assumptions that are themselves not provable from within that system. The question pertaining to the elimination of metaphysics from philosophy must therefore be substituted with another: How is it possible to use metaphysics to inquire into metaphysics?

In answering this question, we are seemingly faced with two possible answers. Either metaphysics is incapable of discovering itself from within, in which case we would need a second-order 'meta-metaphysics' that stands outside of metaphysics. Or, metaphysics must be capable of a kind of self-evaluation that

*Everything Can Be Otherwise Than It Is*          27

does not require recourse to an external explanatory system. The problem with the former option is that we are quite obviously faced with what would quickly become a series of metaphysical explanations *ad infinitum*. The latter, on the other hand, puts us in the unpalatable position of having to accept the ability of metaphysics to justify itself as something 'given' or 'self-evident,' and thus requiring no further explanation. Falling back on this rationale is not without its own pitfalls, however, for it seems to smack of an act of faith, pure and simple— to say nothing of the fact that what meets the standard of incorrigibility has a curious way of changing over time. It is a telling fact that even in his own day, Descartes received a considerable number of objections and replies to his *cogito*, to say nothing of the copious number of challenges and criticisms it has faced since—an odd distinction for a principle that by virtue of its clarity and distinction was supposed to be "necessarily true whenever it is put forward."[28] The point here is this: It is not enough merely to profess the incontestability of any given proposition in order to prove its certitude. Dissent must be a strict and absolute impossibility concerning any matter that is truly incorrigible. By the sheer force of its veracity alone, it would compel all those who understood it to acquiesce to it without exception, which is why self-evidence cannot stand for any one person alone—it must stand for everyone and for all eternity.

The problem of how to account for disagreement concerning fundamental philosophical propositions was one that Wittgenstein seemed to have devoted some amount of thought to. "If the were theses in philosophy," he once told Friedrich Waismann in 1931,

> They would have to be put such that they do not give rise to disputes. For they would have to be put in such a way that everyone would say, Oh yes, that is of course obvious. As long as there is a possibility of having different opinions and disputing about a question, this indicates that things have not yet been expressed clearly enough. Once a perfectly clear formulation – ultimate clarity – has been reached, there can be no second thoughts or reluctance any more.[29]

It is interesting to note that when it was originally released, Wittgenstein considered the propositions of the *Tractatus* to be "unassailable and definitive,"[30] which makes the above comments all the more pertinent given the fact that when he made them, Wittgenstein was beginning to doubt many of the premises on which it had been based. Indeed, the book was hardly greeted with anything resembling the universal assent required to elevate its contents to the level of 'philosophical theses.' Wittgenstein, moreover, was convinced that Russell, Frege, and the Logical Positivists fundamentally misinterpreted the *Tractatus*, a sentiment which he relates to Russell in a letter dated June 12, 1919. It is "galling to think that no one will understand it,"[31] Wittgenstein laments. Despite all this apparent annoyance at not being readily comprehended, he nevertheless seems to have fully expected it, stating in the 1918 introduction to the *Tractatus*, "Perhaps this book will be understood only by someone who has himself already had the thoughts that are expressed in it."[32] The fact that so few did understand the book at its conception is no doubt indicative not only of the novelty of the *Tractatus* but its profundity as well. But one cannot help wondering why it is that the *Tractatus* suffered from so much misinterpretation if in fact it does contain the unassailable truth as Wittgenstein believed it did. It took him many years of laborious thought to craft the propositions of the *Tractatus*, and once he had arrived at them—more importantly: once he had shown others how to arrive at them—his assumption seems to have been that everyone would necessarily say, 'Oh yes, that is of course obvious.' Russell, for one, was not entirely convinced of their truth, as he made clear in his own introduction to the *Tractatus*. "As one with a long experience of the difficulties of logic and of the deceptiveness of theories which seem irrefutable, I find myself unable to be sure of the rightness of a theory, merely on the ground that I cannot see any point on which it is wrong."[33] The concern that Russell expresses here is important, for if the *Tractatus* does indeed contain the irrefutable truth, then it ought to be impossible to raise any objection to it at all, even Russell's relatively minor one.

A related problem to the ones outlined above is that of self-referential incoherence. There are many famous examples of this problem throughout the history of Western philosophy. Plato's objection against the relativism of Protagoras in section 171a of the *Theaetetus*, known as the *peritropê*, or the 'table-turning' argument, is a variation of it and related to it are the liar's paradox and what has come to be known as Russell's paradox. In general, these paradoxes all derive from an assertion that, when applied to itself, contradicts itself. For the statement 'all truth is relative' to be true, the statement 'all truth is relative' must be true for everyone, and thus, truth cannot be relative (or at the very least, there must be one universal truth). My concern with the problem of self-reference is here limited more specifically to instances where a metaphysical proposition is used to deny the impossibility of metaphysics. In modernity, this is perhaps best exhibited by the Logical Positivists. Rudolf Carnap, for instance, once asserted that "in the domain of metaphysics, including all philosophy of value and normative theory, logical analysis yields the negative results that the alleged statements in this domain are entirely meaningless. Therewith a radical elimination of metaphysics is attained, which was not yet possible from the

*Everything Can Be Otherwise Than It Is* 29

earlier antimetaphysical standpoints."[34] The basis of Carnap's assertion is, as he puts it, due to the fact that

> the meaning of a word is determined by its criterion of application (in other words: by the relations of deducibility entered into by its elementary sentence-form, by its truth-conditions, by the method of its verification), the stipulation of the criterion takes away one's freedom to decide what one wishes to 'mean' by the word.[35]

All of this is to say, in other words, that where Carnap is concerned, meaning is stipulated by its verification via empirical criteria and the logical syntax of language in which our observations are conveyed.

The trouble with Carnap's conception of meaning is that it commits the very metaphysical offense that it purports to radically eliminate. In defining how words gain their meaning, he is undertaking a mode of philosophical inquiry that is not altogether dissimilar to the one which Plato used to derive his doctrine of the Forms. This is not to say that Carnap's and Plato's conceptions of meaning are one and the same. However, in attempting to define what meaning is, Carnap is continuing what is a long tradition in metaphysics, one in which Plato has been firmly entrenched for some two and a half millennia. So, how is it possible that Carnap and the Logical Positivists disposed of metaphysics when metaphysics is implicit in their own strategy? In his article "The Metaphysics of Logical Positivism," Feibleman attempts to answer something very similar to this question. According to his suggestion, "Logical positivism mistakenly identifies all metaphysics with (a) a transcendental metaphysics, and (b) an ostensive and explicit metaphysics."[36] This confusion, if Feibleman is correct, would explain why Carnap fails to realize that his critique of metaphysics is self-referentially incoherent. Carnap, by equating metaphysics in general with transcendental metaphysics superficially appears to avoid contradiction. However, he fails to see that his own theory implicitly suggests a metaphysics, because it is not 'ostensive or explicit' in the sense that it openly purports to 'be about' metaphysics. Which is to say, as Feibleman does, that

> Carnap wants, for instance, the position of nominalism without the term "nominalism." That is, he wants the anti-metaphysical position implicit in nominalism, but he does not want it to be called nominalism. In this school, ontology is an ugly epithet, to be reserved for each wing to hurl against the other. He recoils with some horror at the prospect that if variables are to be interpreted realistically instead of nominalistically, physics would imply some degree of Platonic philosophy.[37]

For all intents and purposes, "Logical positivism as it stands contains statements of a metaphysical character. 'Metaphysics is nonsense' is metaphysics."[38]

It should come as no surprise regarding what Carnap terms "metaphysical pseudo-statements"[39] that Heidegger is touted as the practitioner par excellence of such grievances against language. As noted by Martin Puchner,

> Carnap's essay tries to exemplify what it means to conduct a logical analysis of language through a critique of Heidegger's *What is Metaphysics?* (1929). Whatever one might think about Heidegger's philosophy, Carnap's text is less an argued critique than a polemic, for is [*sic*] does not even pretend to reconstruct the concerns and arguments of Heidegger's text, of which it analyzes only a single paragraph. Rather, the logical analysis of language, here, presents itself as a weapon with which one can fire almost randomly at so-called metaphysical sentences.[40]

The polemics that Puchner points to in Carnap's essay are, in no small part, predicated on the ideological supremacy with which the logical and scientific world view was regarded in many intellectual circles during the early twentieth century. While the procedure of logical analysis differs considerably from the etymological methodology employed by Heidegger in *Being and Time*, both are facets in the broader project of the 'linguistic turn.' Each in its way has railed against the concept of philosophy "as a pseudo-science," to quote Richard Rorty. This "linguistic movement in contemporary philosophy," therefore, "Has no animus against the creation of a new art form within which . . . we may carry on in open activity previously conducted behind a façade of pseudo-scientific argumentation."[41] This latter point, however, is one that has—by and large—been lost on the analytic strains of the linguistic turn. If, as Rorty tells us, "Philosophy in the future becomes Heideggerian mediation, or, more generally, becomes the activity of constructing language-games for the sheer joy of it . . . then linguistic philosophers will have nothing left to criticize."[42] What the analytic tradition has failed to realize is that after we have finally turned the linguistic corner, there is no path left to take *except* the artistic one. At the heart of the analytic misreading of Wittgenstein, then, is the mistaken belief that linguistic analysis is the principal end of all philosophical inquiry when in reality it is merely a staging area—one designed for the clearing away of traditional philosophical 'problems' so as to prepare the way for the eventual coming of the 'aesthetic turn.'

Irrespective of the question as to what philosophical results the linguistic turn is supposed to affect, there can be little doubt that it is not only the Heideggerian variety that is engaged in a metaphysical undertaking. In a 1969 article entitled

*Everything Can Be Otherwise Than It Is*

"How is Non-Metaphysics Possible?," John O. Nelson suggests "that every-one who uses a language is in effect engaged in metaphysics, for he is expressing metaphysical theses."[43] His suggestion is well taken, given some of the difficulties pointed out with Carnap's criterion of meaningfulness above. To use a language is to adopt some metaphysical assumption as to how words get their meaning, even if it is only implicitly suggested. Nelson's distinction between "live" and "dead" metaphysics[44] is a useful metaphor to keep in mind here. Not only does he seem to derive the distinction from William James, but the difference between the two bear similarities to what Feibleman referred to as explicit and implicit metaphysics. In the main, Nelson seems correct, save that near the end of his article he quickly falls into what Feibleman calls "an unbridled rational dogmatism or ... uncontrolled empirical scepticism."[45] Clearly, Nelson means his question 'How is non-metaphysics possible?' in a strictly rhetorical sense, for according to him, if we call on Wittgenstein's *Philosophical Investigations*, we will discover

> that ordinary discourse can exist without metaphysics, but metaphysics cannot exist without ordinary discourse. The substance of metaphysics is provided by ordinary discourse ... we err by supposing that because the substance of metaphysics is at least indirectly the substance of ordinary discourse and because this substance is neither given empirically or logically (but is rather the basis for empirical observation and logical intuition) ordinary discourse must be metaphysics.[46]

The problem with Nelson's assertion, as is intimated by Feibleman, is that the dogmatic ascription to ordinary discourse (which smacks of uncontrolled empirical skepticism) is somehow going to absolve us of our metaphysical burdens, but the assertion 'there is only what is ordinary' falls far beyond the confines of ordinary usage and is thus a metaphysical assertion by its own lights. There can be no proof of this statement other than a circular one in which ordinary usage justifies its legitimacy. At best, the examination of everyday discourse is a methodology, which is to say that it is predicated on any number of metaphysical assumptions that cannot themselves be proven true within the system the methodology inaugurates. To deny the very possibility of doing metaphysics is therefore to deny the possibility of any method of inquiry whatsoever, for a methodology is simply a systematization of a set of non-provable axioms that dictate how an inquiry ought to be conducted. If we were to dispose of metaphysics, we would also have to dispose of just these kinds of definitional terms, and without these basic building blocks, no methodology whatsoever could be formed. This means, in other words, that we must come to grips with the realization that all proofs have to end somewhere, and when they do, we must proceed on assumptions alone, none of which are, properly speaking, 'self-evident'. They only ever gain the gravitas of 'truthfulness' when we take them to be aesthetically pleasing—that is, when we take pleasure in them and expect others to acquiesce to them in the same fashion as we do.

The consequence of the above characterization of metaphysics as an essentially assumptive activity has a couple of unavoidable consequences, and one of the most important of these concerns the inability of thought to escape the exercise of fictions. There are indeed any number of examples throughout the history of philosophy that illustrates this only too well, one of the most obvious being that of the Hegelian Absolute (although others abound in plenitude). From at least the time of Parmenides, we have been all too cognizant of the fact that "from nothing only nothing comes,"[47] and nearly four hundred years later, the same basic principle would be reiterated in Lucretius: "Nothing ever springs miraculously out of nothing."[48] But Lucretius, unlike Parmenides, was fully under the influence of Epicurean Atomism, and as such did not find any contradiction in the coexistence of being and the void. Whereas Parmenides was invariably led to the conclusion that "nothing else outside of Being exists or ever will,"[49] Lucretius, working from the same basic premise (nothing begets nothing), held that "the universe in its essential nature is composed of two things, namely matter and the void,"[50] and it is out of this unity of opposites that the seeds of so much modern dialectics were sown. In Kant, it reaches something of a dead end in the antinomies, but in Hegel this fundamental limitation on human cognition is overcome by emphasizing their positive side as opposed to their negative. Thus, for Hegel, the true significance of contradiction is not that it exposes the inadequacies of reason, but rather that it shows how "everything actual contains opposed determinations within it."[51]

The irony in all of this, of course, is that what here looks like a solution is, in the end, nothing more than the recognition of our *aporia* and not the dissolution of it. Merely identifying the contradiction at the heart of reality is not at all the same thing as finally and definitively resolving it, and yet this is precisely what the Hegelian dialectic sets out to accomplish. It does this task by way of three interrelated postulates, the first and most basic of which proceeds on the assumption that contradiction is under a categorical obligation to find resolution in synthesis—that what is opposed *must* (given the right circumstances and enough time) recombine into what is not opposed. Once this much has been taken as axiomatic, the internal logic that undergirds the dialectic may then move on to make its next conceptual leap, namely that the sum of synthetic

*Everything Can Be Otherwise Than It Is* 33

resolutions is not only cumulative but also progressive as well, which is simply to say, as Kojève has already said, that what is negated through the dialectic is nevertheless "preserved in the finished product" in such a way that it "appears in a 'sublimated' or 'mediated' form."[52]

Finally, then, we have the third and perhaps most daring of the predicates on which the whole Hegelian dialectic is based and for which it exists: that being nothing less than the idea of the Absolute itself. The first thing to say here would be the rather obvious point that the Absolute does not spring fully formed from the womb, but rather that it is essentially the result of a process, and therefore it "is what it truly is" only "in the end."[53] As humdrum as this observation may rightly be, it nevertheless belies a crucial axiom that is not itself derived from the notion of the Absolute but is rather presupposed by it. If it is to be possible for the dialectic to produce the Absolute, it must also be possible for the recurrent process of nullification that is at the heart of the dialectic to cease its continual negation of the given so that being may attain its own self-sameness. This is accomplished, of course, when the Absolute is actualized through differences that in the end "are no longer differences,"[54] but the very notion of such a possibility, however, already betrays something of a teleological predilection, without which the dialectic would be free to go on indefinitely. And although Hegel's teleology might be 'infinite' in the sense that it is, as J. N. Findlay puts it, a "purposive activity taken up for its own sake,"[55] it does, nevertheless, depend on the possibility of there being an end, even though it may not preordain what form that end ought to take (as a 'finite' teleology might do).[56] Moreover, this end cannot be purely suppositional or even merely probable; it must be, in some very real sense, an inevitability. The question is not if, but when?

The reader will no doubt recognize the rhetorical nature of these questions, for in each case, the answer is invariably, 'at some undeterminable point in the future,' which means, for all intents and purposes, 'never.' It is a thing that is forever to be put off, never to be actualized, a project always in the making, a goal just beyond reach. The question, therefore, is not so much, 'When will the dialectic result in the actualization of the Absolute?' so much as it is, 'Does the dialectic constitute a form of reality apart from our apprehension of it?' Is it an objective quality of the real that we ascertain via the exercise of our rational or empirical faculties, or is it rather an artifice of the mind that is graphed over the *tabula rasa* of the void, in order to give it the appearance of coherence where there is none? Where the Hegelian dialectic is concerned, then, the problem is not whether it would or would not be capable of producing the Absolute so much as it is whether the dialectic can make a legitimate claim to the truth in any ultimate sense. To have such a guarantee of veracity, it would itself already have to fully embody the Absolute, which would, in turn, negate its *raison d'être*, which was to engender it. And so we are thrown into a line of circular reasoning where the dialectic is a means to justify the Absolute and the Absolute is a means to justify the dialectic.

The lesson to be learned here, as Žižek has put it in his recent *magnum opus* on Hegel, is that the ineffability of the Absolute always "eludes the grasp of our categories," making it possible to say "anything and/or nothing about it," which in the end amounts to nothing more than a kind of "non-substantial reasoning with no connection with reality."[57] Such an assessment of the Absolute, of course, is not without precedent in the annals of philosophy. Hans Vaihinger—whose *Die Philosophie des Als Ob*,[58] despite its perspicacity, has had the grave misfortune of falling out of the good graces of 'fashionable reading.'[59] Therein we find him pulling no punches in his description of the Absolute, which he calls the "greatest fiction"[60] humanity has yet devised. This does not mean, however, that the Absolute—because it is a fictitious conceptual apparatus—is, therefore, a useless one that ought to be discarded without regard as to its potential applications within thought. Indeed, as Vaihinger himself conceded, the Absolute has a "tremendous practical utility"[61] in that it allows us to carry out many functions of thinking that would otherwise be quite impossible without its aid, and it is for this reason that it has a definite pragmatic efficacy.[62] To be sure, it is this service to thought that accounts, at least in part, for whatever value the Absolute might be said to have, and we would do well to bear this fact in mind when pressing it into service, lest we forget, to the detriment of thought, that it has no unmediated correlation to reality in any ultimate sense. In saying this, however, we would do even better to remember that the concept of 'use-value' is just as fictitious a concept as that of the Absolute.

There are, of course, other examples we might point to, one of which is to be found in an idea that played a fundamental role in early modern social and political theory: that of the 'state of nature.' Rousseau was downright frank in his admission that the existence of such a pre-civil mode of life is one that, quite obviously, "no longer exists, perhaps never did exist, and probably never will exist," and yet, so he supposed, it is an idea that is indispensable to the "proper judgment of our present state."[63] The truth of the matter, however, is something quite different than Rousseau seems willing to acknowledge, for if the proper assessment of our present social condition is predicated on what is no doubt a fictive theoretical construct, then how we judge our current state of existence will be irrevocably bound up with how we choose to fashion this fiction. Nowhere

*Everything Can Be Otherwise Than It Is*                                    35

is this made more abundantly clear than in the stark contrast between Rousseau's famous proclamation at the opening of *The Social Contract* that "man was born free,"[64] with the equally indignant polemic of Hobbes that "without a common Power" to keep the competing interests of individuals in check, the state of nature would inevitably degrade into a war of every man "against every man."[65] We need not dwell at any length here on the finer differences between Hobbes and Rousseau, of which much has already been said.[66] All that need concern us, for the time being, is the varying degrees to which Hobbes and Rousseau derived divergent conceptions of the social contract in direct proportion to the incongruities between their respective theories about the state of nature. In the case of Rousseau, the whole purpose of the state is to preserve—as much as is possible given the inherent limitations of civilization in general—the freedom of the individual from the fetters of societal constraints, whereas for Hobbes, the only freedom of any ultimate and indubitable importance is the freedom from bodily harm. Where Rousseau is concerned, the state of nature is an ideal on which to model the construction of society, but for Hobbes, it is its exact antithesis—the thing above all else that civil society must strive to overcome.

The main point in all of this, as should be readily apparent by now, is that the assumptions that undergird a philosophical inquiry will always involve a certain number of inescapable ramifications, some of which may well be quite predictable, some of which are otherwise impossible to foresee in their entirety from the outset.[67] In any given philosophical construct, the ratio between these two extremes will depend, at least in part, on just how closely tied its ends are with its means. Certain kinds of axiomatic presuppositions are bound to produce certain kinds of results; a particular sort of conclusion will follow inexorably from a particular place of origin, and even a slight deviation in first principles can be enough to produce significant discrepancies in the way in which a line of thinking may be extrapolated outwards from its epicenter. We see this quite clearly in Hobbes and Rousseau, where the goals to be *attained* are already *contained*—albeit in a latent form—within their respective conceptions of the state of nature. In Hegel, too, we find that the Absolute must already be in gestation from the very beginning of the dialectical movement of self-consciousness as it comes to be "faced by another self-consciousness."[68] And when, in the preface to the 1888 English edition of the *Communist Manifesto*, Engels took up the task of reevaluating the reception of the text since its publication some forty years earlier, he was quick to reiterate what had already been one of its central underpinnings: in "primitive tribal" societies land was something held "in common ownership."[69] The purpose of the communist state, therefore, would be to bring about a return to the fundamentally communal nature of property—a return, in other words, to a position both posterior and anterior to the instantiation of class warfare; that is, to a form of communism born out of dialectical materialism, one that goes back to a 'primitive' mode of ownership, but in a form that could only come about by way of a synthetic nullification of the competing material interests implicit within class distinctions.

Where each of the above examples is concerned, then, there is an unmistakable way in which a certain metaphysical hypothesis regarding some fundamental feature of nature is both axiomatic in the sense that it must be presupposed in order to commence a philosophical analysis and fictional because it has no ultimate basis in the reality it purports to embody. We could therefore say that the only thing philosophy is capable of 'proving' is what it has already taken as its *a priori* given. This helps explain, as a brief aside, why the so-called 'world-riddles'[70] remain perennially unsolved and indeed unsolvable: They attempt to discover what can only be invented. A methodology that would seek to do the former can only ever hope to pose the very puzzle it would set out to decipher. The insolubility of these problems, therefore, has nothing to do with our inability to devise a suitable means for putting these kinds of riddles to rest. Rather, the failure occurs because we forget that the enigmas of existence invariably involve generative acts of creativity that do not themselves presume the necessity for justification. If we were to inquire after one in spite of this, we would quickly begin to feel as though we could sense some momentous profundity just beyond the periphery of consciousness. In reality, however, the feeling that existence must necessarily be imbued with some higher-order meaning does not occur because our awareness might occasionally brush up against it.[71] No sense-datum—no matter how powerful—is capable of proving the existence of anything external to the mind, and as such, we cannot say for sure whether there is some otherworldly essence just beyond the grasp of intuition that is capable of impressing a fleeting sense of awe upon it. While there may well be a transcendental *raison d'être* for Being, that reason is forever beyond the confines of what is sensible. We cannot, therefore, say with certainty that any of the world-riddles correlate to the ultimate meaning of things—all we can say is that they correlate with a desire to actually discover them once and for all.

Despite this bleak set of circumstances we seem incapable of escaping here, there is at least some reason to remain hopeful. While the world-riddles might ultimately be no more than the fanciful chimeras that we create in the very attempt to solve them, there could, nevertheless, be something significant about them worthy of retention. If the search for some higher meaning is enough to

*Everything Can Be Otherwise Than It Is*      37

produce the meaning that is sought after, then the search for it is, in the end, a worthwhile endeavor, even if it is, properly speaking, not discovered but rather invented. After all, just because the world-riddles are fictitious constructs of the human mind does not mean that they are incapable of serving any conceivable purpose, however great or small. This much, at least, Vaihinger has already given us the tools to understand, and if we heed the lessons of Wittgenstein as well, what practical use there is in 'seeing the world as a riddle' depends, in no small part, on the form of life in which it is embedded. It was, no doubt, an integral component of the form of life Wittgenstein himself lived. Indeed, one might say, the form of life Wittgenstein led would have been quite impossible without the kind of ethico-aesthetic engagement with the mystical that permeated every facet of his being, which in turn manifested itself in his philosophy. Wittgenstein would be the first to admit, as he did in his "A Lecture on Ethics," that "the desire to say something about the ultimate meaning of life" was an "absolutely hopeless" project, but one that he nevertheless could not help "respecting deeply,"[72] a fact that must be kept firmly in mind when reading any of his works that do not appear to have any explicit ethical or aesthetic content.

The idea that a form of life and mode of philosophical thought are deeply interconnected with one another is not a novel one. We can see just this basic premise in Nietzsche's claim that "every great philosophy up till now has consisted of ... the confession of its originator."[73] The germ from which this "species of involuntary and unconscious auto-biography" sprung was to be found in "the moral (or immoral)" purpose that often unwittingly lurked within it. Thus, to "understand how the abstrusest metaphysical assertions of a philosopher have been arrived at," we must first ask what kind of morality they are aiming at. This is why, Nietzsche contended, the "father of philosophy" was not to be found in an "impulse to knowledge," but rather in the moral principles of the person who would set out to philosophize in the first place. It is in this way that the primal metaphysical impetus manifests as a kind of imperious "testimony" that not only tells us how the philosopher in question lived but also how we ought to live as well.[74] There is always "a point in every philosophy at which the 'conviction' of the philosopher appears on the scene,"[75] and this conviction does not correspond to any 'reality' save the one it presupposes for itself. To speak of metaphysics, therefore, as though it were some direct and unmediated inquiry into 'reality qua reality' is to disregard its underlying moral groundwork, one that cannot be ultimately predicated on any other basis save a purely contingent one.

The problem that philosophy must face up to here is one with which it has been intimately familiar since its very inception: To what extent do our theories about the way the world is correspond to the way that it actually is apart from our ruminations on it? In posing this problem of philosophy— this problem of metaphysics—we must inevitably ask how it is we are to judge the accuracy of the theory in relation to the world as it is in itself. One could almost say that the problem of metaphysics is thus the problem of Western philosophy in general, insofar as both have been characterized by the search for the indubitable and unalterable truth at the heart of existence. The inevitable failure with which this inquiry has been met is also a point of importance. It is, in the broadest possible sense, one important aspect of the problem of metaphysics and is typified by two fervently opposed poles. The first of these is the belief that—given enough time—philosophy might reach some sort of eternal truth. Antithetical to this belief is the all too real possibility that this goal might turn out to be unattainable— despite the due course of time and our best efforts. This aspect of the problem of metaphysics, therefore, is implicitly related to a good deal of Wittgenstein's philosophical work. In the *Tractatus*, he presents a theory of language in which propositions must mirror the logical form of the world if they are to have sense. In this very strict conception of meaning, language is defined as what can be said and has a sense (i.e., what can be thought) and that which cannot be said and is senseless (i.e., what cannot be thought). The picture theory, however, quickly runs into many self-referential inconsistencies, for it falls outside of what itself construes as 'meaningful language.' Wittgenstein no doubt realized this and attempted to avoid the self-referential incoherence by making a distinction between what can be said and what can be shown. Whether he was successful in doing so is most certainly up for debate, and given his own disillusionment with his early philosophy, there is good reason for us to be hesitant to accept this distinction. The second rhetorical device that Wittgenstein employs is the 'metaphor of the ladder,' which asks us to imagine the propositions of the *Tractatus* as 'steps' that allow us to transcend the limitations of the picture theory. In so doing, we are meant to see that the *Tractatus* is, strictly speaking, nonsense, but useful nonsense nonetheless. It is no doubt true that at one level, this metaphor allows us to avoid the inherent self-referential incoherence of the picture theory, but then again, there seems to be very little reason for us to implicitly accept this metaphor save that it allows us to escape the inconsistency that is embedded within the picture theory.

In the years after he composed the *Tractatus*, Wittgenstein abandoned philosophy altogether, which is not surprising considering that if he sincerely meant—as he states in the preface—that he had believed himself "to have found, on all essential points, the final solution of the problems."[76] One cannot help but

*Everything Can Be Otherwise Than It Is*     39

notice, however, that these problems are mostly of a metaphysical nature. The unbending belief in logic as a fundamental component of reality, the picture theory of language that develops from that belief, and the mysticism that is the hallmark of the final passages of the *Tractatus*, are all metaphysical responses to metaphysical problems, even though Wittgenstein deployed his early philosophy as a tool to dispatch those very same problems. After his hiatus from philosophy, Wittgenstein, of course, would later find that many of his methods were predicated on indefensible positions, the picture theory not the least of them. In the preface to the *Philosophical Investigations*, dated 1945, Wittgenstein wrote, "For since I began to occupy myself with philosophy again, sixteen years ago, I could not but recognize grave mistakes in what I set out in that first book."[77] This realization would, in part, herald his return to Cambridge in 1929, where he began to work out a new approach to the problems that the *Tractatus* had left unresolved. The *Philosophical Investigations* represents the culmination of much of that effort but was never published during Wittgenstein's lifetime. This is due mainly to Wittgenstein's continuous dissatisfaction with his many attempts at putting together a cohesive work. In actuality, he had, more than once, secured publication of his work only to later withdraw it.[78] His final words in the preface to the *Investigations* are something of a strange admission, considering the longevity and profundity of the book's influence. "I should have liked to produce a good book. It has not turned out that way, but the time is past in which I could improve it."[79]

Much is made of the many points of departure between the *Tractatus* and the *Investigations*. The difference between the respective theories of meaning in each book stands as the most potent example of what is a somewhat superficially stark contrast between the two. The picture theory of the *Tractatus* and the language-games of the *Investigations* offer widely divergent descriptions of how words get their meanings. This is undeniably true, but beyond this difference, which much of the orthodox interpretation of Wittgenstein's work dwells on, there are many startling similarities between his early and late work. Consider his overtly staunch, anti-metaphysical stance in the *Tractatus* and the self-referentially incoherent nature of that stance. Now consider the fact that much the same problem presents itself in the *Investigations*. In that work, Wittgenstein wishes to draw our attention to the varied and multi-faceted nature and usages of language. Often dubbed as an instantiation or a precursor to the ordinary language philosophy that dominated much of the mid-twentieth-century analytic tradition, the *Investigations* implores us to look at how language *is* used, not to think about how it *ought* to be used. Just as the *Tractatus* sought to dispatch with the very same transcendental metaphysics that Feibleman points to, the *Investigations* also attempts to rid philosophy of metaphysics, especially of the idealistic sort. Indeed, in both the *Tractatus* and the *Investigations*, Wittgenstein makes little if any distinction between transcendental or ideal metaphysics and metaphysics in general, just as Feibleman had accused the Positivists of doing. This general lack of distinction leads Wittgenstein to make much the same sort of error in the *Investigations* as he does in the *Tractatus*—that is, he attempts to expunge metaphysics entirely from philosophy while employing various metaphysical techniques in order to do so.

While it is true that part of the overall argument here has to do with the futility of all attempts to escape metaphysical suppositions, this is not, in-and-of-itself, the ultimate point that I aim to make—it is merely the first link in a chain of interlocking contentions that point us to an implication of much more import. If we grant that positivism (i.e., in the anti-metaphysical sense) is a hopelessly doomed endeavor and that there can be no first principle of metaphysics that is beyond the purviews of all doubt (e.g., as the Cartesian project hoped to uncover), then the question inexorably becomes: Why reject some metaphysical suppositions while endorsing others? As I have already suggested in the Introduction, the answer to this question is an aesthetic one: There is no 'why' one way or the other. There is only a subjective preference and a will to universalize that takes pleasure in the thought that this preference can be put forth as a universal maxim.[80] There is, however, a second component to this answer—one that has yet to be stated in terms of a direct formulation. What I have in mind here is the creative side of metaphysics, the main purpose of which is to counterpoise itself to that of the aesthetic. Unlike the latter, the creative function is not concerned with ascribing agreement to everyone else. It is the very antithesis of agreement, by which I do not mean that it amounts to a matter of disagreement, for disagreement does not negate agreement. On the contrary, if we follow Jacques Rancière and take the word 'disagreement' to designate a "speech situation" in which the "contention over what speaking means" constitutes the "very rationality" of the speaking itself,[81] then it follows that disagreement is the very precondition of agreement (and vice versa).[82] Disagreement, therefore, is not opposed to the aesthetic, it is an integral component of it. Creativity, on the other hand, seeks to pose the question of how would things stand in our *weltanschauung* if we were to adopt some other set of precepts on which to predicate it? To what extent is the world imaginable as existing under different conditions of truth and falsity? Is there a boundary beyond which our ability to 'think the alternative' cannot exceed, and if so, is this

*Everything Can Be Otherwise Than It Is*      41

indicative of our rather limited imaginative capacities, or is this a restriction that belongs to reality itself? These are the questions that a creative examination of metaphysics must undertake to answer, and in so doing, it enables us to recognize, as Paul Klee has put it, that the world "in its present shape is not the only possible world," that at one time this world "looked different" than it does currently and that "in the future, [it] will look different again."[83]

There is an important caveat to be made at this point in the discussion concerning Wittgenstein's relative silence on the topics of aesthetics and creativity: what little that exists in his *Nachlass* is not ostensibly concerned with any of the problems outlined thus far. There is little to be found regarding the role of agreement or disagreement in aesthetics, nor is there any consideration of creativity as a means for the adducing of alternative metaphysical hypotheses. It is a curious thing, however, to note the degree to which Wittgenstein's work resonates with just these kinds of interpretive models, so much so that it hardly seems purely coincidental. When he tells us, for instance, in 3.031 of the *Tractatus*, "that we could not say what an 'illogical' world would look like," he is, in many respects, drawing a metaphysical limitation around the creative capacity of thought. Although it may well be a difficult conceptual feat to imagine an illogical world in which something could both be and not be at the same time, the fact that it is unthinkable is not, in and of itself, a valid proof of its veracity. No matter how much we may be wont to ascribe necessity to such 'laws of thought' as that of non-contradiction, the truth is that whatever persuasive force it may be imbued with is due largely to the inability of the human mind to operate according to alternative codes of conduct. This is not to say, we should add, that the limitations of the human mind amount to one and the same thing as the limitations of reality. If quantum mechanics has taught philosophy anything, it is that its 'rules of right reasoning' are just that: rules whose authority only depends upon the extent to which we agree (in the aesthetic sense) to abide by them. Schrödinger's cat is a case in point: The law of the excluded middle can hardly be said to apply to an object in a state of quantum superposition.[84]

I am well aware that a single laconic illustration such as the one provided above hardly constitutes reasonable grounds for the drastically revisionist interpretation of Wittgenstein I am putting forward, which is why others will be produced in the following chapters to help shore up the footing. For the moment, I would only reiterate a point that I have already discussed at some length in the Introduction. Unlike the orthodox and heterodox readings of Wittgenstein's philosophical project, my analysis of his work does not try to explain away its apparently contradictory stance on metaphysics (whether this is accomplished by making exceptions for special kinds of nonsensical statements or by showing that these statements are not nonsensical at all but rather elucidatory). Instead, what I am suggesting is that the contradiction is part and parcel of Wittgenstein's method as a whole and that the numerous objections he raises about the activity of speculative philosophical inquiry are not to be understood as an outright rejection of first philosophy per se but rather as a declaration about what constitutes 'good' and 'bad' forms of metaphysics. Just as someone might reject a particular style of painting as generally bad and another as predominantly good, Wittgenstein can be seen as making a judgment of taste as to what the best and worst ways of philosophizing consist in. His disagreements with certain metaphysical traditions and his endorsement of others are indicative of the kind of groundless assent and dissent implicit in all aesthetic appraisals of value.

For the philosopher, then, just as much as the artist, the project to be undertaken is a creative one, and behind even the most imposing edifice of philosophical rumination, there is always a point at which the system of justification on which it is predicated can no longer legitimize its own method of legitimization. When this point is reached, as it inevitably is, the only way to proceed is through aesthetic substantiation, i.e., through the putting forward of baseless metaphysical assumptions as though they were universally true and incontrovertible. Doing this, however, presents a subsequent difficulty. If there can be no ultimate justification for the propositions of metaphysics we adopt, if our assumptions, and the actions that follow from them, are merely contingent, then we must ask ourselves why it is we choose one premise over another, one belief over another, or one metaphysical construct over another. There can be no answer to this question, but nevertheless, we must choose if we are to move forward. There is nothing before the choice. Nor can there be such a thing as a non-choice, for one must choose not to choose. We therefore must choose without reason, and the act of our choosing one thing over another establishes a preferential hierarchy in the world. In the broadest possible sense, all of our knowledge is based on the necessity of choice and the preference that our decisions bear out, which is to say, again in the broadest possible manner, that the act of choosing is essentially aesthetic in nature. Not only is it subjective, but it is also groundless and yet calls for the universal ascent of everyone. This is the proposed solution to what has been described as the problem of metaphysics, and more specifically, the problem of self-referential incoherence as it is related to this problem. The following chapters will seek to explicate this argument more fully through the lens of Wittgenstein's philosophy.

*Everything Can Be Otherwise Than It Is* 43

## Notes

1 Plato, *The Republic of Plato*, 354b.

2 Marie McGinn, "Between Metaphysics and Nonsense: Elucidation in Wittgenstein's Tractatus," *The Philosophical Quarterly* 49, no. 197 (October 1999): 492.

3 Ibid.

4 Ibid.

5 Ibid.

6 Ibid., 496.

7 Ibid., 497.

8 Ibid.

9 Ibid., 503.

10 Ibid., 509.

11 McGinn, *Between Metaphysics and Nonsense*, 512.

12 A notable exception is to be found in Heidegger's *Kant and the Problem of Metaphysics*, a text that sets out to "lay the foundation of metaphysics in order thus to present the problem of metaphysics as the problem of fundamental ontology" (3). This task is accomplished, Heidegger maintains, by showing that human *Dasein* is an inseparable component of just such a fundamental ontology. Thus, the most "primordial interpretation of the basic problem of metaphysics" must also involve the "question of the finitude in man" (237), which is just another way of saying that every question of metaphysics is also a question of human existence. See *Kant and the Problem of Metaphysics*, trans. James S. Churchill (Bloomington, IN: Indiana University Press, 1965). While my own use of the phrase 'the problem of metaphysics' shares a similar concern for the indissoluble existential quality of all metaphysical questions, it nonetheless differs from it by not necessitating an emphasis on fundamental ontology. One could say, in other words, that where Heidegger dwells on the question of Being itself, I prefer to dwell on the question of the otherwise-than-Being, i.e., on the non-ontological condition of metaphysics.

13 Hartley Burr Alexande *The Problem of Metaphysics and the Meaning of Metaphysical Explanation: An Essay in Definitions* (New York: AMS Press, 1967), 128.

14 Immanuel Kant, *Critique of the Power of Judgment*, ed. Paul Guyer, trans. Paul Guyer and Eric Matthews (Cambridge: Cambridge University Press, 2000), § 17, 5: 231.

15 §1, 5: 203.

16 "When one wants to show the senselessness of metaphysical turns of phrase, one often says 'I couldn't imagine the opposite of that', or 'What would it be like if it were otherwise?'" Ludwig Wittgenstein, *Philosophical Grammar* (Berkeley: University of California Press, 2005), sec. 83. As Wittgenstein seems to imply by this line of thought, the consideration of how things can be otherwise is an important component of circumventing the confusions caused by metaphysical speculation.

For my purposes, however, what I think Wittgenstein misses here is that this 'what if' amounts to a judgment of taste in that it cannot adduce its own grounds and implicitly "ascribes the agreement of everyone," to use Kant's way of putting it (*Critique of the Power of Judgment*, §8, 5: 216). True, one can show the senselessness of any metaphysical phrase if one is willing to accept a state of affairs in which it is rendered senseless, but this demonstration of senselessness only holds if one is willing to accept—without objection—the stipulations set out in the alternative scenario this 'otherwise' puts forth.

17 Ludwig Wittgenstein, *Philosophical Grammar* (Berkeley, CA: University of California Press, 2005), 129.

18 William James, *The Will to Believe and Other Essays in Popular Philosophy* (Longmans, Green, and co., 1896), 1–2.

19 Ibid., vii–viii.

20 Ibid., vii–viii.

21 William James, *A Pluralistic Universe: Hibbert Lectures at Manchester College on the Present Situation in Philosophy* (Lincoln, NE: University of Nebraska Press, 1996), 328.

22 Friedrich Nietzsche, *Beyond Good and Evil* (Lexington, KY: SoHo Books, 2010), sec. 9.

23 Ibid., sec. 260.

24 Ibid.

25 Nietzsche, "The Birth of Tragedy from the Spirit of Music," Preface to Richard Wagner, 17.

26 Ibid., sec. 24.

27 James, *The Will to Believe*, 25.

28 René Descartes, *Meditations on First Philosophy: With Selections from the Objections and Replies*, trans. John Cottingham (Cambridge: Cambridge University Press, 1996), 17.

29 Friedrich Waismann, *Ludwig Wittgenstein and the Vienna Circle: Conversations Recorded by Friedrich Waisman*, ed. B. F. McGuinness (Malden, MA: Blackwell, 1979), 183.

30 Wittgenstein, *Tractatus Logico-Philosophicus*, 2001, 4.

31 Quoted in Ray Monk, *Ludwig Wittgenstein: The Duty of Genius* (New York: Penguin Books), 161.

32 Wittgenstein, *Tractatus Logico-Philosophicus*, 2001, 3.

33 Ibid., xxv.

34 Rudolf Carnap, "The Elimination of Metaphysics through Logical Analysis of Language," in *Logical Positivism*, ed. A. J. Ayer (New York: Free Press, 1959), 61.

35 Ibid., 63.

36 J. K. Feibleman, "The Metaphysics of Logical Positivism," *The Review of Metaphysics* 5, no. 1 (September 1951): 55.

37 Ibid., 56.

38 Ibid., 59.

39 Carnap, "The Elimination of Metaphysics," 69.

40 Martin Puchner, "Doing Logic with a Hammer: Wittgenstein's Tractatus and the Polemics of Logical Positivism," *Journal of the History of Ideas* 66, no. 2 (April 2005): 290.

41 Richard Rorty, *The Linguistic Turn: Essays in Philosophical Method* (Chicago: University of Chicago Press, 1992), 23.

42 Ibid.

43 John O. Nelson, "How Is Non-Metaphysics Possible?," *International Phenomenological Society* 30, no. 2 (December 1969): 222.

44 Ibid., 221.

45 Feibleman, "The Metaphysics of Logical Positivism," 58.

46 Nelson, "How Is Non-Metaphysics Possible?," 237.

47 Parmenides, "On Nature," in *Paramenides of Elea: A Verse Translation with Interpretative Essays and Commentary to the Text*, trans. Martin J. Henn (Westport, CT: Praeger, 2003), l. 115.

48 Lucretius, *On the Nature of Things*, trans. Martin Ferguson Smith (Indianapolis, IN: Hackett Publishing, 2001), ll. 150–1.

49 Parmenides, "On Nature," ll. 157–8.

50 Lucretius, *On the Nature of Things*, ll. 419–21.

51 G. W. F. Hegel, *The Encyclopaedia Logic: Part I of the Encyclopaedia of Philosophical Sciences with the Zusätze*, trans. T. F. Geraets, W. A. Suchting, and H. S. Harris (Indianapolis, IN: Hackett Publishing, 1991), 93.

52 Alexandre Kojève, *Introduction to the Reading of Hegel: Lectures on the Phenomenology of Spirit*, ed. Allan Bloom, trans. James H. Nichols, Jr. (New York: Basic Books, 1969), 211.

53 G. W. F. Hegel, *Hegel's Phenomenology of Spirit*, trans. A. V. Miller (Oxford: Oxford University Press, 1977), 11.

54 Ibid., 350.

55 J. N. Findlay, "Hegel's Use of Teleology," *The Monist* 48, no. 1 (January 1964): 9.

56 According to Findlay, the difference between a 'finite' and an 'infinite' teleology is that the former is dependent on a definite result to be obtained in relation to a definite situation and means of so obtaining it (8), whereas the latter concerns a multiplicity of means, ends, purposes, and contexts, none of which collectively compromise a *causa finalis sui*.

57 Slavoj Žižek, *Less Than Nothing: Hegel and the Shadow of Dialectical Materialism* (London: Verso, 2013), 50.

58 Arthur Fine has made the astute observation that the obvious "disrepute into which [Vaihinger] has fallen" over the course of the preceding century has far outpaced any systematic flaws, inconsistencies, or errors that he may have been guilty of. This is primarily due, as he claims, to the severe criticism leveled at Vaihinger by the Logical Positivists, who succeeded in turning him into a "marginal figure" to be

46     *Wittgenstein and the Problem of Metaphysics*

mocked and discarded while simultaneously ignoring the "originality, quality, or viability of his ideas." See "Fictionalism," *Midwest Studies in Philosophy* 18, no. 1 (1993): 13–14.

59 Indeed, Fine is one of the very few scholars to have even attempted a serious consideration of Vaihinger as of late. One notable exception can be found in Stephen Pollard, who penned an article on his concept of 'as if' as recently as 2010. Although a few other examples can certainly be produced, the relative obscurity to which Vaihinger has been relegated in the secondary literature is unfortunate, especially considering the interest that fictionalism has garnished in the last decade or so (as evidenced in part by a collection of essays put out by Oxford University Press in 2005 and a 2010 book by R. M. Sainsbury). For further reading see Arthur Fine, "Science Fictions: Comment on Godfrey-Smith," *Philosophical Studies: An International Journal for Philosophy in the Analytic Tradition* 143, no. 1 (March 2009): 117–25; Stephen Pollard, "'As If' Reasoning in Vaihinger and Pasch," *Erkenntnis* 73, no. 1 (July 2010): 83–95; Mark Eli Kalderon, ed., *Fictionalism in Metaphysics* (Oxford: Oxford University Press, 2005); R. M. Sainsbury, *Fiction and Fictionalism* (London: Routledge, 2010).

60 Hans Vaihinger, *The Philosophy of 'As If': A System of the Theoretical, Practical and Religious Fictions of Mankind*, trans. C. K. Ogden (Mansfield Center, CT: Martino Publishing, 2009), 77.

61 Ibid., 77.

62 While it may be true that the Absolute is indeed a necessary abstraction "for thought and speech," it does not follow from this that it is also thereby the key to unlocking "the world of reality for us." This, perhaps more than anything, is Vaihinger's main objection against Hegel's speculative method. Whenever we begin to treat abstractions "as special entities invested with life" instead of the useful chimera that they are, "Then we have committed the fundamental error of converting fictions into reality and the elements of a provisional logical scaffolding into real definitive entities" Ibid., 204.

63 Jean-Jacques Rousseau, *Discourse on the Origin of Inequality* (New York: Classic Books America, 2009), 2.

64 Jean-Jacques Rousseau, *The Social Contract*, trans. Maurice Cranston (London: Penguin, 2003), 49.

65 Thomas Hobbes, *Leviathan* (Cambridge University Press, 1904), 85.

66 For a representative sample of the secondary literature, see Peter J. Steinberger, "Hobbes, Rousseau and the Modern Conception of the State," *The Journal of Politics* 70, no. 3 (July 2008): 595–611. Steinberger argues that Hobbes took the state of nature to be essentially pre-political, whereas Rousseau's version of it is typified by its being prior to "all social, not just political, institutions" (597). Unlike many commentators, however, Steinberger is somewhat unique in his emphasis on the

similarities between Hobbes' and Rousseau's conception of the state as a bulwark "against the ever-present threat of a savage and horrific barbarism" (610–1).

67 Levinas puts the matter beautifully in *Entre Nous* when he writes, "In doing what I willed to do, I did a thousand and one things I hadn't willed to do." *Entre Nous: On Thinking-of-the-Other*, trans. Michael B. Smith and Barbara Harshav (New York: Columbia University Press, 1998), 3.

68 Hegel, *Phenomenology of Spirit*, 111.

69 Friedrich Engels, "Preface to the 1888 English Edition," in *The Communist Manifesto* (London: Pluto, 2008), 96.

70 Understood from the broadest possible perspective, all world-riddles are expressions of a latent desire within the human mind to uncover what we might call "the meaning of the earth," to borrow Nietzsche's phrase. Of course we must be cognizant of the all-too-real possibility that this desire may never be fully and finally satiated, to say nothing of the fact that all such "world-enigmas" could, as Ernst Haeckel reminds us, amount to nothing more than the mere "creations of the human imagination." Vaihinger too thought the "riddles of the universe" unsolvable, if for no other reason that they consist in "contradictions created by ourselves." It is, he continues, therefore ridiculous to desire an understanding of the world "for all understanding consists in an actual or imaginary reduction to the known," and this 'known' can always, in the end, turn "out to be something 'unknown.'" See *Thus Spoke Zarathustra* (Cambridge: Cambridge University Press, 2006), 6; *The Riddle of the Universe*, trans. Joseph McCabb (London: Watts & Co., 1934), 250; *The Philosophy of 'As If*,' 38, 171.

71 In saying as much, however, I do not necessarily wish to disparage—in the way Freud did—this "oceanic" feeling of "an indissoluble bond, of being one with external world as a whole"(12). Even if we were to grant that the roots of this "ego-feeling" can be traced back to an "early phase" (19) of our development in which we failed to distinguish between the self and the external world, this would not necessarily warrant an outright dismissal of it. If anything, all that Freud has shown is that this artifact of "infantile helplessness" (ibid.) out of which this oceanic feeling grew is a purely fictive one. Whether this feeling is one worthy of retention in the well-adjusted adult is a question that is certainly up for debate, even though Freud was quite clearly concerned about its potential for the "restoration of limitless narcissism" (ibid.). See Sigmund Freud, *Civilization and Its Discontents*, trans. James Strachey (New York: W. W. Norton & Company, 1962).

72 Ludwig Wittgenstein, "A Lecture on Ethics," *The Philosophical Review* 74, no. 1 (January 1965): 12.

73 Nietzsche, *Beyond Good and Evil*, sec. 6.

74 Ibid.

75 Ibid., sec. 8.

76 Wittgenstein, *Tractatus Logico-Philosophicus*, 2001, 4.

77 Wittgenstein, *Philosophical Investigations*, 4.

78 P. M. S. Hacker and Joachim Schulte, eds., "The Text of the Philosopische Untersuchungen," in *Philosophical Investigations*, 4th ed. (Oxford: Wiley-Blackwell, 2009), xviii–xxiii.

79 Wittgenstein, *Philosophical Investigations*, 4.

80 The pleasure taken in assertions of this sort can be compounded when others in their turn acquiesce to them, thus producing conditions favorable for the development of what we habitually term as 'truths.' That is to say, in other words, that given enough agreement amongst a sufficiently large number of people, the subjective origin of a commonly held judgment of taste can become obscured by the collective accord in which it is held, thus giving it the appearance of being objectively universal when in reality, however, they belong to the class of fallacies known as *argumentum ad populum*.

81 Jacques Rancière, *Disagreement: Politics and Philosophy*, trans. Julie Rose (Minneapolis, MN: University of Minnesota Press, 2004), xi.

82 We may find a parallel here to Wittgenstein's treatment of tautologies and contradictions in the *Tractatus*, which are, he tells us, "Not pictures of reality" in that "they do not represent any possible situations" (4.462). A tautology leaves the whole of reality open whereas "a contradiction fills the whole of logical space leaving no point of it for reality" (4.463). Tautologies and contradictions do "not stand in any representational relation to reality" (4.462) and thus they constitute "the limiting cases" of reality (4.466). In terms of our current discussion, we might say that for any being to exist, it must be possible for it also to not exist.

83 Paul Klee, "On Modern Art," in *Art in Theory, 1900–2000: An Anthology of Changing Ideas*, ed. Paul Wood and Charles Harrison (Malden, MA: Blackwell, 2003), 367.

84 W. V. Quine once famously suggested that "no statement is immune to revision" in the face of new empirical evidence, and that modifications of "the logical law of the excluded middle" may be required "as a means of simplifying quantum mechanics." See "Main Trends in Recent Philosophy: Two Dogmas of Empiricism," *The Philosophical Review* 60, no. 1 (1951): 40.

2

# The Rest Is Silence

One of the principal difficulties one must overcome if one is to undertake an inquiry into Wittgenstein's metaphysics is that he seemingly disavows the very possibility of doing it in the first place. A significant portion of the *Tractatus* is devoted, after all, to developing the idea that the fundamental structure of the world must, by necessity, seamlessly coincide with the laws of logic. This premise, of course, would lead him to the unavoidable conclusion that for language to be adequately meaningful, it must share the logical form of that which it depicts. As such, he says, the only true method of philosophizing would be the following:

> To say nothing except what can be said, i.e. propositions of natural science—i.e. something that has nothing to do with philosophy—and then, whenever someone else wanted to say something metaphysical, to demonstrate to him that he failed to give a meaning to certain signs in his propositions. Although it would not be satisfying to the other person—he would not have the feeling that we were teaching him philosophy—*this* method would be the only strictly correct one.[1]

Whatever the merits or demerits of this method, one thing is abundantly clear: Wittgenstein himself did not—perhaps could not—practice it. However assiduous and vehement his rebuttal of the metaphysical impulse might be, the severity of it does not adequately disguise just how much he was prone to indulge in the very compulsion he would demonize. Rather, it only serves to arouse suspicions as regards the hidden motivations that undergird those protestations—a phenomenon that in the psychoanalytic parlance is termed 'reaction-formation.' To take the renunciation at face value, however, is to invite the possibility of glossing over the numerous metaphysical suppositions that abound in Wittgenstein's early work.

Take, for example, the following claim made by Wittgenstein in his *Notebooks* from the years 1914 to 1916,[2] "The logic of the world is prior to all truth and falsehood."[3] Although it may come off as something of an innocuous declaration, it is hardly devoid of metaphysical allusions, the most obvious of which concerns the nature of existence generally: The world has an order, and that order is logical. This world-logic both precedes and enables all delineations between truth and falsehood and thus not only says something about what reality is (it is logical), it also tells us how it is structured (it is hierarchical). This latter point is, for all intents and purposes, nothing all that novel in the annals of philosophy: Wittgenstein—like so many others before him—would appear to be claiming that we must first gain some metaphysical clarity about what there is before it is possible to proceed onto the epistemological question of what can be known. One of the principal goals of so much of Wittgenstein's early work is not, therefore, to displace the whole of metaphysics from philosophy, but to put the *correct* metaphysical method clearly within our view and thereafter remain silent about it. This is the cure to our philosophical ailments: to not talk about them— to repress them so that they no longer trouble us. The problem with this tactic, however, is that it rarely, if ever, succeeds—the more pronounced the repression, the more marked the reaction to it. We see this quite clearly in much of Wittgenstein's early philosophy: Despite all his best efforts, he could not refrain from saying what he claimed could not be said.

It is not surprising, then, that a self-referential inconsistency should present itself here. According to Wittgenstein, any proposition that does not accurately correspond to the logical structure of that which it pictures must necessarily be categorized as metaphysical nonsense. However, in so doing, we would also have to reject the picture theory itself, for it too does not depict the logical structure of anything and is, as such, metaphysically nonsensical according to its own rules. We thus have a conundrum to consider. On the one hand, we ought really to do as Wittgenstein suggests and keep quiet about metaphysics, but on the other, we need to speak metaphysically if we are going to establish our need to keep quiet about metaphysics. In an attempt to dissolve the problem, Wittgenstein offers the following metaphor:

> My propositions serve as elucidations in the following way: anyone who understands me eventually recognizes them as nonsensical, when he has used them—as steps—to climb up beyond them. (He must, so to speak, throw away the ladder after he as climbed up it.) He must transcend these propositions, and then he will see the world aright.[4]

Exactly what Wittgenstein was alluding to in this by now much disputed example has spawned a veritable cottage industry of speculative interpretation

*The Rest Is Silence*

with little by way of accord amongst the various disputants. One thing, however, seems all but incontrovertible: Whatever import the ladder metaphor might have for the overall scope of the *Tractatus,* it most certainly does not fall under the rubric of a meaningful proposition, and one wonders how a statement devoid of sense can be elucidatory in any way, shape, or form. There is no clear-cut solution to this problem (even Wittgenstein was somewhat at a loss in his effort to formulate one), but a significant component of it must lie in the difference between 'saying' and 'showing,' a topic we will consider in more depth later on in this chapter. Suffice it to say, for now, Wittgenstein's solution to his metaphysical difficulty can be summed up thusly, "What *can* be shown *cannot* be said."[5] Thus we must take the *Tractatus* as an endeavor to *show* us the correct method of metaphysics and not to tell us about it.[6]

Some of the difficulties outlined above have been the subject of ongoing debate within Wittgensteinian scholarship since the *Tractatus* was first published in 1921. Among the early positivistic interpretations, A. J. Ayer's 1934 essay "Demonstration of the Impossibility of Metaphysics" is an excellent example. It is an essay that, by its author's admission, was inspired by the work of Wittgenstein,[7] which is readily apparent in terms of the essay's heightened anti-metaphysical sentiment—a sentiment that Ayer no doubt picks up, at least in part, from the *Tractatus.* Unlike Wittgenstein, however, Ayer places a much higher premium on the role of experience in establishing a criterion for demarcating metaphysical propositions from meaningful ones. As Ayer puts it, "Metaphysical propositions are by definition such as no possible experience could verify, and as the theoretical possibility of verification has been taken as our criterion of significance, there is no difficulty in concluding that metaphysical propositions are meaningless."[8] Ayer's criterion of verification via experience would, as he believes, show metaphysical propositions to be meaningless if, that is, he had some method for demonstrating that his criterion for identifying them is correct. But the criterion as Ayer formulated it, is, by way of its own rule, meaningless metaphysics, simply because no possible experience can verify that the correct method of verification is via experience. Thus the assertion 'no future experience will confirm any metaphysical assertion' is itself an assertion that cannot be confirmed by any experience, past, present, or future.

In general, then, we can say that the definition of a metaphysical proposition is one that cannot provide for itself the basis of its own verification. What is immediately made evident by this definition, however, is that metaphysics is indispensable to philosophy, despite Ayer's rigorous attempt to discard it. If anything, he makes an admission to this of sorts.

# 52    *Wittgenstein and the Problem of Metaphysics*

> In our criterion we have something that is presupposed in any . . . philosophical enquiry. . . . For the business of philosophy is to give definitions. . . . We must adopt some rule according to which we conduct our enquiry, and by reference to which we determine whether its conclusions are correct. In formulating our criterion we are attempting to show what this rule should be. We cannot do more.[9]

Ayer is quite right, of course. We can do no more than to adopt some rule or definition by which we must conduct an inquiry. However, whether we are justified in so doing is not verifiable by experience or by any other self-evident criterion whatsoever. Such criteria of verifiability, even Ayer's, are thus metaphysical 'pseudo-propositions,' as he calls them. In all fairness to Ayer, we should take care to note that he anticipates this objection with no uncertainty:

> If we admit that the proposition in which we attempt to formulate our criterion of significance is nonsensical, does not our whole demonstration of the impossibility of metaphysics collapse? We may be able to *see* that metaphysical propositions are nonsensical and by making a special set of nonsensical utterances we may induce others to see it also.[10]

As Ayer no doubt recognized, his proof of the impossibility of metaphysics, if it is to be successful, must admit the following proviso: In order for the proof not to contradict itself, it must admit of a 'special set' of 'sensible' nonsensical utterances. The assertion, however, that we need a special set of nonsensical utterances to avoid the paradox of denying nonsensical utterances is just another in an ever-increasing line of metaphysical propositions. Ayer could have just as easily cut his losses and admitted to only one metaphysical proposition (his criterion of verifiability) and been done with it. Instead, he attempts to give credence to his criterion by evoking the claim that it is a member of a special set of propositions and therefore not under the jurisdiction of its own rules, which at best only serves to shift the metaphysical burden of proof from one proposition to another, and at worst threatens us with the possibility of a string of metaphysical propositions *ad infinitum*.

What hope is there for Ayer's project then if every attempt to disprove metaphysics necessitates the use of metaphysics? In his article "The Myth of the Metaphysical Circle: An Analysis of the Contemporary Crisis of the Critique of Metaphysics" Herbert De Vriese advances a potential solution to this impasse. His argument centers on the claim that the contemporary discourse on metaphysics suffers from a "widespread and virtually unchallenged acceptance in contemporary philosophy of an inescapable circular relationship between metaphysics and its critique."[11] This "unchallenged acceptance" takes one of four forms. The first is the assertion that "critique is metaphysical,"

> Which reflects the view that criticism is an immanent part of metaphysical thinking.... The core of their argument is that metaphysics is, essentially, a self-critical discipline. Engaging in this way of thinking requires self-criticism; it means exploring the question of what metaphysics is supposed to be and justifying every decision taken. Criticism, in short, is identified by definition as part of metaphysical thinking.[12]

The second of these suggests that "critique produces metaphysics." This

> strategy is close to the first. It espouses the view that critiquing metaphysics is an immanent part of the history of metaphysics. The underlying thought here is, not that a particular type of criticism is *ipso facto* part of some metaphysical project, but that critique is the driving force behind the historical development of the metaphysical tradition.[13]

The third of these interpretations "holds that every critique of metaphysics necessarily departs from metaphysical premises.... This view is expressed in ... exposing the hidden metaphysical assumptions of renowned opponents of metaphysics."[14] The last strategy that De Vriese identifies is "the wholesale rejection of metaphysics as such.... These approaches essentially come down to the observation that the absolute rejection of metaphysics must be relativized, because such criticism is either a purely self-serving, self-defeating, or self-overestimating argument."[15]

Part of the problem, as De Vriese sees it, is that the vicious circle that we seem to have fallen into depends on a broadly conceived notion of what metaphysics is. As such, the belief that "the critique of metaphysics cannot free itself from metaphysics"[16] must necessarily include a radical anti-metaphysical metaphysics without contradicting itself. "If it is true that metaphysics can only be contested by metaphysics," De Vriese asks, "Why not take seriously the 'metaphysical' rejections of the entire history of metaphysics?"[17] The answer to the question is that such ways of thinking have become "philosophically illegitimate"[18] for contemporary metaphysicians. De Vriese's point is valid in as much as it is currently *en vogue* to eschew most positivistic leaning philosophies within the greater corpus of metaphysical research. In truth, one cannot deny the possibility of anti-metaphysics any more than one can do likewise for metaphysics. One can only point to the fact that anti-metaphysics is self-referentially incoherent and leave it at that. This does not, however, *prove* anti-metaphysics to be untenable; it simply requires us to abide by a contradiction.

54  *Wittgenstein and the Problem of Metaphysics*

In an attempt to shore up what it is we mean by 'metaphysics', De Vriese offers his own definition based on its traditional historical aims (which he admits is "too broad to comprehensively capture the nature of metaphysics"[19]).

> The field of metaphysics can be delimited by reference to five major tendencies: an idealistic tendency to consider thought-objects ... as a primary, underived reality; a speculative tendency to acquire or develop knowledge beyond the limits of experience; a systematic tendency to reduce difference to unity within the framework of a rational order; a foundational tendency to provide ultimate grounds for knowledge and reality; and a totalizing tendency to think in terms of wholes.[20]

According to this definition, De Vriese argues that historical challenges to metaphysics, such as Hume's skeptical critique, and Wittgenstein's later linguistic criticism, do not properly belong to the field of philosophical inquiry that has usually been understood by the moniker 'metaphysics.' Even according to this definition, Hume's skepticism of metaphysics, based as it is in his commitment to empiricism, must assume that experience is self-evidently the 'correct' philosophical foundation. Experience does not show this, however, and Hume's philosophy is thus 'metaphysics' even according to De Vriese's definition, simply for the reason that the dogmatic ascription to empiricism constitutes 'knowledge beyond the limits of experience.' As for the metaphysical implications of Wittgenstein's later philosophy, that is a topic that will be dealt with more fully in the next chapter. Although De Vriese claims that the "general statement of the inescapability of metaphysics is nothing but an assumption, and the radical consequences to which it leads show that it is a highly improbable assumption,"[21] one cannot help but notice a few of his own assumptions at work. The first of these, no doubt, is that 'radical consequences' produce 'highly improbable assumptions.' Take Einstein's special theory of relativity, for example, the second axiom of which asserts "the constancy of the velocity of light, from which follows the relativity of spatial and temporal measurements."[22] The 'assumption' that this axiom makes, namely that the speed of light in a vacuum is constant for all observers in all frames of reference, is not 'highly improbable' in the sense that all hitherto experimental data has confirmed it (though one must admit that it is nevertheless an assumption because it is in principle 'falsifiable' in Popper's sense). From such a relatively indubitable assertion, we are, of course, led to the 'radical consequence' that there can be no such thing as 'absolute' time and space in the classical Newtonian sense. The point being: There is no necessary connection between 'radical consequences' and 'highly improbable assumptions.'

*The Rest Is Silence* 55

Beyond this initial objection, we can see still other assumptions that dog De Vriese's reasoning. His attempt to "demonstrate that the categorical assertion of a circular relationship between metaphysics and critique cannot be logically justified"[23] is a case in point. Let us consider what 'logically justified' means for him: self-evidence, or at least the possibility of discovering it. Therein he is clearly reverting to a metaphysics that is playing possum, inasmuch as the 'search for the indubitable' has been one of the primary goals of metaphysicians throughout history (one which he fails to identify). De Vriese's claim that there is no 'logical justification' of the 'metaphysical circle' leads us not away from the circle but directly into it. The justification for entering this circle is not that the 'critique of metaphysics' produces metaphysics, but rather that there can be no ultimate validation of any axiomatic assertion whatsoever and that any mode of argumentation, whether it be critique or otherwise, must be predicated on such unfounded metaphysical definitions. Simply forestalling the justification via an appeal to self-evidence—whether through the use of logic or some other method—will only shift the burden of proof from one assumption to another.

The difficulty one inevitably encounters when attempting to definitively substantiate a definition is well known to anyone acquainted with even the most basic principles of geometry. It is a "familiar fact," as Hans Reichenbach notes in his essay "The Philosophical Significance of the Theory of Relativity," that all units of measurement are "a matter of definition."[24] Whether or not a meter is really equivalent to 1/299,792,458 of the distance traveled by light in a vacuum over the course of one second is not a question that can be answered without arguing in circles. This also applies, as Reichenbach goes on to observe, to "the comparison of distances," which is also "a matter of definition." To say that one distance "is congruent to another distance situated at a different place" is not a proposition that can "be proved to be true; it can only be maintained in the sense of a definition." Indeed, the only way we can speak of equivalence in this situation is "after a definition of congruence" has been given.[25] We must take care to remember, however, that the "definitional character of fundamental concepts" is always arbitrary, and that along with a "change of ... definitions" comes any number of alternative "descriptional systems."[26]

One of the things that the Theory of Relativity teaches us, therefore, is that it makes no sense to say—in absolute terms—that two separate distances are proportionate without postulating what would count as 'congruence' in a given situation. While various definitional systems may be devised for making divergent standards of measurement "equivalent to each other" via "a suitable transformation,"[27] we should not make the mistake of inferring from this, as

Reichenbach does, that these descriptions, therefore, amount to nothing more than different ways of expressing "the same physical content."[28] By definition, 1 inch is roughly equal to 2.54 centimeters. That this is true is easily shown by applying a formula of conversion—namely 1/0.39370. To assume, however, that they consequently refer to different but equivalent physical lengths is to adopt quasi-Newtonian absolutism. It cannot be proven whether 1 inch and 2.54 centimeters refer to the same physical length without resorting to an arbitrarily accepted definition that tells us as much. In other words, the definition cannot be separated from the physical content and vice versa. We therefore cannot infer that 'commensurate descriptions' express the same 'physical content' without begging the question. We may only surmise that the length of 1 inch can be converted into a number of centimeters that approximates a physical equivalency—which no more amounts to a proof than does the claim to self-evidence.

The above considerations are made in order to set the tone of this chapter. The argument being put forth here is that Wittgenstein's philosophical development can be read as an attempt to escape the vicious metaphysical circle that we seem to have fallen into and that the way to do so is through the poetic gesture. This chapter will be devoted to a reading of Wittgenstein's *Tractatus Logico-Philosophicus*. In that book, there is no doubt that Wittgenstein takes up a partially anti-metaphysical position, but it is also just as certain that Wittgenstein employs his own metaphysical strategies in substitution of those he rejects. This does not, however, lead him into a vicious circle—there is no self-referential inconsistency in denying one metaphysical assertion in favor of another (this is simply the way in which aesthetics functions as the determining apparatus of our metaphysical axioms). The vicious circle arises not from an overt critique of metaphysics but because a primary implication of Wittgenstein's metaphysics is that metaphysics itself cannot be given any meaning within language. The whole endeavor of the *Tractatus*, as far as it is an attempt to use metaphysics to explicate the senselessness of metaphysics, is an attempt to say what language will not allow us to say. This is certainly not unbeknownst to Wittgenstein. Given the logical frame of reference that he postulates as the primary metaphysical structure of reality, it is all but obvious. His solution to the problem of metaphysics, that logic shows its sense, is an attempt to avoid the contradiction inherent in his theory. As I will argue, however, Wittgenstein's doctrine of showing is simply a reiteration (albeit in a new form) of an old philosophical hat: indubitability.

Though the *Tractatus* was published in 1922, it had "received its final form" in the summer of 1918.[29] In truth, Wittgenstein had been doing work in philosophy after his arrival at Cambridge in 1911, the accumulated effort of which would result in the highly condensed propositions of the *Tractatus*. The fact that Wittgenstein's thinking underwent such long periods of maturation with no tangible finished product to show for it was a scholarly habit born out of his self-perceived inability to give his thoughts the degree of polish that he desired. This was a character trait that Bertrand Russell noted. "He has the artist's feeling that he will produce the perfect thing or nothing – I explained how he wouldn't get a degree or be able to teach unless he learnt to write imperfect things."[30] The laborious care that he took in formulating the *Tractatus* is evident in its placid and pristine sequence of numbered statements, which often do not provide the background against which they may be understood and without which it can be difficult to glean their intended meaning. It is also, therefore, difficult to apprehend the problem with which Wittgenstein concerns himself. This is perhaps one of the reasons Wittgenstein eventually came to reject the picture theory—it does not take into consideration the malleability of language according to the context in which it is given meaning. His realization of this oversight is recounted in an anecdote Wittgenstein told to both Norman Malcolm and G. H. von Wright. It recalls an exchange that took place between himself and the Italian economist Piero Sraffa

> in which Wittgenstein insisted that a proposition and that which it describes must have the same 'logical form'. . . . Sraffa made a Neapolitan gesture of brushing his chin with his fingertips, asking: 'What is the logical form of *that*?' This, according to the story, broke the hold on Wittgenstein of the Tractarian idea that a proposition must be a 'picture' of the reality it describes.[31]

A seemingly ancillary contention to those that have thus far been suggested is that Wittgenstein's philosophy does not entirely make sense unless we read him, first and foremost, as an artist. Many of the people who knew or met Wittgenstein have remarked that his temperament was artistic in inclination, including Rudolf Carnap. "His point of view and his attitude toward people and problems, even theoretical problems, were much more similar to those of a creative artist than to those of a scientist; one might almost say, similar to those of a religious prophet or a seer."[32] Although the *Tractatus* is concerned almost entirely with logic, Wittgenstein remarks in a letter to Ludwig von Ficker, "My work consists of two parts: the one presented here plus all that I have *not* written. And it is precisely this second part that is the important one."[33] What is left out of Wittgenstein's book, of course, is the ethical and the aesthetic. While there is certainly a degree of truth to this bifurcated division of the *Tractatus*—inasmuch as there is an ethical and aesthetic component to remaining silent for

Wittgenstein—it is not as silent on those topics as he might suggest. First of all, the *Tractatus* is as much a work of art as it is a work of philosophy and taken as such, it shows us (more than it tells us) what Wittgenstein's conception of art was like: minimalistic but beautiful. Second, even though it is not possible to say what cannot be said, there is an ethical virtue in the attempt itself. We are also therefore given a glimpse into Wittgenstein's ethics: striving to do what cannot be done.

The larger part of this chapter, more specifically, will be given over to an exegesis of the implicit metaphysics of the *Tractatus*. There can be little doubt that Wittgenstein, from the very first lines of the text, is giving us what amounts to a conception of the true nature of reality as he believes it to be:

1 The world is all that is the case.
1.1 The world is the totality of facts, not of things.
1.11 The world is determined by the facts, and by their being *all* the facts.
1.12 For the totality of facts determines what is the case.
1.13 The facts in logical space are the world.

What is fascinating about Wittgenstein's style of argumentation is the axiomatic quality of the assertions he makes. Like Nietzsche's aphorisms, the propositions of the *Tractatus* offer little by way of evidence in their favor. They are simply stated, though with such aesthetic force, that any evidence that might be offered in their favor seems as if it would be either an unnecessary afterthought or, worse, a detriment to their beauty (which is, of course, their chief appeal). In truth, however, no evidence is given because none can be given. Axioms, by their very nature, are not provable. We either accept them, or we do not. This, however, is what metaphysics chiefly consists of: axioms. Wittgenstein, unlike many other philosophers, dispenses with the charade of presenting 'evidence' for metaphysical propositions and instead puts them forth without any such support.

Beyond this initial point, there are still other examples in the *Tractatus* where we can see Wittgenstein engaging in what seems to be speculative first philosophy. Take, for example, the assertion that "the completely general propositions can all be formed *a priori*,"[34] which is one of the central themes of the *Tractatus*. I would even go so far as to argue that it forms the metaphysical crux of his whole argument. The entire edifice of Wittgenstein's logic rests on the possibility of such general propositions *a priori*, and he sees their possibility as being essentially bound to what he believes is our ability to analyze simple propositions from complex ones. "It seems that the idea of the SIMPLE is already to be found contained in that of the complex and in the idea of analysis, and in such a way that we come to this idea

*The Rest Is Silence*                                                                 59

quite apart from any examples of simple objects, . . . and we realize the existence of the simple object—*a priori*—as a logical necessity."[35] Although Wittgenstein is intellectually committed to this doctrine, he does tentatively explore the possibility that simples are not logically necessary in his *Notebooks*. "*Is it*, A PRIORI, *clear that in analysing we must arrive at simple components—is this, e.g., involved in the concept of analysis—*, or is analysing *ad infinitum* possible?—Or is there in the end even a third possibility? . . . Nothing seems to speak against infinite divisibility."[36] Wittgenstein raises an interesting metaphysical question here. If nothing logically prevents us from infinitely analyzing components into smaller and smaller constituents, why should we settle on the supposition that there are such things as 'simple components' that may not be further analyzed at all? Yet, if we do not settle on this supposition, it becomes difficult to make the case that 'the world is the totality of facts, not of things,' for there would be no possibility of a 'totality of facts' if each fact could be infinitely divided into other facts. In short, we are faced with two differing views about the nature of existence. One holds it to be finite and the other infinite. One is constrained by boundaries; the other is not. It is clear that Wittgenstein holds the former metaphysical supposition to be true, but of course there is a substantial difference between a supposition and a fact, and telling the difference is no small feat.

At base, Wittgenstein is struggling to devise a demonstration of the necessity of simple facts that cannot be further analyzed into still further facts, but such a proof is extraordinarily difficult to formulate, and Wittgenstein, in the end, is ultimately unable to do so, but can only admit that "*it keeps on* forcing itself upon us that there is some simple indivisible, an element of being, in brief a thing."[37] This, then, is the only proof that Wittgenstein may fall back on: self-evidence, i.e., the force of the idea itself. Does this, then, amount to a demonstration of its necessity? This is a metaphysical question that proves much more troublesome to answer. Wittgenstein was not deterred by the fact that no one had yet to discover some "simple, indivisible element" of a proposition.

> It does not go against our feeling, that *we* cannot analyse PROPOSITIONS so far as to mention the elements by name; no, we feel that the WORLD must consist of elements. And it appears as if that were identical with the proposition that the world must be what it is, it must be definite. Or in other words, what vacillates is our determinations, not the world.[38]

The feeling of certitude that Wittgenstein is describing above is most notably marked by his conviction that, no matter what happens, a change of mind is all but impossible to conceive of. The failure to demonstratively point out any example of basic propositional units, for instance, was not reason enough for Wittgenstein to disregard their necessity. In truth, however, basic propositional units are only necessary for the kind of philosophical inquiry that Wittgenstein wishes to make. They are not necessary to all philosophical inquiry *a priori*. Rather, it is Wittgenstein's desire to see the world as definite rather than indefinite that is the cause of his certitude. After all, if it is our determinations that vacillate and not the world, then the determination that the 'world is definite' would similarly be subject to an alteration of opinion. The 'feeling of being unconditionally right' is not a result of the accuracy of one's determinations; the feeling can occur even if a determination turns out to be incorrect. Rather, what leads us to the experience of certitude is an aesthetic sensibility that allows us to universalize the feeling of pleasure and expect that others ought to comport to that feeling as well. In other words, the belief that 'I am correct' does not arise from a proof but rather from the conviction that things would be better off one way as opposed to another. In Wittgenstein's case—at least in his early philosophy—his aesthetic inclination moved him towards the belief that the world must be definite. The fact that he changed his mind about the nature of language in his later work is not due to the discovery of an error but rather to a change in his aesthetic preference wrought by the creative instinct that things can always be different than they are.

Although Wittgenstein makes a few brief references to aesthetics in the *Tractatus*, the aesthetic underpinnings of its metaphysics are not in any overt treatment of the subject but rather in the treatment of logic itself as the *prima facie* condition of existence. Wittgenstein's unalterable belief in logic as constituting the fundamental nature of existence—and his faith that this structure could be mirrored in language—was not brought about by some definitive proof but by his aesthetic inclinations. This is seen in propositions such as 2.012, for instance, where he states, "In logic nothing is accidental: if a thing can occur in states of affairs, the possibility of the state of affairs must be written into the thing itself."[39] Logic does not deal in potential or actual states of affairs, but rather in the possibility of them. Thus, in 2.0121 we read, "Logic deals with every possibility and all possibilities are its facts." To put it in other words, logic is tautological; it says nothing about what exists, only about what can exist. Because existence is barred to anything that is illogical, logic represents the very horizon of existence itself, a point that is made in 3.031. "It used to be said that God could create anything except what would be contrary to the laws of logic.— The truth is that we could not *say* what an 'illogical' world would look like." Not only could we not say what an illogical world would look like, the intimate relationship between thought and language for Wittgenstein prevents us from even thinking about it. "Thought can never be of anything illogical, since, if it were, we should have to think illogically."[40]

We cannot think illogically because to do so is to think about what cannot—under any circumstances—be a state of affairs. This would amount to 'thinking about what cannot exist.' If it is possible for a state of affairs to be thought of, it is also thereby possible for that state of affairs to come about. This, then, is how we arrive at the picture theory of language: whatever can exist can also be meaningfully represented in thought.

| 2.1 | We picture facts to ourselves. |
|---|---|
| 2.11 | A Picture presents a situation in logical space, the existence and non-existence of states of affairs. |
| 2.12 | A picture is a model of reality. |
| 2.141 | A picture is a fact. |
| 2.151 | Pictorial form is the possibility that things are related to one another in the same way as the elements of the picture. |
| 2.1511 | *That* is how a picture is attached to reality; it reaches right out to it. |
| 2.16 | If a fact is to be a picture, it must have something in common with what it depicts. |
| 2.17 | What a picture must have in common with reality, in order to be able to depict it—correctly or incorrectly—in the way it does, is its pictorial form. |

The possibility of pictorial form, like the possibility of existence or non-existence of a state of affairs, is written into the pictorial form itself. There can therefore be no such thing as a pictorial form that correctly depicts an impossible state of affairs (i.e., an illogical one), for there would be no form that a picture could share with it. Pictorial form, as a mode of representation, is limited to the realm of possible states of affairs, as is indicated by 2.171. "A picture can depict any reality whose form it has." What pictorial form cannot depict, however, is its own form; but it can show it. It cannot, in other words, state in logical form the proposition 'this is the logical form of picturing.' In order to do so, pictorial form would have to step outside of itself in order to picture itself. That is because the logical form of picturing involves the concept of exteriority—the picture of a state of affairs must be outside of the state of affairs that it is representing. We cannot, therefore, say what pictorial form is because in order to do so, we would require the use of pictorial form. Wittgenstein does, however, make it clear that pictorial form does display its structure. The basis for the distinction between saying and showing is first laid out in propositions 2.172–2.174.

2.172 A picture cannot, however, depict its pictorial form: it displays it.

2.173 A picture represents its subject from a position outside it. (Its standpoint is its representational form.) That is why a picture represents its subject correctly or incorrectly.

2.174 A picture cannot, however, place itself outside its representational form.

Representation, according to the above definition, must always be external to that which it depicts. Since a picture must stand outside of what is pictured, a picture cannot depict the logic of its own form. Just as a painting of a tree is not the same thing as a painting of a painting of a tree, a picture of a state of affairs is not the same thing as a picture of a picture of a state of affairs. Even if one were to construct such a second-order 'picture of a picture,' it is not as if this would amount to a picture that pictured its own form. Although the logical form of the first picture would be contained in the second, the second picture would nevertheless not be a picture of itself. Rather, a picture of a state of affairs shows its form simply by way of its being a picture. It shows its sense; it does not depict it. Just as we do not need a painting of a painting of a tree to understand what a painting of a tree is, we likewise do not need a picture of a picture of a state of affairs to understand what a picture is. If we understand the sense of what 'representation' means—that it stands outside of that which it depicts—we also understand that a second-order representation becomes extraneous, indeed, even impossible. We cannot represent the 'form of representation,' for that would require us to step outside of representation in order to do so. In other words, a picture is a picture, and we cannot say any more about it than that.

One of the most crucial realizations Wittgenstein would come to in his early work was the foundational role that both tautologies and contradictions played in logic. Even Russell was willing to admit that his attempt to give a logical basis to mathematics was indebted to it. In his 1919 book *Introduction to Mathematical Philosophy*, he notes, "The importance of 'tautology' for a definition of mathematics was pointed out to me by my former pupil Ludwig Wittgenstein."[41] In a letter written to Wittgenstein in August of the same year, Russell says of the *Tractatus*, "I am convinced you are right in your main contention, that logical prop[osition]s are tautologies, which are not true in the sense that substantial prop[osition]s are true."[42] Although this is certainly one of Wittgenstein's points in the *Tractatus*, it is by no means the main one, as Wittgenstein was quick to point out to Russell.

Now I am afraid you haven't really got hold of my main contention, to which the whole business of logical prop[osition]s is only a corollary. The main point is the theory of what can be expressed (gesagt) by prop[osition]s – i.e. by language – (and, which comes to the same, what can be *thought* ) and what can not be expressed by prop[osition]s, but only shown (gezeigt); which, I believe, is the cardinal problem of philosophy.[43]

The cardinal problems of philosophy arise, so Wittgenstein thinks, because philosophers throughout history have attempted to say what can only be shown and to think what cannot be thought. Wittgenstein's unassailable and definitive solution to these problems, therefore, is to clarify those things which can only be shown so that we may thereafter be silent about them. Of course, the *Tractatus* is anything but silent about such issues. It says a great deal, for instance, about such things as simple indefinable elements of being—and quite lucidly, at that—which, according to its own tenets, should not be possible at all. Yet, surely one can read its propositions and understand them. This tension in the *Tractatus* is never quite resolved, and Wittgenstein's attempt to deflate it by claiming that simples show their sense instead of saying it is only a reformulation of the metaphysical appeal to self-evidence. This is, of course, despite the fact that Wittgenstein thought that the idea of 'self-evidence' was completely superfluous in logic. In 5.4731, he writes, "Self-evidence, which Russell talked about so much, can become dispensable in logic, only because language itself prevents every logical mistake.— What makes logic a priori is the *impossibility* of illogical thought." Certainly, we may recognize that, in theory, illogical thought is metaphysically impossible, for this amounts to saying only that what cannot be a possible state of affairs cannot also not be meaningfully spoken of in language. In practice, however, we must be able to distinguish between a proposition with and without a sense. For it is not impossible to say something illogical; it is only impossible to give an illogical proposition a meaning. Wittgenstein, in 6.3751, gives us an example of what a logical impossibility might look like. "The simultaneous presence of two colours at the same place in the same visual field is impossible, in fact logically impossible, since it is ruled out by the logical structure of colour." While it may be logically impossible for the same place in the visual field to be two colors simultaneously, this does not prevent us from saying it, and so, the job of philosophy for Wittgenstein is to eliminate from language what cannot be meaningfully said. To do this, we must understand that simples are indefinable but that we can nevertheless know, with certainty, what they are, or at the very least, that there are such things as simples. Such simples would, in fact, be tautologies, but we would nonetheless be able to understand their meaning without being able to define it in language. This is, of course, not very far from admitting that simples must be objects with which we can be intuitively and self-evidently acquainted. We need to know how to tell the difference between propositions that are meaningful and those that are not, and the only way to do this, without attempting to contradict ourselves by saying what cannot be said, is to acknowledge that 'showing' practically amounts to the same thing as 'self-evidence.'

There is also something of an echo of G. E. Moore's use of "indefinable simple notions" in Wittgenstein's conception of showing. In *Principia Ethica*, for example, Moore poses the following question:

> If I am asked 'What is good?' my answer is that good is good, and that is the end of the matter. Or if I am asked 'How is good to be defined?' my answer is that it cannot be defined, and that is all I have to say about it.... My point is that 'good' is a simple notion, just as 'yellow' is a simple notion; that, just as you cannot, by any means, explain to any one who does not already know it, what yellow is, so you cannot explain what good is. Definitions of the kind that I was asking for, definitions which describe the real nature of the object or notion denoted by a word, and which do not merely tell us what the word is used to mean, are only possible when the object or notion in question is something complex.[44]

Moore's definition of good is, of course, tautological and therefore cannot be a definition in any appreciable and positive sense, which is exactly his point: definitions must end somewhere. At some base point in an analysis, one can only name the constituent simples, but that is as far as one can go. In the strictest sense, the only thing we may say about them is that they are what they are, and if you do not already know what they are, there is no way to explain it. Just as no amount of explanation will suffice in elucidating what it is like to see yellow to someone who has never had an experience of that color, likewise there is no appreciable way to explain what good is to someone who does not, in some sense, already know. One might imagine that the same would be applicable to the concept of logical simples. Since one cannot meaningfully define them, it is also quite impossible to meaningfully speak of them. If one did not already know that logical analysis required logical simples, one would not gain this knowledge definitionally. One must be acquainted with what the notion of a logical simple is, which is to say, more directly, that the idea of logical simples must be the logical simple *par excellence*, from which the possibility of logical simples derives. But this raises an important question: If language does not permit unmediated access to the existence of logical simples, how can we know that there are such things to begin with? The only possible answer, it would seem, is that logical analysis provides the basis for logical simples and that if one is acquainted with logical analysis, it must also be self-evident that logical analysis demands the existence of logical simples. It is difficult to avoid this conclusion without either trying to administer further proofs of the necessity of logical simples or admitting that they are an arbitrary requirement of logical analysis, which is not the same thing as a demonstration of logical necessity in general.

While it is well known that the concept of logical simples was an essential one for Wittgenstein in his early work, it is worth noting, as Julius Weinberg has, that it was also "fundamental to the philosophy of Logical Positivism."[45] Despite the similarity in their respective doctrines, Wittgenstein was by no means a logical positivist. While he interacted with the members of the Vienna Circle, he did so only loosely and reluctantly. When Wittgenstein met with some of those affiliated with the group, especially those close to the German philosopher Moritz Schlick, "To the surprise of his audience, Wittgenstein would turn his back on them and read poetry . . . as if to emphasize to them . . . that what he had *not* said in the *Tractatus* was more important that what he had."[46] Not only is poetry the sort of thing that is outside the confines of meaningful propositional language (i.e., the language of natural science), so too is the nature of logical simples. One cannot say what simples are, but one knows that there are such things, not because one has discovered them, but because analysis demands that they must be there. "The doctrine that ultimate simples exist is," as Weinberg rightly suggests, "Required to ensure the completeness and uniqueness of any given analysis. The doctrine can either be assumed, or demonstrated, or introduced as an arbitrary postulate (convention) to be justified by the success of the system employing it."[47] Of course, it is here that Weinberg has put his finger on the metaphysical pulse that not only drives the logical positivists but Wittgenstein's *Tractatus* as well. For no one has yet to empirically demonstrate a specific instance of a logical simple, and we therefore cannot use this as the basis of our belief in their existence. One might retort that this is entirely beside the point, that an empirical demonstration would only be a confirmation of a logical necessity. In reality, however, logical simples are only necessary to certain kinds of analysis. Thus if one wants to do the sort of analysis that requires the concept of logical simples, one can hardly do away with it. If one adopts this form of analysis as 'self-evidently' correct, the need for logical simples will take on the aura of being necessary in itself. Let us not forget that logical analysis does not, nor could it, prove that logical analysis is the correct form of analysis *a priori*. Starting from the premise 'logical analysis is the only correct kind,' we will seem to arrive, as if by necessity, at the idea that logical simples are actual constituents of reality. This 'proof,' however, is only predicated on our unquestioning acceptance of logical analysis as self-evidently correct. This is how Wittgenstein was able to arrive at the conclusion that self-evidence was completely unessential to the project of logical analysis. He took for granted the postulate that logical analysis must necessarily be the only possible correct one, and forgetting this fact; it seemed as if logical analysis was able to bypass the need for self-evidence. In truth, the whole endeavor of logical analysis depends on an 'arbitrary postulate,' to use Weinberg's words once again. Whether the success of such a system is used as a justification for it is quite beside the point; its success—or lack thereof—is not a demonstration of its truth or its falsity.

At base, Wittgenstein's conception of language is dependent on a definition of tautology, and for good reasons. A tautology, insofar as it is an expression of the law of self-identity, seems to bypass the need for self-evidence because it makes no other claim save for a purely formal one: Everything is whatever it is. Even though this is an empty truism, it is nevertheless the boundary of existence—not because it has content, but rather because it does not. It only tells us what is logically permissible to exist, not what actually does exist (the latter is the realm of the natural sciences). Of course, this depends on our willingness to accept the law of self-identity as incontestably true. That a thing is the same as itself is an axiom that is by no means provable beyond the possibility of doubt. We may either say that it is self-evident—which is not a proof of its truth, but rather a declaration that we will not doubt it—or we may acknowledge that no ultimate proof may be given and that our belief in the law of self-identity is an arbitrarily adopted convention that makes certain kinds of methodologies possible. It is not true unconditionally, but only contingently true according to the kind of analysis one wishes to make. In the case of logical analysis, the need for a definition of tautology is indispensable to its cogency, as is the existence of logical simples. Both are assumed by the methodological constraints of logical analysis.

The epigraph with which Moore begins *Principia Ethica* comes from Bishop Butler's oft-quoted witticism, "Everything is what it is, and not another thing."[48] Wittgenstein, too, was fond of this phrase, and as Ray Monk notes in his biography of Wittgenstein, he thought of using it "as a motto for *Philosophical Investigations*."[49] Doubtless, it would serve equally well as a motto for the *Tractatus*. Logic, insofar as it is concerned with what must be self-evidently the case in all possible worlds, is concerned only with what is tautological. This much is stated by Wittgenstein in 6.1 and 6.11.

6.1 The propositions of logic are tautologies.

6.11 Therefore the propositions of logic say nothing. (They are the analytic propositions.)

Accordingly, a tautology, on the face of it, is only meant to convey the idea that "if $p$ then $p$."[50] Even though a tautology, strictly speaking, 'says nothing,' it can nonetheless be used, oddly enough, to say many other things besides. Dorothy Emmet makes several interesting points about the various ways in which tautologies are sometimes anything but silent.

> Philosophers have questioned whether any proposition true in virtue of its form of words alone can be factually informative. There are problems here in the notion of necessary truth and of synonymity. But it would seem as though the lowest, simplest form of a tautology 'A is A' could not possibly be informative. Yet there are ways in which it may be sensible to assert this, and in which 'A is A', though vacuous in what it directly asserts, may be communicative in what it indirectly conveys.[51]

Emmet details several of these uses, such as the "'This is what matters' use.... Close to this, but I think distinct from it, is the use of a tautology to remind us of the generic meaning of an idea."[52] Besides this, there are also, as she calls them, "'Shut up' tautologies,"[53] which she claims is the sense that Moore uses it in. The use of a tautology in this sense "is invoked when the analysis is becoming so artificial as to lack a sense of proposition."[54] This also, seemingly, is the sense in which Wittgenstein uses the term. It is, in effect, meant to convey to us that things are what they are, and that is the end of the matter. The conclusion of the *Tractatus*, it might be said, which entreats us to pass over what we cannot say in silence, is one of the most grandiose 'shut up' tautologies ever devised. Its sole purpose is to put an end to the conversation or, more directly, to put an end to the possibility of philosophy as traditionally understood.

Emmet's consideration of the various non-vacuous uses of tautologies is a view that Wittgenstein seems not to have shared, or possibly not even considered. The fact that a phrase like 'no means no' has an entirely different (and meaningful) connotation than its tautological form allows shows the inevitable inadequacy of Wittgenstein's *Tractarian* linguistic theory. No doubt, it was instances similar to this that led Wittgenstein to have second thoughts about his first book. Nevertheless, there is something inexorably important about the use of tautology in the *Tractatus*, not just for logic but in metaphysics in general. An essential component of a tautology, after all, is that it stands in for a logically simple object. Such objects, as Wittgenstein remarks in 3.221, "Can only be *named*. Signs are their representatives. I can only speak *about* them: I cannot *put them into words*. Propositions can only say *how* things are, not *what* they are." In 3.26, he goes on, "A name cannot be dissected any further by means of a definition: it is a primitive sign." In this respect, names serve a basic metaphysical function in the *Tractatus*; they are the necessary components that allow us to construct definitions in the first place. One immediately sees the problem that this creates. If a name is what allows us to give definitions, then how is it that we can give a definition to 'names' in general? If we have defined 'names' as 'that which allows us to give definitions,' are we not saying something to the effect that names are both the cause and effect of names? This, however, cannot be accepted as valid. A definition of 'names' must be given prior to its application in determining other definitions.

In a move that is an uncanny foreshadowing of the *Investigations*, Wittgenstein seems to be attempting to resolve this issue in passages 3.262–3.3:

> 3.262 What signs fail to express, their application shows. What signs slur over, their application says clearly.
>
> 3.263 The meanings of primitive signs can be explained by means of elucidations. Elucidations are propositions that contain primitive signs. So they can only be understood if the meanings of those signs are already known.
>
> 3.3 Only propositions have sense; only in the nexus of a proposition does a name have a meaning.

The idea of 'elucidations' seems to provide Wittgenstein a means of escaping the vicious circle described above. Primitive signs, which are not definable, but only nameable, are completely meaningless by themselves. They are purely tautologies, and nothing follows from them save for other tautologies. Simple, primitive signs, therefore, gain their sense in combination with other primitive signs. Their meaning is illustrated by their use in a proposition. A proposition cannot say what the use of a primitive sign is, but if one understands the sense of a proposition, one can see the sense of the primitive signs contained therein. The importance of the application of primitive signs that Wittgenstein places in the above quotation bears some resemblance to a concept that pervades the discussion of language in the *Investigations*: Meaning is bound up with use. The difference, however, is that where the *Tractatus* is concerned, 'the nexus of a proposition' shows that the meanings of simple names are fundamentally set in stone. Not only does the *Investigations* take the completely opposite view (names are not fixed constants), the very notion of primitive signs is taken into serious question. It is, of course, a shortcoming of the *Tractatus* that it can give no real justification for why we need to suppose the existence of primitive signs to begin with. If their existence is due to methodological constraints, there seems to be little reason to assume that this implies their necessity. Furthermore, if primitive signs are known only by way of their application within the context of propositions, they are a superfluous addition to Wittgenstein's theory of language. In other words, the assertion, 'what signs fail to express, their application shows,' implies that we need not understand signs at all. This is despite the fact that Wittgenstein claims that propositions 'can only be understood if the meanings of those signs are already known.' From here, however, we are once again led back to the problem of cause and effect. If we can only understand the meaning of a primitive sign by its application in a proposition, and if we can only understand the meaning of a proposition if we understand the meaning of the primitive signs of which it is composed, it would be impossible for us to understand either without first understanding the other.

It is at this point that Wittgenstein's metaphysics come into a more focused consideration. Not only does the notion of primitive symbols make an assertion about the nature of language, it also sets conditions on the nature of existence. Although the world, in a certain sense, is entirely separate from its depiction in language—which is to say that we may correctly or incorrectly mirror any particular state of affairs in language—in another sense entirely, "*The limits of my language*," as Wittgenstein states in 5.6, "Mean the limits of my world." If it is not possible for something to be meaningfully said in language, it is not possible for it to exist either (and vice versa), for there would be no possible logical form that language and reality could have in common. More importantly, this point provides the key to the problem of solipsism for Wittgenstein. "For what the solipsist means is quite correct; only it cannot be *said*, but makes itself manifest."[55] What makes itself manifest is the 'metaphysical subject,' as Wittgenstein calls it. Michael Hodges, in his book *Transcendence and Wittgenstein's Tractatus*, asks why it is that Wittgenstein felt it necessary to introduce such an idea into a conception of language that is rigorously realistic, as the picture theory undoubtedly is. The answer, he says,

> has to do with representation: if one fact (a sentence) is to represent another fact (a state of affairs), there must be a subject. A fact merely as a state of affairs and a fact as a representing sentence are logically distinct. Only for a subject can one fact represent another. Without subjectivity there would be merely an unarticulated totality of facts. Thus subjectivity is a *logically* necessary condition for the possibility of representation.[56]

A picture, in other words, is always a picture for someone, and so it is quite true that the possibility of representation is predicated on there being a subject to whom the representation is presented. "I am my world,"[57] Wittgenstein remarks.

From this realization, we see that "solipsism, when its implications are followed out strictly, coincides with pure realism."[58] It does so because the metaphysical subject is not a part of the world; it is the limit of it. It is, as Wittgenstein says, "Exactly like the case of the eye in the visual field. But really you do *not* see the eye. And nothing *in the visual field* allows you to infer that it is seen by an eye."[59] Just as the eye does not see itself in the visual field, but is nevertheless the mechanism by which the visual field is seen, so too is the metaphysical subject the mechanism by which the world—my world—exists. The metaphysical subject, although it is not in any appreciable sense, a part of the world, is the prerequisite for it, just as a picture requires a viewer in order to be a picture. This is the real metaphysical consequence of the picture theory. If we start from the premise that language is essentially representational (and this, of course, is not the only one from which we may begin), then it is quite impossible to avoid the consequence of the metaphysical subject.

This, however, is only one particular consequence of the metaphysics that belies the *Tractatus*. In truth, its basis is simply the idea that arbitrary decisions produce necessary results. From a given set of axioms, one must derive a given set of corollaries. One cannot justify adopting any particular axiom without further recourse to still other axioms, in which case it ceases to be an axiom and becomes a corollary. This is to say that metaphysical propositions, by their very nature, are analogous to the axioms and laws of logic. Though we may appeal to a claim of self-evidence when our ability to produce further proofs exhausts itself, doing so does not suffice as a guarantor of truth. The only thing it demonstrates with any modicum of certainty is our unwillingness to disbelieve it—to hold it as universally true in spite of the fact that nothing compels us to do so except for our own aesthetic preferences. Thus even the most obvious seeming axioms are, in the end, entirely arbitrary in that their validity is based solely on the will to believe them. This distinguishes a metaphysical proposition from other kinds of propositions: it cannot be proved because it cannot be derived from other propositions. The same, of course, applies to logical propositions. Let us hasten to add that this is not at all Wittgenstein's main point in the *Tractatus*, but something like it is hinted at in 3.342. "Although there is something arbitrary in our notations, *this* much is not arbitrary—that *when* we have determined one thing arbitrarily, something else is necessarily the case. (This derives from the *essence* of notation)." This is certainly an important point. For although notational rules are arbitrary, once established, one must abide by them or discard them in favor of other rules. This fact, so I contend, is the essential feature of metaphysics.

To be sure, however, there is no notational rule *a priori* that allows us to determine which types of elementary propositions exist. Rather, it is in "the *application* of logic," Wittgenstein says, that "decides what elementary propositions there are. What belongs to its application, logic cannot anticipate. It is clear that logic must not clash with its application."[60] In another anticipation of the *Investigations*, the above passage calls into question the idea that logic may be separated from its application. If one cannot determine what elementary propositions there are without the application of logic, then it becomes suspect to assert that there is such a thing as elementary propositions apart from how they are used. Although it is fairly obvious that what Wittgenstein is referring to above are elementary propositions that are actually the case and not potentially so, given the assertion that 'the application of logic decides what elementary propositions there are,' there can be no such thing as 'potential elementary propositions that are not actually the case,' because to discover such an elementary proposition would require an application of logic, and the application of logic decides what elementary propositions there are. In 5.5571, Wittgenstein remarks, "If I cannot say a priori what elementary propositions there are, then the attempt to do so must lead to obvious nonsense." This means, roughly speaking, that there is no 'logic before logic,' or, more precisely, there is no logic before its application. The attempt to say what logic is apart from its application, therefore, leads to nonsense. It is endeavoring to say what cannot be said.

There has been some attention given to Wittgenstein's metaphysics within the corpus of the secondary literature, but mostly it has been concerned with the ontological aspects of the *Tractatus*. While ontology is most certainly a topic of interest within metaphysics, it is by no means the only one. As I have previously suggested, the problem of metaphysics can best be typified by what amounts to a crisis of justification. One can only give reasons for one's suppositions up to a certain point, at which point validation must come to an end. The inability to justify an assertion is thus the condition by which it is to be considered 'metaphysical.' Therefore, ontology need not be synonymous with metaphysics, inasmuch as ontological propositions may be derived from non-ontological ones. Metaphysics, in the above sense, simply means 'first philosophy.'

In *The Metaphysics of the Tractatus*, Peter Carruthers has remarked that "Wittgenstein, like Frege, took logic and semantics to be prior to metaphysics and ontology."[61] There are certainly good textual reasons to suppose that Wittgenstein derived his conception of ontology from his logical methodology in general. This is seen most evidently in the doctrine of simple and indefinable elements of being. His use of logic, as discussed above, requires such an ontology, but Carruthers' contention that logic is also prior to metaphysics is, I would argue, untenable. There are certainly aspects of Wittgenstein's thinking in the *Tractatus* that adopt a metaphysical tenor. The emphasis on mysticism is but one instance (which is also derived from his use of logic). Logic, therefore, does not precede metaphysics; it is metaphysics—at least it is in this particular case. Carruthers also notes that "Wittgenstein wants his simples to have necessary existence."[62] We need only answer the question of how this necessity is to be achieved. The answer, not surprisingly, is that Wittgenstein's logic necessitates the existence of simples. However, this leaves us with yet another unanswered question: How is logic to be validated as the necessarily 'correct' methodology to the exclusion of all others? There is no answer to this question unless one wishes to resort to self-evidence, which it seems Wittgenstein unwittingly does. The truth is, however, that Wittgenstein never gives any attempt at a justification of logic whatsoever. It is merely assumed without question. This is precisely the point at which aesthetics enters into his metaphysical considerations: where reasons fail, and conjecture is the only viable option in establishing any basis for his assertions.

Where the topic of ontology in the *Tractatus* is concerned, there has been some interesting debate within the secondary Wittgensteinian scholarship as to what sort of theory is suggested therein. On this, there are several divergent and irreconcilable interpretations. John W. Cook, in *Wittgenstein's Metaphysics*, asserts that by 1916 Wittgenstein "had embraced that version of empiricism that William James called 'radical empiricism' and Bertrand Russell later called 'neutral monism.' From that date until his death his fundamental views changed very little."[63] The radical feature of neutral monism, as Cook describes it,

> Is that, unlike idealism, it does not hold that everything is mental or *in* a mind. On the contrary, it claims to eliminate altogether the (Cartesian) mind or ego, thus doing away with the subjectivity of experience. In this view, then, there is nothing that is subjective (or private) and therefore there is nothing that is unknowable.[64]

There are certainly elements of neutral monism in the *Tractatus*, and Cook does an admirable job in drawing them out. Wittgenstein's assertions in 5.621, "The world and life are one," and 5.63, "I am my world. (The microcosm.)," are enough to demonstrate this point. However, like Wittgenstein's use of logical simples, the elements of neutral monism that pervade the *Tractatus* are necessitated by the dictates of his logic. The picture theory requires, as noted above, the 'metaphysical subject.' I am the boundary of my world, and thus there can be no difference between my experiences of the world and the corporeal world. They are one and the same.

This is, as Cook noted, more or less a reiteration of James's concept of radical empiricism, which is a central tenet of his famous essay "Does 'Consciousness' Exist?":

> My thesis is that if we start with the supposition that there is only one primal stuff or material in the world, a stuff of which everything is composed, and if we call that stuff 'pure experience,' then knowing can easily be explained as a particular sort of relation towards one another into which portions of pure experience may enter. The relation itself is a part of pure experience; one of its 'terms' becomes the subject or bearer of the knowledge, the knower, the other becomes the object known.[65]

Wittgenstein adopts much the same argumentative apparatus in the *Tractatus*. The world is essentially one sort of thing: 'facts,' which stand in a given set of logically possible relationships to one another. Accordingly, 'subject' and 'object' are not two separate substances, as an idealistic leaning dualist might hold, but rather a relationship between facts. In Hodges' account of the *Tractatus*, he describes how "Wittgenstein proposes an ontology of facts . . . as well as a theory of meaning that takes the propositions as the basic unit."[66] This, along with Cook's interpretation of the neutral monism of the *Tractatus*, goes a long way towards giving the *Tractatus* a monistic slant. If the world is reducible to basic units called 'facts,' then it follows that the world is constructed of facts and nothing else, despite whatever illusion of corporeality it might have. Furthermore, if the world is 'my world'—the totality of facts and not things—then we should acknowledge, as Cook does, that "the world of the *Tractatus* is a phenomenal world."[67]

The above interpretation, however, does little to account for the mystical and transcendental aspects that abound in the later passages of the *Tractatus*. Carruthers, in the preface to his book on *The Metaphysics of the Tractatus*, tells his reader:

> I shall say nothing about Wittgenstein's remarks on value and on mysticism. . . . It is, in my view, clearly unnecessary to take any particular stance on the *TLP* [*Tractatus Logico Philosphicus*] doctrine of the Ethical in order to interpret and assess the semantic and metaphysical doctrines which make up the body of the work.[68]

This, however, seems to be a difficult assertion to give credence to. It is, at the very least, indicative of the sort of oversight reminiscent of the early positivistic interpretations of the *Tractatus*—especially given the importance that Wittgenstein put on the subjects of transcendence, mysticism, ethics, and aesthetics in the latter pages of his first book. It is precisely these interests that give the text something of a dualistic flavor. It should be noted that where Wittgenstein can be made out to be a dualist, he bears little resemblance to the dualism of someone like Descartes, for example. For Wittgenstein, the world is made up essentially of facts, all of which may be meaningfully expressed in language. However, what lies beyond language (i.e., what is transcendental, mystical, ethical, aesthetic, etc.) is curiously present in the world nonetheless (it shows itself). Unlike Descartes—for whom mind was more 'real' than the body—Wittgenstein does not implicitly favor either the world of facts or the transcendental as being more 'essential' than the other. Both are equally 'real' in the sense that the world of facts is predicated on the transcendental and vice versa.

The metaphysical subject, although it is not a fact about the world, must, in a loosely conceived sense, 'exist' if there is to be a world at all. It is in this way, too, that Wittgenstein believes logic to be transcendental. In 5.61, he remarks:

> Logic pervades the world: the limits of the world are also its limits. So we cannot say in logic, 'The world has this in it, and this, but not that.' For that would appear to presuppose that we were excluding certain possibilities, and this cannot be the case, since it would require that logic should go beyond the limits of the world; for only in that way could it view those limits from the other side as well.

We cannot go beyond the limits of the world, for this would require us to think the other side of the boundary of the world, in which case it would cease to be a boundary at all. The attempt to go beyond this boundary is what typifies all metaphysical tendencies for Wittgenstein, and thus all metaphysics is 'transcendental.' In 6.13, he states, "Logic is not a body of doctrine, but a mirror-image of the world. Logic is transcendental." Logic, understood thusly, is virtually synonymous with the metaphysical subject, as can be inferred from 5.641.

> Thus there really is a sense in which philosophy can talk about the self in a non-psychological way. What brings the self into philosophy is the fact that 'the world is my world'. The philosophical self is not the human being, not the human body, or the human soul, with which psychology deals, but rather the metaphysical subject, the limit of the world—not a part of it.

Since 'the world is my world' and both the metaphysical subject and logic are its 'boundaries,' it would seem to follow that the two must implicitly coincide with one another. Thus, there is the world: that which is bounded by the logical-metaphysical self; and there is the transcendental: that which lies on the other side of the world's boundary.

*The Rest Is Silence* 75

This partly explains why Wittgenstein believes that all facts are on the same level in logical space, as can be seen in 5.556, "There cannot be a hierarchy of the forms of elementary propositions;" and in 6.42, "Propositions can express nothing higher." Accordingly, we may gather that the world is composed only of facts that may be mirrored in propositions and that they cannot express anything which is not a fact, i.e., what is transcendental or beyond the boundary of the world. This, of course, lends itself to the neutral monism interpretation advocated by Cook. However, in 5.5561, Wittgenstein goes on to say, "Hierarchies are and must be independent of reality," which again points towards a dualist interpretation, for it implies that there are such things as 'higher propositions,' although they must necessarily be independent of reality. Even though 'the world,' according to Wittgenstein, is essentially made of facts and nothing else, he nevertheless makes a dualistic distinction between what is logically permissible (the boundary of the world) and what is the case (the subset of facts that constitute the world in its current state). The former decides what can and cannot be a possible state of affairs; e.g., there is nothing 'illogical' about unicorns even though none exist. The latter is the realm of the natural sciences. Though the existence of unicorns is not logically restricted, the natural sciences do not deal with them because only the "totality of true propositions is the whole of natural science."[69] Thus, even if we dismiss the implicit dualistic divide between logic and mysticism in the *Tractatus*, we can still infer a quasi-dualism in Wittgenstein's distinction between logic and natural science.

I would here like to take a brief segue and say something about the possibility of reading the *Tractatus* from the pluralist point of view. Even if we were to grant the monist's main contention—that the world consists of facts and nothing else—the possibility of an alternative pluralistic interpretation based on this supposition is not thereby eliminated. Supposing that the world is everything that is the case and that all facts stand on the same level, this does not necessarily imply that these facts may be reducible to one grandiose 'metafact' which all other facts are derivatives of (analogous to the Form of the Good in Plato's metaphysics). This is the conclusion to which monism would seemingly lead us. There can only be one thing and one thing only; the appearance of difference is an illusion. William James, whose doctrine of radical empiricism supposed "a world of pure experience," remarks that his theory "is essentially a mosaic philosophy, a philosophy of plural facts."[70] The same may be said of Wittgenstein's facts in the *Tractatus*. It might well be the case that the monistic interpretation is correct, that the only true fact is that the world is the totality of facts, that "everything, whether we realize it or not, drags the whole universe along with itself and drops nothing,"[71] as James puts it. It might also be the case that the multitude of facts that make up reality are non-reducible to any single metafact, thus giving us a pluralistic world consisting of a plurality of facts.

In an interesting way, James's pluralism anticipates the same exact turn that Wittgenstein would make in the *Investigations*. "For pluralism," James says, "All that we are required to admit as the constitution of reality is what we ourselves find empirically realized in every minimum of finite life. Briefly, it is this, that nothing real is absolutely simple."[72] Wittgenstein, in a certain sense, must have come to something of the same conclusion because one of his main points of self-criticism in the *Investigations* is leveraged against the very idea of a 'simple, indivisible element of being' as a logical necessity which is at the heart of the *Tractatus*. As a result, there is a shade of pluralism that colors the *Investigations* as well, the reason being that a pluralistic universe does not allow for the possibility of any simple and indivisible element of being. Accordingly, multiple interpretations are always nascent. The metaphysical subject—the boundary of the world—is the pluralistic subject: no account of it is forever fixed in place.

The topics with which the *Tractatus* deals—especially those of logic and language—present us with a quandary not easily solved. There is no question that Wittgenstein prescribes a theory that attempts to clearly demarcate the boundaries of meaning, and thereby the boundaries of the world. The question is whether he is successful in so doing. The picture theory, while it gives us a way of identifying a meaningful proposition from a pseudo-proposition, falls noticeably flat in one way: it breaks its own rules. It says what can only be shown. Russell, in his introduction to the *Tractatus*, makes this very same point. "Mr Wittgenstein manages to say a good deal about what cannot be said, thus suggesting to the sceptical reader that possibly there may be some loophole through a hierarchy of languages, or by some other exit."[73] Wittgenstein, writing to Russell on April 4, 1920, expresses his dissatisfaction with the latter's introduction. "There's so much in it that I'm not quite in agreement with – both where you're critical of me and also where you're simply elucidating my point of view. But that doesn't matter. The future will pass judgment on us – or perhaps it won't, and if it is silent, that will be a judgment too."[74] This final remark, regarding the judgment of silence, is a poignant one, for the future has been anything but silent about the *Tractatus*, least of all where it beseeches us to remain silent. Despite Wittgenstein's dislike of the book's introduction, there is no definitive way for him to respond to Russell's observation concerning his supposed ability to say a good deal about what cannot be spoken.

Russell, of course, picked up on Wittgenstein's division between saying and showing in his introduction. A proposition is a picture of a fact via a shared logical structure that the two must have. "It is this common structure which makes it capable of being a picture of a fact, but the structure cannot itself be put into words, since it is a structure *of* words, as well as of the facts to which they refer."[75] One of the contentions that I have attempted to make in this chapter is that Wittgenstein, apart from his criticism of the need for self-evidence in logic, in the end must resort to a form of it (as is seen in his conception of showing). For his part, Wittgenstein seems to have recognized the issues surrounding self-evidence—a theory is inherently weak if it must resort to it—and Wittgenstein's use of showing, as the theoretical basis of logic, is meant to sidestep this weakness. He is, for example, particularly hard on Frege in 6.1271 for his recourse to it. "It is remarkable that a thinker as rigorous as Frege appealed to the degree of self-evidence as the criterion of a logical proposition." Part of the problem with self-evidence is that disputes may easily arise about exactly what does and does not count as 'true beyond doubt.' The purpose of showing in the *Tractatus* is to avert this difficulty. It does so, or at least it attempts to do so, by making mistakes in logic impossible. It is not possible—even for God—to think contrary to the laws of logic, and therefore the laws of logic are manifest in the world because reality is logical. This is how "propositions *show* the logical form of reality. They display it."[76] Wittgenstein's doctrine of showing is thus an attempt to remove the 'self' from self-evidence. There can be no disagreement in logic because illogical thought is impossible, and therefore we are constrained by logic to think logically. Logic thus shows itself in the world because there can be no such thing as an illogical world, even if the logical form of reality cannot be meaningfully put into words.

Wittgenstein's attitude towards self-evidence, was, as we have seen, to disregard it as completely unnecessary in logic. But in making this claim, one cannot help feeling that he is talking out both sides of his mouth. In 5.551, he remarks, "Our fundamental principle is that whenever a question can be decided by logic at all it must be possible to decide it without more ado." The same may be said, however, of self-evidence: When one appeals to it, one does so as an indication that no further ado is considered possible. This is exactly the kind of quality Wittgenstein assigns to the questions of logic: There can be no arguing about them. This sort of attitude towards logic is seen in many of the propositions of the *Tractatus*, all of which implicitly suggest self-evidence as their basis. Take 6.1265 as an example. "It is always possible to construe logic in such a way that every proposition is its own proof." A proposition that was its own proof would show this fact. So too would a self-evidential one, and thus one might rightly wonder what method could here be devised for distinguishing between the certainty of a logical proposition and a proposition that derives its certitude from its being purportedly self-evident.

In 5.1363, Wittgenstein asserts that "if the truth of a proposition does not *follow* from the fact that it is self-evident to us, then its self-evidence in no way justifies our belief in its truth." Wittgenstein's point seems to be that if the truth of a proposition does not logically follow from our belief that it is self-evident, then it is not a proof of its truth. One may believe a proposition to be self-evident, and yet the proposition may nevertheless turn out to be false. The same does not apply to a proposition of logic, however. In theory, a correctly posited logical statement is true whether we believe in it or not—a sentiment that perhaps figured into Wittgenstein's rejection of self-evidence as a criterion of judging logical validity. While this may no doubt be true, the real difficulty is in formulating such a proposition without recourse to some sort of ungrounded assumption or belief. Take, for example, one of the central ideas of the *Tractatus*: 'logic shows its sense.' Surely, this proposition is not logical in any appreciable sense, for it is neither analytical nor true *a priori*. We can believe it to be true, we can assume its truth to ensure that the structural coherence of the text is not weakened, but no amount of assumption or belief is ever going to amount to anything like the rigorous sort of proof required by logic. More to the point, Wittgenstein's concept of showing itself requires us either to accept it as an axiomatic principle which cannot be proven but is nevertheless methodologically useful or to declare that it is self-evidently certain that self-evidence is superfluous in logic, in which case self-evidence would be anything but superfluous to logic—a self-referential incoherence. While Wittgenstein seems to have intended his doctrine of 'showing' as a means for dispatching the need for self-evidence, the former is merely a redressing of the latter on all main points. We could just as easily say that 'a tautology shows its sense' as we could say 'a tautology is self-evident.'

It is no surprise, then, that Wittgenstein would place such a high degree of importance on the tautology in the *Tractatus*:

5.142    A tautology follows from all propositions: it says nothing.
6.1264  Every proposition of logic is a modus ponens represented in signs. (And one cannot express the modus ponens by means of a proposition.)

Given the fact that logic is entirely composed of tautological propositions and that tautologies say nothing, whenever we speak about logic, we are, of course, saying nothing. In this sense, the *Tractatus* remains dutifully silent. It is also in this sense that it is most appreciably a book that treats a metaphysical topic: logic, which according to Wittgenstein, "*is prior* to every experience."[77] We cannot, however, determine that logic is the correct metaphysical construct *a priori*. This would require us to use logic to justify logic. It also requires that we make many presuppositions about the nature of reality, as is suggested by Wittgenstein in 6.124 (which rather succinctly sums up the whole of the *Tractatus*).

> The propositions of logic describe the scaffolding of the world, or rather they represent it. They have no 'subject-matter'. They presuppose that names have meaning and elementary propositions sense. . . . It is clear that something about the world must be indicated by the fact that certain combinations of symbols . . . are tautologies. This contains the decisive point. We have said that some things are arbitrary in the symbols that we use and that some things are not. In logic it is only the latter that express: but that means that logic is not a field in which *we* express what we wish with the help of signs, but rather one in which the nature of the absolutely necessary signs speaks for itself. If we know the logical syntax of any sign-language, then we have already given all the propositions of logic.

Metaphysics, as it is expressed in the context of Wittgenstein's logic, must make certain assumptions that cannot be proved in any appreciable sense, including not only the belief that names have a meaning and elementary propositions a sense but also the belief that logic is the only form of legitimate metaphysics. Logic in the *Tractatus* does not prevent us from metaphysical speech; it is a form of it. This self-referential inconsistency is only reinforced by the fact that Wittgenstein says so much about what cannot be spoken of, which is yet further evidence suggesting that logic is the metaphysical backbone of the *Tractatus* (logic can no more be meaningfully spoken of than metaphysics).

Some things are arbitrary in logic, just as in metaphysics, and some things are not. For what is arbitrarily selected, no justification can be given except for an aesthetic one. As for necessity and its relation to logic, let us note that a great many things must be presupposed before that can even be a consideration for us, but once they have been made, many things will inexorably follow. The source of Wittgenstein's certitude—that logic provided him the unassailable truth to the problems of philosophy—does not, to be sure, result from its indubitability, but rather the aesthetic belief that the world *must* conform to it. This is all the more evident when Wittgenstein changes his mind about many of his early assurances in the *Tractatus*, which is not so much a refutation of his early work as it is indicative of creativity's capacity for seeing everything with new eyes.

## Notes

1 Wittgenstein, *Tractatus Logico-Philosophicus*, 2001, sec. 6.53.
2 Much of the material in these notebooks would later be culled by Wittgenstein in the composition of the *Tractatus*.
3 Wittgenstein, *Notebooks 1914–1916* (Chicago: University of Chicago Press, 1984), 14.
4 Wittgenstein, *Tractatus Logico-Philosophicus*, 2001, sec. 6.54.
5 Ibid., sec. 4.1212.
6 Whether this is a successful solution to the problem of self-referential incoherence is a matter of some debate, as is evidenced quite clearly by the secondary literature on Wittgenstein's *Tractatus*.
7 A. J. Ayer, "Demonstration of the Impossibility of Metaphysics," *Mind* 43, no. 171 (July 1934): 335.
8 Ibid., 343.
9 Ibid.
10 Ibid., 344.
11 Herbert De Vriese, "The Myth of the Metaphysical Circle: An Analysis of the Contemporary Crisis of the Critique of Metaphysics," *Inquiry* 51, no. 3 (June 2008): 315, https://doi.org/10.1080/00201740802120772.
12 Ayer, "Demonstration of the Impossibility of Metaphysics," 316.
13 Ibid.
14 Ibid., 318.
15 Ibid., 319.
16 De Vriese, "The Myth of the Metaphysical Circle," 326.
17 Ibid.
18 Ibid.
19 Ibid., 328.
20 Ibid.
21 Ibid., 330.
22 Aloys Wenzl, "Einstein's Theory of Relativity, Viewed from the Standpoint of Critical Realism, and Its Significance for Philosophy," in *Albert Einstein: Philosopher-Scientist*, ed. Paul Arthur Schilpp, 4th printing. (New York: Tudor Publishing Company, 1957), 586.
23 De Vriese, "The Myth of the Metaphysical Circle," 323.
24 Hans Reichenbach, "The Philosophical Significance of the Theory of Relativity," in *Albert Einstein: Philosopher-Scientist*, ed. Paul Arthur Schilpp, 4th printing. (New York: Tudor Publishing Company, 1957), 294.
25 Ibid.
26 Ibid., 295.
27 Ibid.

28 Ibid.

29 Monk, *Ludwig Wittgenstein*, 154.

30 Quoted in ibid., 57.

31 Ibid., 260–61.

32 Rudolf Carnap, *The Philosophy of Rudolf Carnap*, ed. Paul Arthur Schilpp (La Salle, IL: Open Court, 1997), 25.

33 Quoted in McGuinness, *Wittgenstein: A Life: Young Ludwig 1889–1921*, 288.

34 Wittgenstein, *Notebooks*, 12.

35 Ibid., 60.

36 Ibid., 62.

37 Ibid.

38 Ibid.

39 Wittgenstein, *Tractatus Logico-Philosophicus*, 2001, sec. 2.012.

40 Ibid., sec. 3.031.

41 Bertrand Russell, *Introduction to Mathematical Philosophy*, 2nd ed. (London: G. Allen & Unwin, 1920), 205.

42 Brian McGuinness and Georg Henrik von Wright, eds., *Ludwig Wittgenstein, Cambridge Letters: Correspondence with Russell, Keynes, Moore, Ramsey, and Sraffa* (Oxford: Blackwell, 1997), 121.

43 Ibid., 124.

44 G. E. Moore, *Principia Ethica* (Mineola, NY: Dover Publications, 2004), 6–7.

45 Julius Weinberg, "Are There Ultimate Simples?," *Philosophy of Science* 2, no. 4 (October 1935): 387.

46 Monk, *Ludwig Wittgenstein*, 243.

47 Weinberg, "Are There Ultimate Simples?," 337–38.

48 Joseph Butler, *Five Sermons, Preached at the Rolls Chapel and A Dissertation Upon the Nature of Virtue*, ed. Stephen L. Darwall (Indianapolis: Hackett Publishing, 1983), 20.

49 Monk, *Ludwig Wittgenstein*, 451.

50 Wittgenstein, *Tractatus Logico-Philosophicus*, 2001, sec. 5.101.

51 Dorothy Emmet, "'That's That'; Or Some Uses of Tautology," *Philosophy* 37, no. 139 (January 1962): 15.

52 Ibid.

53 Ibid., 16.

54 Ibid.

55 Wittgenstein, *Tractatus Logico-Philosophicus*, 2001, sec. 5.62.

56 Michael Hodges, *Transcendence and Wittgenstein's Tractatus* (Philadelphia, PA: Temple University Press, 1990), 76.

57 Wittgenstein, *Tractatus Logico-Philosophicus*, 2001, sec. 5.63.

58 Ibid., sec. 5.64.

59 Ibid., sec. 5.633.

60 Ibid., sec. 5.557.

61 Peter Carruthers, *The Metaphysics of the Tractatus* (Cambridge: Cambridge University Press, 2009), 20.

62 Ibid., 143.

63 John W. Cook, *Wittgenstein's Metaphysics* (Cambridge: Cambridge University Press, 1994), xv.

64 Ibid., 8.

65 William James, "Does 'Consciousness' Exist?," *The Journal of Philosophy, Psychology and Scientific Methods* 1, no. 18 (September 1904): 478.

66 Hodges, *Transcendence and Wittgenstein's Tractatus*, 30.

67 Cook, *Wittgenstein's Metaphysics*, 31.

68 Carruthers, *The Metaphysics of the Tractatus*, xii.

69 Wittgenstein, *Tractatus Logico-Philosophicus*, 2001, sec. 4.11.

70 "A World of Pure Experience," in *Essays in Radical Empiricism* (Radford VA: Wilder Publishing, 2008), 23.

71 James, *A Pluralistic Universe*, 323.

72 Ibid., 322.

73 Bertrand Russell, Introduction to *Tractatus Logico-Philosophicus*, by Ludwig Wittgenstein (London: Routledge, 2001), xxiii.

74 Quoted in McGuinness and Wright, *Ludwig Wittgenstein, Cambridge Letters*, 152.

75 Russell, Introduction to *Tractatus Logico-Philosophicus*, xxiii.

76 Wittgenstein, *Tractatus Logico-Philosophicus*, 2001, sec. 4.121.

77 Ibid., sec. 5.552.

# 3

# The Humble Origin of Words

For all his protestations to the contrary, the Wittgenstein of the *Tractatus* would seem to have no shortage of insights into metaphysics. His early philosophy, as we have seen, is rife with them, and this fact—in combination with his vehement rejection of metaphysics—produces a discord in his work that is never fully resolved. Not even the division between saying and showing was, in the end, able to justify these two diametrically opposed points of view. Thus it would appear that, on a fundamental level, the *Tractatus* fails to do what it set out to do: demarcate the boundaries of meaningful language. Perhaps this also explains why Wittgenstein eventually became so dissatisfied with the conclusions of his first book and why he decided to make a second attempt at finding an alternative method for displacing metaphysics from philosophy. In §97 of the *Philosophical Investigations*, for example, we not only see him pushing back against some of the flawed assumptions that underpinned the *Tractatus*, but also putting forward a re-worked conception for how metaphysics can be cleaved from philosophy.

> We are under the illusion that what is peculiar, profound and essential to us in our investigation resides in its trying to grasp the incomparable essence of language. That is, the order existing between the concepts of proposition, word, inference, truth, experience, and so forth. This order is a *super*-order between – so to speak – *super*-concepts. Whereas, in fact, if the words "language", "experience", "world" have a use, it must be as humble a one as that of the words "table", "lamp", "door".

The problem with Wittgenstein's use of logic in the *Tractatus* is that it attempts to encapsulate the 'incomparable essence' of language and the 'super-order' between 'super-concepts' that makes signification possible in the first place. By the time of the *Investigations*, this tendency in Wittgenstein had run its course. Whatever meaning words like 'language', 'experience', and 'world' might have, it must be a completely ordinary one, thereby eliminating all traces of metaphysics from philosophy once and for all.

Or at least this is what it would purport to do. As I will aim to show in this chapter, however, the recourse that the *Investigations* makes to the ordinary must still own up to the problem of metaphysics in general; that is, it needs to provide us some reason as to why we ought to adopt the methodological turn to the 'humble' origin of words. Yet in order to provide such a convincingly irrefutable justification, it would require the use of the same sort of super-concepts that Wittgenstein was attempting to escape. There is, one could say, something of an extraordinarily unshakable faith in the explanatory power of the ordinary in the *Investigations*. Despite his best efforts, Wittgenstein can no more show that this method is any less prone to metaphysical interpretations than was the *Tractatus*, and faced with the inability to give his methodology any sound and unshakable footing, Wittgenstein is forced into making any number of assumptions that have an unavoidable metaphysical tenor.

No doubt there are objections that might be leveled against the above reading. What Wittgenstein really meant to do, one might retort, was to show that metaphysics amounts to a misapplication of words—a divorcing of the meanings that words ordinarily possess from their use in language. Clearly, Wittgenstein wants us to forgo such questions as 'What is the essence of language?' and to instead look at how language is used in context. Metaphysics, according to Wittgenstein, is the attempt to say what language will not allow us to say. All words are equally modest from the very outset—there are no higher, essential, or super-order words—only words as they are used in language. Thus, the only cure for our metaphysical misunderstandings is never to lose sight of the application of language. This diagnosis does not, however, equate to a metaphysical doctrine in any appreciable sense of the word. On the contrary, it is an argument that is stridently anti-metaphysical while avoiding the self-referential inconsistencies that had plagued Wittgenstein for so long.

While I would not argue with the supposition that the professed goal of the *Investigations* was to discover a theory that afforded no possibility of any metaphysical implications, I would disagree with the idea that it is any more successful in the attempt than was the *Tractatus*. Wittgenstein may well have become much more adept at hiding the metaphysical underpinnings of his later work, but, as we will see, some of the most central doctrines of the *Investigations* are anything but metaphysically neutral.

The first point to make about the metaphysics of the *Investigations* is not all that different than the one we made about the *Tractatus* in the previous chapter. Just as the latter is not written in the 'logically perfect language' of the sort that it expounds, it is difficult to see the former as an exercise in a language that is altogether 'humble' or within the context of 'ordinary use,' which is Wittgenstein's criterion of meaningfulness in the *Investigations*. Part of the trouble behind this criterion is that there is the tendency to assume that what is 'ordinary' is metaphysically 'neutral,' a point that is not lost upon Penelope Mackie in her essay "Ordinary Language and Metaphysical Commitment,"[1] in which she is decisively critical of this view as it is propounded in Peter van Inwagen's book *Material Beings*.[2] "The central tenet of van Inwagen's metaphysics," she writes,

> Is that there are no tables, chairs, rocks, stars, or any other visible material objects except living organisms. Yet he maintains that this theory is consistent with what ordinary people mean when, in everyday life, they say things like ... 'There are rocks that weigh over a ton.' This ... thesis is defended by an appeal to the metaphysical neutrality of ordinary language. Van Inwagen holds that the everyday utterances are sufficiently free of metaphysical commitment to be insulated from conflict with his metaphysical denial of the existence of chairs, rocks, etc.[3]

Mackie's objection to van Inwagen seems centered on the observation that his metaphysics *requires* a metaphysically neutral ordinary language to avoid a blatant contradiction that arises from the fact that ordinary language refers to the existence of all sorts of material objects. First of all, there is no obvious reason to suppose ordinary language to be metaphysically neutral. Second of all, it would take a more convincing proof of metaphysical neutrality besides the requirement of the revisionist metaphysics that van Inwagen has produced. The most convincing argument available is that any appearance of ontological commitment in ordinary language is "simply the product of a misleading idiom."[4] Of course, if ordinary language sometimes 'misleads' us into ontological commitments that are not accurate, one may be inclined to wonder how metaphysically neutral it really is. For ordinary usage to be truly metaphysically neutral, it would have to avoid all appearances to the contrary. Otherwise, we would have to assume that behind those apparent ontological commitments, there is no actual commitment either way, which hardly seems 'metaphysically neutral' in any appreciable sense. As Mackie observes, "In the absence of further argument, we should take it that, in this respect, things are as they appear to be."[5]

Gordon Baker, on the other hand, defends the idea of metaphysical neutrality. He asserts that Wittgenstein "used 'metaphysical' in a traditional way, namely, to describe philosophical attempts to delineate the essence of things by establishing necessities and impossibilities. On his conception, 'everyday' simply means 'non-metaphysical.'"[6] The first point that Baker makes here seems to me undoubtedly correct. When Wittgenstein does mention metaphysics by name, he

86  *Wittgenstein and the Problem of Metaphysics*

unquestionably means to evoke a traditional conception of the sort alluded to in the quotation above. But even if we grant this point without any hesitation, it does not necessarily imply that the *Investigations* is a metaphysically vacuous text. Towards the end of his paper, Baker suggests that we should see Wittgenstein as "trying to do justice to individuals' metaphysical uses of words by bringing to light what motivates their utterances."[7] This is a very interesting statement indeed. Does Baker mean to suggest that metaphysical utterances are by their very nature motivated by some particular interest and as a consequence cannot be 'true' precisely because they lack 'objectivity' or 'neutrality?' If we take 'motivation' as our signification of 'metaphysical utterances,' then all of Wittgenstein's writings are ripe with rhetorically motivated assertions, the *Investigations* not the least among them.

Whether or not Wittgenstein asserted that 'ordinary language is metaphysically neutral' is debatable. Marjorie Perloff, for instance, remarks that "Wittgenstein's *ordinary* is best understood as quite simply *that which is*, the language we do *actually* use when we communicate with one another."[8] Understood in this light, the ordinary takes on the guise of a quasi-realistic ontology, which would clearly not make it metaphysically neutral. Again, we may feel inclined to question whether or not Wittgenstein was a realist of any sort, quasi or otherwise, but what Wittgenstein does tell us to do is to look at how our language is used and to avoid thinking how it ought to be used, as can be seen quite clearly in §66 of the *Investigations*. Even still, we do not escape metaphysical implications wholesale. If we want to know how language is used, so Wittgenstein thinks, the correct method for doing so is not going to be an analytical one, such as he used in the *Tractatus*. The right one is going to be something like an 'empirical descriptivism.' Not only does this suggest an epistemological theory, but Wittgenstein seems to be taking such a theory as his first philosophical principle that forms the basis of his entire inquiry.

The second point to be made is that there is a certain fundamental 'belief' that Wittgenstein holds to in the *Investigations* that can only be adequately characterized as an 'aesthetics of the ordinary.' This becomes all the more important if George Leonard is correct, and we can trace "the art of the commonplace" to its origins in the early nineteenth century. One of the central contentions of his book *Into the Light of Things* is

> that the turn against the art object [which] ... Emerson and Whitman make was inevitable, given their credo that paradise, perfection can be found in the "simple produce of the common day," the commonplace, the "eternal picture which nature paints in the street," in "mere real things." Does not the very existence of

the separate term "art object" imply a class of things which aren't identical to mere real "objects"?[9]

Leonard also suggests that Whitman and Emerson's elevation of the common, and the attack on art objects in general, "Were not anomalies . . . but the necessary outcome of what M. H. Abrams cautiously termed 'a new intellectual tendency' in Western culture around 1800, 'Natural Supernaturalism.'"[10] This new intellectual tendency, the argument could be made, was just as prevalent in philosophy as it was in literature and art. Thomas Carlyle's *Sartor Resartus*—as much a work of literature as philosophy—is an exemplar of this tendency, and from which the term "Natural Supernaturalism" is derived.[11] It is, in no small part, a rather oblique lampooning of German Idealism:

> Philosophy complains that Custom has hoodwinked us, from the first; that we do everything by Custom, even Believe by it; that our very Axioms, let us boast of Free-thinking as we may, are oftenest simply such Beliefs as we have never heard questioned. Nay, what is Philosophy throughout but a continual battle against Custom; an ever-renewed effort to *transcend* the sphere of blind Custom, and so become Transcendental?[12]

This 'complaint of philosophy' which Carlyle identifies—that custom throws a veil over ultimate reality, just as clothes conceal the body—is also implicitly rejected by the ironic overtone of his style. By making an artificial distinction between 'appearance' and 'reality,' it is philosophy that has hoodwinked us and not custom. Transcendence, then, is not a matter of rising above appearances. Rather, it is about seeing mere nature as itself transcendent. There is no truth behind appearances—there are only the appearances themselves.

If, in a sense, we might speak of the 'transcendental' in Wittgenstein's later philosophy, it would be because he places such a high premium on how language functions within the context of everyday usage. That is to say, in other words, that there is no compelling reason for us to subscribe to Wittgenstein's conception of language as opposed to that of the idealist, for, in either case, the account provided is incapable of substantiating the axiomatic postulates on which it is predicated. More troublesome still is the fact that all explanations, no matter how detailed, can never definitively separate between conformity and deviation, a problem that is intimated by §201 of the *Investigations*—commonly known as the rule-following paradox.

> This was our paradox: no course of action could be determined by a rule, because every course of action can be brought into accord with the rule. The answer was:

if every course of action can be brought into accord with the rule, then it can also be brought into conflict with it. And so there would be neither accord nor conflict here.

The quandary that Wittgenstein alludes to above is one that is especially applicable to the problem of metaphysics insofar as it offers us a compelling example of the futility involved in devising rules *ad infinitum*. All axioms, by their very nature, are groundless suppositions: They cannot be determined according to a rule, for they are the mechanism by which the formation of rules is made possible in the first place. It makes no sense, therefore, to speak of an axiom as something that does or does not accord with a rule. To do so would not produce a justification or explanation of the axiom in question, it would only result in one axiom being supplanted in favor of another that is equally baseless. Understood as such, philosophy cannot help but fall into the fallacy of *petitio principii*: It always assumes the point, it always begs the question, and it always fails to prove its most fundamental principles. Thus, all attempts to sidestep the problem of the transcendental only ever succeed in reaffirming it as an inescapability. At the terminus of justification—where all propositions transcend the rules that they themselves lay down—the only justification left to us is that of the subjective universalization implicit to judgments of taste.

Before proceeding further, I should mention that the above reading of the rule-following paradox is about as far from that of Wittgenstein's as is possible to get. There is a number of excerpts from the *Investigations* that clearly show how Wittgenstein believed this paradox to be indicative of the sort of misunderstanding into which philosophy is capable of leading us. The chain of reasoning responsible for our confusion, so he contends, comes about because of our desire to "place one interpretation behind another, as if each one contented us at least for a moment, until we thought of yet another lying behind it."[13] The rule-following paradox is untenable for Wittgenstein because it contradicts what we actually do in practice. "There is a way of grasping a rule which is *not* an interpretation, but which, from case to case of application, is exhibited in what we call 'following the rule' and 'going against it.'"[14] There are many obvious instances we could think of here, and Wittgenstein gives us one. "Imagine a game of chess translated according to certain rules into a series of actions which we do not ordinarily associate with a *game* – say into yells and stamping of feet."[15] What would we make of such an interpretation of the rules of chess? Quite likely, we would say that if anyone were to "yell and stamp instead of playing the form of chess that we are used to"[16] they would not be playing chess at all. We could, of course,

The Humble Origin of Words 89

translate the rules of chess into yells and stamps so that something like a game of chess was produced, but nevertheless, it would be a reinterpretation of those rules, and thus, it would—in a certain sense—no longer be a game of chess.

The pivot point, on which the rule-following paradox hinges, Wittgenstein tells us, is a misconception of what 'interpretation' means. "There is an inclination to say: every action according to a rule is an interpretation. But one should speak of interpretation only when one expression of a rule is substituted for another."[17] There is, of course, nothing that stops us from placing one interpretation of a rule behind another indefinitely, but there is also nothing that stops us from abiding by a rule without interpreting it. If we did not, there would be no such thing as following a rule at all, and clearly, there is such a thing. This brings us to Wittgenstein's main point and his solution to the paradox. "'Following a rule' is a practice. And to *think* one is following a rule is not to follow a rule. And that's why it's not possible to follow a rule 'privately'; otherwise, thinking one was following a rule would be the same thing as following it."[18] Just as following a rule is a practice, so too is interpreting a rule, one that follows its own set of rules, and if we were to reinterpret the rules by which we interpret, we would no longer be 'interpreting' in the sense in which we are accustomed to thinking of it. In other words, the practice of following a rule must consist in our being contented not to interpret *ad infinitum*, to "exorcise the insidious assumption that there must be an interpretation that mediates between an order,"[19] as John McDowell says. It is not a "choice between the paradox that there is no substance to meaning, on the one hand, and the fantastic mythology of the super-rigid machine, on the other."[20]

The interpretation of §201 I proffered above also differs notably from what is perhaps the best-known elucidation of the predicament found in the secondary literature. I have in mind here, of course, Saul Kripke's divisive *Wittgenstein on Rules and Private Language*. Therein he characterizes the rule-following paradox as "the central problem of *Philosophical Investigations*"[21] and credits Wittgenstein with the invention of "a new form of skepticism." He even goes so far as to call the rule-following paradox "the most radical and original sceptical problem that philosophy has seen to date,"[22] one that seems to suggest that "there can be no such thing as meaning anything by any word."[23] That this skeptical conclusion should be the ultimate moral of the paradox is, as Kripke notes, "Insane and intolerable," and any rebuttal to it must be dependent on the "argument against 'private language.'"[24] In §243, Wittgenstein characterizes such a language as that which refers to "what only the speaker can know," i.e., "his immediate private sensations" which other people do not have access to and therefore "cannot understand." Within the confines of a private language, so it is supposed, one may represent ideas to oneself concerning one's sensations, emotions, etc., but if one were to attempt to translate this private language of sensation into a shared public language, the act of the translation from private to public would diminish the representational authenticity of the sensations that one is attempting to express.

The problem here for Wittgenstein is that the whole notion of a private language rests on an untenable conception of meaning that is predicated on the representational accuracy of a sign to its referent—a concept of meaning that was at work in the *Tractatus* and one that Wittgenstein went to great lengths to dismantle in the *Investigations*. Thus, we see Wittgenstein asking in §244, "How do words *refer* to sensations?" And in §245, "How can I even attempt to interpose language between the expression of pain and the pain?" The question—and the answer to the question—is even more directly stated in §246.

> In what sense are my sensations *private*? – Well, only I can know whether I am really in pain; another person can only surmise it. – In one way this is false, and in another nonsense. If we are using the word "know" as it is normally used (and how else are we to use it?), then other people very often know if I'm in pain.... This much is true: it makes sense to say about other people that they doubt whether I am in pain; but not to say it about myself.

The conception being attacked here is not that sensations are wholly deprived of what we might call a perspectival subjectivity, i.e., the feeling of 'what it is like' to have an experience. Nor is the argument meant to show that these sensations do not—despite all the appearances to the contrary—'belong' to me and not to someone else. Rather, the target of Wittgenstein's critique is the belief that the subjective closeness of personal experience permits me to represent it to myself in a language that is equally private, knowable only by me, and about which I cannot be mistaken. Indeed, it would seem that one of the primary reasons that Wittgenstein takes such a keen interest in this problem is precisely because it portends to make a claim to absolute epistemic certainty, and in this regard, it is not all that dissimilar from the Tractarian treatment of tautologies. One cannot say that one knows that a tautology is true because a tautology is, by definition, true in all possible worlds. It is the *a priori* logical-metaphysical condition of existence and is as such not an epistemological proposition but rather the boundary of all possible epistemological propositions. The realm of the knowable is, therefore, strictly delimited to the propositions of natural science, i.e., those statements that might turn out to be either true or false in the due course of experience. A tautology is always true, and hence it can never be construed as a genuine piece of knowledge, let alone one that has any special claim to absolute indubitability. Much the same argument would apply, of course, to the supposed certitude attributed to private sensations. If it is senseless for one to doubt that 'I am in pain' when one has just stubbed one's toe, then it is also just as senseless to say that 'I know that I am in pain' when used as a philosophical expression of infallibility.

The principal lesson we learn from Wittgenstein's examination of the rule-following paradox and the private language argument may be summed up as follows: There is no such thing as ultimate accordance with a rule precisely because there is no such thing as ultimate representational accuracy. Even the portrayal of our private sensations—which is supposed to be the exemplar of a supremely precise language, albeit in an incommunicable form—is subject to the same vagrancies of application and interpretation as the more run-of-the-mill public varieties. Careful observation of our so-called private language reveals that it is the public that antecedes the private and not the other way around. Anything that can be expressed clandestinely to oneself can be expressed communally and with no less degree of certitude. From the first-person point of view, it may appear that action and justification are so closely intertwined that it would seem all but impossible to misattribute the one to the other, but the proximity afforded by the perspective of subjectivity hardly constitutes anything like privileged access or a demonstration of necessary causation. Thus, "The entire point of the sceptical argument is," Kripke contends, "that ultimately we reach a level where we act without any reason in terms of which we can justify our action. We act unhesitatingly but *blindly*."[25] This does not mean, however, that there is no such thing as being justified in how one acts, but the justification does not lie at the level of the individual but rather the collective. The solution to the skeptical problem presented by the rule-following paradox must, therefore, be met with an equally skeptical solution, and for Kripke, the whole thing "turns on the idea that each person who claims to be following a rule can be checked by others."[26] In the case of private sensations, the criterion on which others must base their judgments is on outward behavior or first person avowals. "No further 'justification' or 'explanation' for this procedure is required."[27]

It should come as no surprise, given its prominence within the literature, that this account of the rule-following paradox has garnished its fair share of detractors[28] and, to a much lesser extent, some proponents as well.[29] Baker and Hacker, for instance, rebuke Kripke for attributing "a variety of views" to Wittgenstein that "he never held" while imposing a whole host of interpretations on his writings "for which there is no licence."[30] I find a chastisement of this sort a bit perplexing, however. What, if anything, is the rule-following paradox supposed to teach us if not that the legitimization of interpretation is never something ultimately decided upon? To be sure, the validity of any given judgment is a question that may always be brought before the scrutiny of the community, of which Baker and Hacker are certainly members. They do not, however, have any more right than anyone else in determining the final and definitive form that the correct reading of Wittgenstein ought to take. Nevertheless, it is precisely this authority they apparently attribute to themselves when they claim to be able to sharply differentiate "between Wittgenstein's argument as it struck Kripke"[31] and the argument that Wittgenstein actually made. It is as if Baker and Hacker think themselves capable of producing an interpretation of Wittgenstein "that takes us outside of the writing toward a psychobiographical signified."[32] This method of "doubling commentary," as Derrida has called it, is typified by the tranquil assurance in the ability of exegesis to leap "*over the text toward its presumed content, in the direction of the pure signified.*"[33] Certainly, one could contend that the attainment of something like the pure signified was exactly what Wittgenstein set out to achieve in the *Tractatus*, but the same could hardly be said of the *Investigations*. To read it, then, as if that were a possibility, is not even to read it at all, let alone understand it.

To be sure, the airing of the above qualm does little by way of justice to the overall concerns voiced by Baker and Hacker in their article. In all fairness to them, they do not claim to offer an incontrovertible proof "that the core question of the [*Investigations*] is not a sceptical one, nor that the solution is not a 'sceptical solution.'"[34] One of the things they do claim to do, however, is to disprove Kripke's assertion that "the real private language argument is to be found in the sections preceding §243. Indeed, in §202, the conclusion is already stated explicitly.... The sections following §243 are meant to be read in the light of the preceding discussion."[35] While Baker and Hacker agree that "the private language argument is indeed built" on the discussions that precede §243, they are not blind to the fact that this discussion includes not only the rule-following paradox but also questions "of ostensive definitions, samples, meaning, understanding, and explanation."[36] On this point, I find myself in agreement. It seems to me incongruent with the general spirit of the *Investigations* to consider any one component of it separately from the context of the whole. The rule-following paradox is, no doubt, closely enmeshed with the argument against private language, but so too are such ideas as the 'language-game,' the 'form of life,' and 'family resemblance,' amongst many others. If the *Investigations* warns us of anything, it is the danger of contemplating an idea in isolation from the interconnected web which gives it life. Baker and Hacker's rejoinder to Kripke can thus be lauded for the way in which it reminds us of what Wittgenstein considered to be "the upshot" of all "these considerations," namely that it enables us to "see a complicated network of similarities overlapping and criss-crossing: similarities in the large and in the small."[37]

While I perfectly well grant that Baker and Hacker raise many valid misgivings about Kripke's conjoining of the rule-following paradox and the private language argument, there is one point in particular about which I could not disagree more fervently: that what Wittgenstein's critique of private language is meant to demonstrate is "the nonprimacy of the mental, the 'inner', the subjective."[38] Indeed, this rather one-sided emphasis on the importance of the public sphere is a problem that is, to a certain extent, endemic to Kripke as well, and one that is entirely detrimental to the role the subjective plays in the formation of justifications. So when Baker and Hacker write, for example, "If something can be a justification for me, it must also be capable of functioning as a justification for others,"[39] I would respond by asking, 'And how does one bridge the gap between the two?' As they rightly note, "My 'seeing that this is so' cannot function as a justification," a point that Wittgenstein similarly makes in *On Certainty*, "'I know' often means: I have the proper grounds for my statement. So if the other person is acquainted with the language-game, he would admit that I know."[40] To say that one has a claim to knowledge, of course, implies that one can also produce a justification for that claim, and this means that it cannot be a justification for me alone but must in principle be capable of sufficing as a justification for someone else as well. There can thus "be no technique of applying a 'private rule'. Such a rule really would 'hang in the air', and there would indeed be no distinction between thinking one is following a rule and actually following it."[41] It is here, if I am not mistaken, that Baker and Hacker inadvertently touch on a key component of the private language argument. Justification, it is true, cannot be predicated on a private criterion, for in that case it would cease to have any grounding whatsoever. It would indeed 'hang in the air' and as such would not qualify as a justification precisely because it would have no ground on which to stand. What this means, in other words, is that all justification is public in nature. In acquiescing to this point, however, we have hardly admitted that the subjective has no primary function as regards justification. No matter how universally accepted a criterion of judgment might be, there is no such thing as one that would mandate our assent. Each of us is subjectively free to either accept or reject a principle that is generally regarded as sound in the public arena. So while justification may not hang unsupported in the air, aesthetic judgment always does.

94        *Wittgenstein and the Problem of Metaphysics*

Let me return now to the question I posited just a moment ago: How is it possible to move from the subjective postulation of a judgment to the communal implementation of a rule that can subsequently be transformed into a principle according to which conformity or dissent may be assessed? In responding to this question, the first place to look would be to Kant, who has already supplied us with a partial answer. "One thinks," as he says, that the beautiful "has a necessary relation to satisfaction," but this "necessity is of a special kind." It is not a "theoretical objective necessity" that enables us to cognize *apriori* "that everyone will feel this satisfaction." Nor is it "a practical necessity" that serves as a rule "for freely acting beings," which would signify "nothing other than that one absolutely (without further aim) ought to act in a certain way." Rather, aesthetic judgments "can only be called exemplary" and are thus emblematic "of a universal rule that one cannot produce" but which nonetheless ascribes "the universal assent of all."[42] As such, Judgments of taste do not provide us any rule that applies without exception to everyone, but it does, one might say, provide us an example of what such a rule *might* look like. They are, as Henry Allison tells us, "rule-giving" judgments whose normativity is predicated on "the feeling of pleasure and displeasure."[43] The source of this normativity is not, therefore, to be found in "the nature of nature" but instead "in the nature of *judgment*" itself. So although aesthetics is—and must—be based wholly in the subjective, the fact that "we allow no one to be of a different opinion" when "we declare something to be beautiful"[44] already imparts to us the possibility of traversing the space between the individual judgment and the collective justification. The only difference between the two is that a justification has gained a sufficiently wide degree of acceptance amongst a sufficiently large number of people. This does not mean, however, that justifications are incontestable, only that there are any number of social consequences for so doing (depending, of course, on the justification in question and how it is being contested).

The second thing to say as regards the above transition between the private and the public is that judgments of taste do not, by any means, constitute the sole method for conveying the aesthetic preference of the individual to the collective verdict of the community. Indeed, explicit avowals of aesthetic judgments have a relatively confined function within the context of our day-to-day comings and goings. Certainly, they play a role within just about any form of human life, but the overuse of it would make cohabitation amongst other people difficult, if not impossible—a phenomenon that Freud was already well aware of in *Civilization and Its Discontents*. To have any hope of existing together in even a moderately cohesive fashion requires, as he notes, that a majority can come "together which is stronger than any separate individual and which remains united against all separate individuals."[45] This is why, in other words, that in the vast majority of cases, it is our actions that bear the weight of the subjective universal ought and not any outright demand for accord that we might make of others. Whenever we take action—be it intentional or otherwise—we are implicitly suggesting to other people that they ought to do the same.[46] Each time I choose to commit myself to a course of action I do not commit myself alone. "If I decide to marry and have children," Sartre writes, "I am committing not only myself, but all of humanity"[47] to the idea of matrimony and the begetting of children as the correct form of human life. It goes without saying, of course, that other people may accept or reject this imperative that my action lays upon them, but that is precisely the point: Our actions function like judgments of taste insofar as they expect but do not absolutely mandate the acquiescence of others. The important point to remember, however, is that this freedom from outside injunction belongs not only to the collective, but also to the subjective as well. While it is true that all of our actions "contribute to making us"[48] who we have been, "each one" of them, "Even the most trivial, is entirely free" in the sense that the action in question "could have been other than what it is."[49]

The primary point I aim to get across in the somewhat tangential considerations above is that the private language argument and the rule-following paradox are both indicative of the larger problem of metaphysics, which is, so I contend, the central problem of Wittgenstein's philosophy. Each of them, in their way, treat questions that concern the difficulties surrounding the quest for foundational justifications and ultimate indubitability, and what each of them reveals—again after their fashion—is that what counts as being validated in one's actions and sure in one's ability to abide by a rule are public affairs that are nevertheless subject to the unjustifiable judgment of every individual. In the end, what we learn is that there is no such thing as a self-evident axiom of metaphysics that can be proved as true beyond any shadow of a doubt, and this is, Wittgenstein well knew, precisely "the position in which someone finds himself in ethics or aesthetics when he looks for definitions that correspond to our concepts."[50] This applies, I would add, just as much to first philosophy as it does to ethics and aesthetics. When one searches for definitions in metaphysics, one is quickly forced to admit that there is no such thing as a principle beyond the purview of suspicion. There never was, nor will there ever be, such a thing as an axiom of metaphysics that forces our capitulation. We are thus inexorably led back to the groundlessness of aesthetic judgments, which not only avoid the regress of justification implicit to every claim of dogmatic irrefutability but also provide us with the means for establishing rules that implore adherence while permitting descent.[51] This is to say, in other words, that the way to grasp a rule without falling into a regress is through the act of aesthetic assent.

As we can see, then, the *Investigations* is just as much dependent on the subjective universalization inherent to judgments of taste as is the *Tractatus*, which is not to say that the two are therefore predicated on anything like the same conceptions of language. The evolution from the picture theory of meaning to that of the language-game shows us just how effective the creative impulse is at overcoming the tyrannical compulsion of the aesthetic towards homogenization. In his mature work, Wittgenstein ceased to look at meaning as a shared logical form between picture and pictured. Rather, he began to see language as loosely defined, always open to interpretation and intimately tied to how it was used. Seen in this light, language is a way of interacting with the world as opposed to a tool of analysis. It is this re-conceptualization that leads Wittgenstein to what is perhaps one of the most central ideas of his later philosophy: "What we call the meaning of the word lies in the game we play with it."[52] Just as "our language contains countless different parts of speech,"[53] it also contains countless different uses and meanings in the context of countless different games. If we fail to realize this, we make a fundamental error (as Wittgenstein did in the *Tractatus*). "When we study language, we *envisage* it as a game with fixed rules. We compare it with, and measure it against, a game of that kind."[54] In reality, this is only one of the various possible ways in which we might think of it.

Such a conception of language is what Wittgenstein refers to as a 'primitive' game, in which there "are ways of using signs simpler than those in which we use the signs of our highly complicated everyday language."[55] Language-games of this sort are useful, for example, when "we want to study the problems of truth and falsehood ... without the confusing background of highly complicated processes of thought."[56] When we take any one primitive language-game as the 'essence' of our highly complex one, we get an overly simplistic model of language that cannot possibly account for the vagaries of our everyday language. Wittgenstein's criticism of the Augustinian theory of language, which "does not mention any difference between kinds of word,"[57] is in a similar vein. "Augustine, we might say, does describe a system of communication; only not everything that we call language is this system."[58] We must be careful when thinking about the multitude of possible language-games not to lose sight of the "whole, consisting of language and the activities into which it is woven."[59] Language, and the activities that accompany it, are inseparable from one another. When this fact is forgotten—especially in philosophy—it produces "misunderstandings concerning the use of words, brought about, among other things, by certain analogies between the forms of expression in different regions of our language."[60]

One of the most important aspects of a game is that it can be 'played,' which is why Wittgenstein places such an emphasis on his examination of rules. They can be precisely codified, such as in chess, or vague and amorphous, such as when a child bounces a ball for amusement. This is also part of the reason that the metaphor of the language-game is so powerful: Games are as diverse as language is, and both consist in the performance of certain kinds of actions. Furthermore, there is no one type of game any more than there is one thing in which language consists. There is no one thing "that is common to *all.*" Instead, there are "similarities, affinities, and a whole series of them at that."[61] In §67 of the *Investigations*, Wittgenstein writes, "I can think of no better expression to characterize these similarities than 'family resemblances'; for the various resemblances between members of a family – build, features, colour of eyes, gait, and so on and so forth – overlap and criss-cross in the same way." What is most strikingly implicit within this concept is its seemingly staunch anti-Platonic stance. As David Finkelstein notes, "Typically, Wittgenstein's response to platonism is not, 'What you're saying is *false,*' but rather, 'What you say is all right; only there's nothing queer or magical about it.'"[62] One might, under certain circumstances, have occasion to claim that all games have something in common. One could easily say that by definition, a 'game' is something that can be 'played.' While this tells us nothing about what games are, insofar as no definition of 'playing' has yet to be given, nevertheless a game that was not playable is categorically not a game. A point of this sort might even be useful when instructing someone on the meaning of the word 'game.' This is no reason to suppose, however, that there is a corresponding Form to which the term 'game' must refer, which is why Finkelstein goes on to say, "Most of the platonist's words can be uttered innocently by someone who doesn't try to view signs apart from the applications that living beings make of them – apart, that is, from 'the weave of life.'"[63]

According to this view, the orthodox Wittgensteinian is simply trying to demystify our views of language. In so doing, we are meant to see that words have no meaning apart from their application in our lives, thereby ridding ourselves of idealist metaphysics—and metaphysics in general. A similar reading of Wittgenstein is also expounded by Alice Crary. "For Wittgenstein, . . . questions about whether particular forms of criticism are metaphysically suspicious or innocent are questions which cannot be answered apart from investigations of how these forms of words are being *used.*"[64] Interestingly enough, both Crary and

Finkelstein use the word 'innocent' to describe sans-metaphysical language, as if 'ordinary use' was somehow void of any metaphysical corruption. One could argue, however, that the Wittgensteinian who ascribes to such a theory of language is engaging in metaphysics just as certainly as the Platonist is. Both are making 'fundamental' claims about the nature of 'reality.' The former says that words get their meaning from their use, the latter says that the use of words is determined by their correspondence to an idea. There is, therefore, no 'bringing' words back from their 'metaphysical' to their 'everyday' usage because the very idea of the 'everyday use' is just as metaphysically loaded as the idealism of the Platonist. What allows us to move past the metaphysical, however, is the ability to *stop* the interpretation of rules without further ado. "The real discovery," Wittgenstein says in §133 of the *Investigations*, "is the one that enables me to break off philosophizing when I want to. – The one that gives philosophy peace, so that it is no longer tormented by questions which bring *itself* in question."

The concept of family resemblance—like that of the language-game—is one that Wittgenstein no doubt employed as an antidote to Platonic idealism and universals in general. Stanley Cavell notes a similar tendency in the way in which Wittgenstein seems to offer "the notion of 'family resemblance' as an alternative to the idea of 'essence.'"[65] But as Cavell goes on to write, "For a philosopher who feels the need of universals to explain meaning or naming will certainly still feel their need to explain the notion of 'family resemblance.'"[66] It is worth noting that a point very similar to this is made by Wittgenstein in §65 of the *Investigations*. "Here we come up against the great question that lies behind all these considerations. – For someone might object against me: 'You make things easy for yourself! You talk about all sorts of language-games, but have nowhere said what is essential to a language.'" His response to this imagined accusation is, interestingly, more of a reiteration of his position on family resemblance than it is an answer to the charge. "Instead of pointing out something common to all that we call language, I'm saying that these phenomena have no one thing in common in virtue of which we use the same word for all – but there are many different kinds of *affinity* between them."[67] The problem, however, is that Wittgenstein's response to his imagined interlocutor is not an answer to the allegation at all, for we could simply continue to reiterate the objection that the concept of 'family resemblance' amounts to nothing more than the universal 'essence' of all language. While there may be no way to overcome this objection ultimately, Cavell makes a compelling point when he suggests "that all that the idea of 'family resemblance' is meant to do, or need do, is to make us dissatisfied with the idea of universals as explanations of language."[68]

At most, all that Wittgenstein can admit to is that he and the idealist are simply operating according to differing metaphysical constructs that are in principle irreconcilable. He cannot prove idealism incorrect but can only attempt to show us that "universals are neither necessary nor even useful in explaining how words and concepts apply to different things."[69] Such a strategy would, Cavell points out, only need to demonstrate "that the grasping of universals cannot perform the function it is imagined to have" and once we realize this, "the idea of a universal no longer has its *obvious* appeal, it no longer carries a *sense* of explaining something profound."[70] The implication here—though not directly stated by Cavell—is that what the metaphor of family resemblance lacks by way of argumentative force is more than made up for by the persuasive power of its eloquence. By making universals lose their 'obvious appeal,' Wittgenstein is, in a very real sense, attempting to make them 'ugly' and therefore 'unworthy' of belief, which in the end turns out to be a much more effective rhetorical strategy than even the most convincing proof. For the Greeks, as Nietzsche well knew, ugliness was not only "an objection in itself," but was also "almost a refutation."[71] The best 'proofs,' then, are not the ones that 'demonstrate the truth' beyond any shadow of a doubt but rather the ones that are fashioned to be as aesthetically pleasing as possible in order that we might accept them without reservations.

One of the key features of language-games for Wittgenstein is the context in which they are played; just as the architecture of a building is altered by the landscape surrounding it, so too are the meanings of words altered by their use in the language-game. Wittgenstein calls this linguistic background the 'form of life' to highlight the fact that language and life are inseparably bound up with one another. It is also a term that, despite its importance for Wittgenstein's philosophy, does not occur with great frequency in his work.[72] One such occurrence can be found in §19 of the *Investigations*. "To imagine a language means to imagine a form of life." Another is to be found in §23. "The word 'language-*game*' is used here to emphasize the fact that the *speaking* of language is part of an activity, or a form of life." Both of these quotations make it clear that the kind of life in which language is used is the foundational basis for our understanding of a language in the first place. That is why when we think of imaginary language-games, especially primitive ones, we are imagining a primitive form of life that corresponds to it. In other words, a simplistic form of language equates to a simplistic form of life, whereas a more complex form of language affords us the possibility of a more complex form of life. When we, therefore, imagine primitive language-games as a way of distilling our complex language into manageable theoretical components, we will not arrive at any one theory that accounts for it in its entirety.

100 *Wittgenstein and the Problem of Metaphysics*

Wittgenstein shows us a few different instances of the irreducible complexity of our language-game. For example,

> One can imagine an animal angry, fearful, sad, joyful, startled. But hopeful? And why not? . . . Can only those hope who can talk? Only those who have mastered the use of language. That is to say, the manifestations of hope are modifications of this complicated form of life.

We cannot say that an animal 'hopes' because the only sense of that word we understand is tied to the kind of life we live. We do not share a common form of life with a dog, and therefore we cannot know what being 'hopeful' would be like for such a creature. It is not a matter of possessing language that separates our form of life from other animals, such as Aristotle suggested in 1.2 of the *Politics*.[73] Our form of life, however—whether it is essentially political or not—does not result from the fact that we possess language but the other way around. This is why Wittgenstein goes so far as to state, "If a lion could talk, we wouldn't be able to understand it."[74] It is not a commonality of language that forms a basis for communication but rather a form of life. The fact that we have language and animals do not is an entirely irrelevant distinction to make. Communication is possible only in those respects where the form of life is similar enough to permit it (this is the case even amongst people who share the same language but have different ways of life).

Newton Garver has taken the opposing view to the one outlined above, which he refers to as the misleading "orthodox reading" indicative of the widespread assumption "that Wittgenstein spoke of a plurality of human forms of life . . . [and] that each language-game . . . determines a separate life distinct from that determined by any other language-game."[75] This contention is centered on the observation that Wittgenstein almost always uses the singular German term *Lebensform* (form of life) and not the plural *Lebensformen* (forms of life).[76] Keeping this fact in mind, Garver concludes "that the correlation between *Sprachspiel* [language-game] and *Lebensform* is many to one rather than one to one. Each language-game does constitute or determine a special form, namely, a form of activity or behavior, not a form of life."[77] Garver, of course, does not base his assertion solely on the fact that Wittgenstein more frequently used *Lebensform* as opposed to *Lebensformen*. Although he does acknowledge that breakdowns in communication do occur, "They result from not having learned the practices [of other people] rather than not having the capacity to learn them. Therefore they do not connote any differences in form of life."[78] While it is certainly true that we possess the capacity to learn the customs and practices of other people, such that difficulties in communication are minimized, there is an implicit metaphysical claim in Garver's reading of Wittgenstein.

> Now it is a very general fact that speakers all have the same form of life. They are all human. What determines this form of life is the capacity to use language. So it is the same form of life which I imagine no matter which linguistic activity or which language I think of. This form of life is presupposed by a language or a language-game, that is, by the speaking of a language, because it is presupposed by the activities of the speakers.[79]

Garver's assertion above—that this form of life is determined by the ability to use language—amounts to a basic reiteration of the Aristotelian definition. Because we all have this capability (to a greater or lesser extent) and because no other animal shows the obvious signs of possessing anything like the 'complex' language that we employ, it is concluded that what ultimately distinguishes humans from other animals is language. From this supposition, it is further asserted that if no other animal besides us possesses language, then the ability to use it must be the necessary and sufficient condition according to which inclusion under the classificatory heading 'human being' is determined.

The consequences of this interpretation, which Garver can hardly avoid, seem to run contrary to the general theme of Wittgenstein's work in the *Investigations*. In §25, for example, we read, "It is sometimes said: animals do not talk because they lack the mental abilities. And this means: 'They do not think, and that is why they do not talk.' But – they simply do not talk. Or better: they do not use language." Wittgenstein's point in this passage is twofold. First of all, when we observe animals, the only thing that we see is that they do not use 'language' (meaning 'human' language). Second of all, this observation does not provide any convincing reason to assume that animals do not 'think' in the way that humans think. It is thus the application of a descriptive model—for the purpose of species classification—that brings us to the conclusion that 'language use' delineates humans from other animals. It is not, therefore, an empirical observation that language use is the essential feature that all humans share and animals do not. The only thing that we actually *see* is that animals 'simply do not talk.' The rest is, of course, gratuitous inference. Whether the 'human' form of life is essentially defined by the 'capacity to use language' is quite beyond the pale of empirical observation, and so too is the assertion that 'animals do not think.'

In addition to running contrary to the methodological themes of the *Investigations*, Garver's reading of the form of life metaphor, more importantly, contradicts Wittgenstein's emphatic and continuously repeated warning against misunderstanding "the role played by the ideal in our language."[80] By dismissing the possibility of "a plurality of human *Lebensformen*,"[81] Garver is, in some sense, doing exactly this. His interpretation points to the existence of something like an 'essence' of humanity. There certainly may be many characteristics that all humans similarly share, but it is a misguided endeavor to single out one thing as that which makes us human (such as language). Granted, humans, when taken collectively, share many 'family resemblances,' one of which is the preponderant tendency towards the use of complex language. It does not follow, however, that language use is what makes us human—it is but one feature of many. There are no hard and fast boundaries that separate this human form of life from that of a lion or a dog (there are family resemblances, even amongst differing species). Likewise, there are no hard and fast boundaries that prevent multiple forms of human life.

The point of all this is merely to remind ourselves that the meaning of the word 'human,' like all words, is inseparable from how it is used in the language-game. There are many instances where one might rightly speak of 'humanity' in quasi-essentialist terms, e.g., a biologist may speak of a 'human' species as a distinct and unitary form of life—perhaps in relation to our genetic make-up. In this situation, 'human' serves a classificatory function in the language-game, and its meaning is tied up with that use. A sociologist, on the other hand, might use the term 'human' in less distinct terms. The culture of ancient Egyptians, one might say, is significantly different from that of a modern industrial society so as to constitute a genuinely different form of human life. The meaning of the word 'human' in this context would be much more permeable and less rigid. From these two uses, two quite differing metaphysical conceptions of 'humanity' may arise. Neither is true or false in an absolute sense. They are true or false only in relation to their use. There is no way to determine whether the biologist's use of the word 'human' is any more correct than that of the sociologist. There are thus instances where one can rightly speak of both a singular form of life and a plurality of forms of life. Sometimes, given the correct circumstances, imagining a language is to imagine a form of life or, indeed, *forms* of life.

As with the rule-following paradox and the private language argument, the discussion concerning the form of life is partly meant to show us just how fruitless the metaphysical endeavor is when stripped of all its supposed profundity. The truth of the matter, however, is that Wittgenstein rarely dealt directly with the topic of metaphysics in the *Investigations*. In fact, the word 'metaphysics' appears in the book only twice, once in §58 and once in §116. In the former passage, Wittgenstein's view of the relationship between meaning and reality is explicitly laid out.

"I want to restrict the term '*name*' to what cannot occur in the combination 'X exists'. – And so one cannot say 'Red exists', because if there were no red, it could not be spoken of at all," – More correctly: If "X exists" amounts to no more than "X" has a meaning – then it is not a sentence which treats of X, but a sentence about our use of language, that is about the use of the word "X".

Wittgenstein's proposed restriction on the use of names in the language-game seems designed to head off any possible metaphysical conflagrations before they even have a chance to begin. It is also a direct assault on the metaphysical doctrine of the *Tractatus*, i.e., that only 'simple elements of being' have 'names'. This is exactly the kind of philosophical contagion which the ordinary language treatment is meant to cure: the disease of our understanding. Later in §58, Wittgenstein attempts to head off a potential misunderstanding.

It looks to us as if we were saying something about the nature of red in saying that the words "Red exists" do not make sense. Namely, that red exists 'in and of itself'. The same idea – that this is a metaphysical statement about red – finds expression again when we say such a thing as that red is timeless, and perhaps still more strongly in the word "indestructible". But what we really *want* is simply to take "Red exists" as the statement: the word "red" has a meaning.

The problem with a phrase like 'red exists' is that it very often tempts us into applying the grammatical model of 'object and name'[82] to cases that are incompatible with it.[83] When we do this, we are often led to conclude that for the word 'red' to have meaning, it must be because it is the name we assign to the ideal and eternal 'form of red' which gives reality to individual instances of that color. This is not to say, however, that one could not imagine circumstances in which the statement 'red exists' might have some meaningful use in the language-game, but it would not be in the philosophical sense which posits various universal categories of being. The only thing, therefore, that a philosophical statement like 'red exists' can mean is "that something exists that has that colour."[84]

Nietzsche—in a remarkably similar fashion to Wittgenstein—thought the idea of a 'true and apparent world' to be virtually devoid of any substantive meaning. If the world is anything, it "is essentially a world of relationships; under certain conditions it has a differing aspect from every point."[85] The very notion of the 'in itself' was for Nietzsche, as it would later become for Wittgenstein, an extraneous and misleading philosophical trope born out of the misunderstandings bred by language. In a passage from the *Will to Power*, it is remarkable to note how Wittgensteinian Nietzsche sounds (or, more precisely, how Nietzscheian Wittgenstein would later come to sound). "Language depends on the most naive prejudices. Now we read disharmonies and problems into things because we think *only* in the form of language."[86] For both Nietzsche and Wittgenstein, the traditional problems of philosophy were results of our inability to disengage with forms of language we habitually use, and the form of language that is particularly culpable for forcing the idea of the *ding an sich* upon us as a metaphysical necessity is that of signifier and signified. Much the same confusion between various forms of language was, for Wittgenstein, responsible for the unduly high degree of veracity we seem willing to ascribe to our inner experiences. Indeed, the private language argument is one that Nietzsche very nearly anticipates in many of its main points. "'Inner experience' enters our consciousness only after it has found a language the individual understands—i.e., a translation of a condition into conditions familiar to him—; 'to understand' means merely: to be able to express something new in the language of something old and familiar."[87] The mistake philosophers often make, however, is to express the understanding of old and familiar things in terms of something new and unfamiliar, as is the case when we attempt to express familiar sensations—such as those of pain—in terms normally reserved for the signification of physical objects.

To be sure, Nietzsche was a great destroyer of the metaphysical underpinnings of European 'herd morality,' but he did not do so in the name of nihilism. He did not seek the destruction of metaphysics in general (which cannot be done anyhow, for even the nihilist must operate from a 'metaphysics of nihilism'), but the destruction of life-stultifying metaphysics. His goal was to put a 'metaphysics of art' in its place—a soil in which life could flourish. Wittgenstein—in his own way—attempted to accomplish the same basic task in nearly all phases of his own work: the supplanting of one metaphysical construct in favor of another. In both the *Tractatus* and the *Investigations*, however, there is still a kind of latent positivist rhetoric that undergirds their anti-metaphysical sentiments. Each operates under the assumption that it remains possible to demonstrate the superfluity of metaphysics. All that is required to do so is the proper sans-metaphysical conception of language—a project that proved just as untenable in the late work as it did in the early.

Those familiar with the development of Nietzsche's thought will recall the positivistic turn it took towards the middle of his career. It encompasses his work from the *Untimely Meditations* to *The Gay Science* and is marked by his supposed "use of science to criticize metaphysics."[88] By the time *The Genealogy of Morals* was written, we see instances of Nietzsche criticizing science for falling into many of the metaphysical tropes that he once used it to criticize. "For all its detachment and freedom from emotion, our science is still the dupe of linguistic habits; it has never yet got rid of those changelings called 'subjects.' The atom is one such changeling, another is the Kantian 'thing-in-itself.'"[89] He did not, of course, discard science entirely in his later works. In *Beyond Good and Evil* he calls for a return to psychology "as the queen of the sciences, for whose service and equipment the other sciences exist. For psychology is once more the path to the fundamental problems."[90] According to Robert Pippin, this passage, amongst others, suggests that Nietzsche viewed "psychology, not metaphysics or epistemology, ... as playing a role very much like what Aristotle called first philosophy."[91] Taking up psychology as first philosophy has its advantages for Nietzsche, particularly as a means of explaining how we came to the Judeo-Christian metaphysics in the first place. The certainty that has attached itself to this metaphysics has not done so by way of its inherent truth but by our psychological will to believe it. Nietzsche's psychological first philosophy is thus both a critique and a replacement for Christian metaphysics.

This brief foray into Nietzsche's philosophy is undertaken to set the stage for a kind of analogy. Wittgenstein, like Nietzsche, went through a quasi-positivistic stage, and both would, to some extent, abandon it. There is in the *Investigations*, for instance, still something of a tension between the metaphysics that it critiques and the metaphysics that it suggests. The latter is never fully acknowledged by Wittgenstein, which was something that he at least did in the *Tractatus*, if only implicitly, as can be inferred from its closing passages. This kind of acknowledgment, however, never really occurs in the *Investigations*, and if we take this as one possible indication of latent positivism, then the *Investigations* is a more positivistic text than the *Tractatus*. All though this is something of a hyperbolic statement, it is meant to call attention to the extent which self-referential incoherence occurs in the *Investigations*. Many of its most central and important themes, e.g., ordinary language, meaning is use, family resemblance, and the form of life, have a flavor that one might describe as 'anti-philosophical.' Indeed, throughout the *Investigations*, we see Wittgenstein railing against the misconceptions into which philosophizing leads us. Sections 119 through 131 offers us excellent examples both of the kind of philosophy Wittgenstein wishes for us to avoid and the kind he advocates. Take §121, for example. "One might think: if philosophy speaks of the use of the word 'philosophy', there must be a second-order philosophy. But that's not the way it is; it is, rather, like the case of orthography, which deals with the word 'orthography' among others without then being second-order."[92] The problem at issue with Wittgenstein is not that we cannot engage in such second-order philosophizing, but rather that is indicative of the fact "that we don't have an *overview* of the use of our words. – Our grammar

106 *Wittgenstein and the Problem of Metaphysics*

is deficient in surveyability."[93] Second-order philosophy has no real explanatory power in Wittgenstein's view—it does not add anything 'useful' to our understanding of grammar or language.

> In giving explanations, I already have to use language full-blown ... this is enough to show that I can come up only with externalities about language. Yes, but then how can these observations satisfy us? – Well, your very questions were framed in this language; they had to be expressed in this language, if there was anything to ask.[94]

This poignant exchange between Wittgenstein and his interlocutor highlights an important consequence of the former's line of thinking: All philosophy is the philosophy of language—a view that is expressed in both the *Tractatus* and the *Investigations*. The belief in a second-order 'metaphilosophy' is predicated on the belief that the 'essence' of things can be apprehended outside the confines of language. It is further assumed that once this essence is discovered, it can be recapitulated in language without any loss of accuracy. Simply put, the thing-in-itself is not the same as the thing-in-language. If we could discover something outside language it would not be possible to say it in language. It is thus impossible to speak of a 'second-order' philosophy that steps outside language and views it from afar.

This is a source of tension in Wittgenstein's philosophy. For him, philosophical problems are characterized by our inability to get an overview of our grammatical structure. "The concept of a surveyable representation is of fundamental significance for us. It characterizes the way we represent things, how we look at matters. (Is this a 'Weltanschauung'?)"[95] This last question is an interesting one, for it seems that the idea of 'representation' and the importance that we attach to it forms the boundary of how we can view the world. Of course, we cannot exceed this boundary, and thus we can never quite reach the point where our grammar is no longer deficient in its surveyability. There is no all-encompassing point of view, which is why "a philosophical problem has the form: 'I don't know my way about.'"[96] And since there is no hope of achieving this vantage, there is also no hope of purging metaphysics from philosophy either. The best that we can hope for is the 'correct' perspective that makes philosophical problems evaporate. "It is not the business of philosophy to resolve a contradiction ... but to render surveyable ... the state of affairs *before* the contradiction is resolved."[97] Two senses of 'philosophy' are obviously at work here: one that always manages to baffle us and one that allows us to have peace—to be silent, as the *Tractatus* instructs us. In a passage that could have just as easily fit in his first book, Wittgenstein remarks in §126 of the *Investigations*, "Philosophy just puts everything before us, and neither explains nor deduces anything. – Since everything lies open to view, there is nothing to explain. For whatever may be hidden is of no interest to us."

In this sense, philosophy is, as it was in the *Tractatus*, that which treats of the *a priori*. "The name 'philosophy' might also be given to what is possible *before* all new discoveries and inventions."[98] The key difference, however, between the sense of the *a priori* in the *Tractatus* and the *Investigations* is that the former takes logic as *a priori*, and the latter takes grammar. In other words, grammar in the *Investigations*, much like logic in the *Tractatus*, serves as the metaphysical frame of our understanding. "Wittgenstein's most basic conception of grammar," Michael Forster says, "is that it consists in rules which govern the use of words and which thereby constitute meanings or concepts."[99] Given this sense of what Wittgenstein means by the term, we can immediately infer that the role of logic in the *Tractatus* presupposes the grammar of the *Investigations* because logic is itself based on its own kind of grammar; i.e., logic is a kind of language-game that is predicated on a particular set of rules which may or may not be valid within other language-games.

Some forms of grammar are irreconcilable with each other, which is shown by the fact that philosophical misunderstandings can occur due to the misapplication of one grammatical procedure in an incompatible context. This is, of course, precisely what happened in the *Tractatus*. Wittgenstein took the logic of 'picture' and 'pictured' as the *ideal* form of grammar—the form in which all meaningful language must be cast. What followed from this premise, the later Wittgenstein would come to realize, was a conception of logic as "something sublime." The "peculiar depth" and "universal significance" embodied by logic gave it the appearance of being "at the foundation of all the sciences."[100] It would thus seem, as Baker and Hacker put it, that "The rules of grammar, by contrast with the rules of logical syntax, are not universal. They are rules of particular languages at particular times, characteristic of particular forms of representation."[101] The point here, as it seems to me, is one that is more in tune with the spirit of the early Wittgenstein than it is the later one. In §521 of the *Investigations*, for example, we see him testing out the idea that logical possibility might depend "wholly on grammar," a suggestion that is immediately followed by the objection, "But surely that is arbitrary! – Is it arbitrary?" On one level, of course, it is quite obvious that every system of signification is, to some degree, arbitrarily constructed—be it syntactical, grammatical, or symbolic. Presumably, this applies even to logic, which is not to say that the syntax of logic is not 'universal,' but rather that its universality applies to only a small subset of all possible language-games. The quality of 'being universally applicable' is one that does not properly belong to every conceivable situation in which language might be employed. Universality, in other words, is one of the rules by which the language-game of logic is conducted, and it is just as susceptible to the vagaries of particular times and forms of representation as is any other language-game. At most, we might say that it *sometimes* makes sense to speak of logic as universal, whereas at other times, it does not. The syntax of logic is, like all rules of grammar, arbitrarily selected for the function it performs in a particular language-game, a quality that Baker and Hacker duly acknowledge. "The rules of grammar are not answerable to reality for truth or correctness.... In that sense they are, as Wittgenstein puts it, 'arbitrary'. They are not answerable to the 'laws of thought', but constitute them.... Grammar is, in an important sense *autonomous*."[102]

The autonomist nature of grammar, in combination with its arbitrarily decided rules, is very much like the picture of metaphysics that has been developed up to this point. It is autonomous because language cannot proceed unless based on a grammatical structure of some sort and arbitrary because there is no *a priori* justification for selecting grammatical rules. Justification exists only insofar as agreement exists. In this light, it would seem appropriate to suggest that grammar is very much the metaphysical construct of the *Investigations*—it determines what can and cannot be meaningful, and also, in a very real sense, what the nature of existence is. Pain, for instance, is not a corporeal object like a chair. Thus, we cannot apply the grammar of physical things to it without causing a good deal of confusion as to what pains are. Particular forms of grammar, however, can be difficult to break free from, so difficult in fact that we cannot imagine what it would be like outside of it. "A *picture* held us captive," Wittgenstein remarks in §115 of the *Investigations*. "And we couldn't get outside of it, for it lay in our language, and language seemed only to repeat it to us inexorably." In hindsight, however, Wittgenstein did break free from the siren song of pictorial grammar, which during his *Tractatus* period would have no doubt seemed a categorical impossibility for him. This brings up an important point. To prove that something is impossible is quite a different thing from its seeming to be impossible. Kant, for instance, claimed that space was a necessary and *a priori* condition of all our external intuitions. His reason was that "One can never represent that there is no space, although one can very well think that there are no objects to be encountered in it"[103] His inability—or anyone else's—to imagine a representation of nonexistent space does not qualify as a proof of its impossibility, or that space is an *a priori* condition of our intuition. It only shows that we are, at the present moment, incapable of so imagining the nonexistence of space. It says nothing about how we might one day view space or that we might even devise a way to represent nonexistent space. From its seeming impossible to me now does not equate to its being impossible categorically.

Wittgenstein's sense of the function of grammar, as potent as it might be, does run into one particular snag in regards to its treatment of philosophy as a deviation from grammatical 'norms.' Wittgenstein is harsh towards philosophy throughout the *Investigations* and particularly so at the end of §194. "When we do philosophy, we are like savages, primitive people, who hear the way in which civilized people talk, put a false interpretation on it, and then draw the oddest conclusions from this." Philosophical problems for Wittgenstein are always as a result of some error we make in the application of our grammatical rules, which results from our inability to get a clear view of its overall structure. The only task philosophy has—according to Wittgenstein's conception of it—is "to show the fly the way out of the fly-bottle."[104] There is, however, at least one potential difficulty that may be drawn from this stance. If philosophical problems result from a misapplication of rules, we must, of course, be able to tell the difference between what counts as 'correctly' and 'incorrectly' following a rule. We must be able to correctly tell the difference between a 'primitive' and a 'civilized' interpretation of language, i.e., between a 'philosophical' and a 'non-philosophical' interpretation—and Wittgenstein seems to have believed that we were in some sense capable of doing just that. The fact that the philosophical use of language is purportedly riddled with mistakes presupposes that we have the ability to distinguish between correct and incorrect uses. In other words, if philosophical misunderstandings exist, they exist because we have lost sight of the grammatical functions of our everyday language. Granted, the rules by which everyday language gets its meaning are not set in stone—they are always within the context of the form of life in which they occur. A difficulty remains in divining the criterion by which we are to measure any such deviations from this context. What counts as a deviation and what does not? Does it depend on the context of the language-game in which it occurs?

In order to attempt an answer to the above questions, one point should be made first. Wittgenstein does not, I would argue, adequately acknowledge that the activity of doing philosophy is as much a part of our form of life as anything else. Indeed, it is one of the most enduring components of human life. In what sense, then, can we speak of it as a grammatical deviation when it is tied up with the form of life we live? Philosophical problems are discussed by people every day. They have actual consequences in regards to the world views we adopt and to the interpretations we give. Why, then, is this considered a deviation from the norm? In response to Wittgenstein's criticism of philosophy, one might retort that the application of ordinary language grammar to the grammar of philosophy creates just as much misunderstanding as when we apply philosophical grammar to our everyday grammar. Philosophical problems are not misunderstandings of language according to its own lights. Why then should we take the rules of one language-game and apply them to another where they do not belong? One might retort to this question that the language-game of philosophy is a derivative of the broader language-game that is its home, and therefore the latter takes precedence over the former. Even if we grant this point, we do not thereby give a justification for dismissing philosophical grammar as a 'misunderstanding.' This would be like calling the use of the word 'king' in chess a 'misuse' because it does not conform to the sense that the word has in relation to the traditional head of a monarchy. We might similarly say that calling a pain an 'object' is not a misuse according to the grammar of certain kinds of philosophical language-games, even though this grammar may be derived from that of corporeal objects. In such a case, it makes perfect sense to view a pain as 'mine alone' and to assert that I 'know it' with absolute certainty. Different language-games have different rules, and different rules produce different meanings.

This, then, is the problem of metaphysics as it occurs in the *Investigations*: There is no way to justify the validity of the rules that comprise one language-game as opposed to another. We might have a preference for how one language-game is played when compared to others. We might even be of the opinion that certain kinds of language-games are composed entirely of hopelessly meaningless misunderstandings, but we cannot prove that the grammar on which any of these language-games is based is itself either right or wrong. And if we cannot do this, how can we assert that philosophical problems are 'misunderstandings' of our ordinary language? It is a self-referential inconsistency to assert that the meaning of a word is based on its use in the language-game and then deny outright that certain kinds of words, in certain kinds of language-games (i.e., philosophical ones), are meaningless, despite how they are used in the context of that language-game. To be coherent, this doctrine would have to admit that there are no such things as misunderstandings in an absolute sense, only misunderstandings in relation to the context of various language-games, some of which may be based on incompatible grammatical forms.

One of the central purposes of the *Investigations*, we could thus say, is to give us a method for disentangling the grammatical confusions that give the problems of philosophy their perplexing airs. It should come as no surprise, then, that when we successfully accomplish this task that we also cease to do philosophy precisely because it is predicated on the desire to see the otherwise ordinary uses of language as something deep and mysterious. Indeed, "Some philosophers," as Wittgenstein notes in *Zettel*, "suffer from what may be called 'loss of problems.'" To them, "everything seems quite simple," and the "deep problems" that so often mark the traditional philosophical discourse no longer "seem to exist." In such cases, "the world becomes broad and flat and loses all depth, and what they write becomes immeasurably shallow and trivial. Russell and H. G. Wells suffer from this."[105] This affliction, I think it safe to say, is one that Wittgenstein himself never suffered very severely from, neither in his outlook on life nor in his philosophical writings. This would, of course, appear to be the source of a somewhat conflicting perspective on his part. So much of Wittgenstein's work as a philosopher, after all, is predicated on his belief that the perennial philosophical problems consist only in the jumbled grammatical rules of our ordinary language-game. One would think that it would be the shallowest and most trivial philosophers that deserved the bulk of Wittgenstein's praise, but it is the opposite that is in fact true.[106] So despite all his various calls for ridding philosophy of its dilemmas, the problem for Wittgenstein—and a very deep one at that—was how to avoid the trivialization of philosophy. Perhaps this explains why the question of the value of philosophy is one that Wittgenstein never strays very far from: In order to avoid the petty bickering over semantics that mars so much of what makes philosophy important, Wittgenstein had to rein in its scope as a discipline in order to make room for what was enigmatic in it.[107]

This is also, in part, an account of the motivation behind Wittgenstein's anti-philosophical tone in the *Investigations*. It is not as if he definitively succeeds in demonstrating the premise that philosophy amounts to no more than a misunderstanding of grammar. Nor does he offer us any ultimately convincing reasons as to why the only correct mode of philosophizing is the one that endeavors to clear up the misunderstandings that philosophy itself causes. He assumes such a position precisely because the problem of how to view philosophical problems as unproblematic gives his thought so much depth. In general, Wittgenstein's attitude towards philosophy in the *Investigations* should no doubt strike us as being remarkably similar to that of the *Tractatus*. Both seek to limit what we can do with philosophy—especially in the realm of metaphysics. As with the *Tractatus*, the *Investigations* hardly avoids the topic, however forcefully, Wittgenstein rails against it. While it is true that many of the blatantly metaphysical ideas of the *Tractatus*—e.g., the doctrine of the 'simple elements of being'—are dispensed within the later work, the *Investigations* nevertheless allows us the possibility of imagining various language-games in which it *does* makes sense to speak *as if* simple elements were the basic constituents of physical

112       *Wittgenstein and the Problem of Metaphysics*

reality. And this is exactly what the strength of the text consists in: its creative capacity for imagining the innumerable forms of life that would imbue virtually any idea with the context necessary to be meaningful. What we learn along the way is that there is no such thing as a rule that would apply unilaterally to every conceivable language-game, nor a procedure for determining what constitutes following a rule in an absolute sense.

No doubt there are many other valuable lessons to be gleaned from a close reading of the *Investigations*, but perhaps one of the most important ones is not textual but rather methodological; that is, not in the content of any one of the examples Wittgenstein enumerates but rather in the way he goes about approaching them. This is not to say that the considerable wealth of perspectives in the text are not valuable in and of themselves, but it is to say, I think, that the style in which they are fleshed out actually contains the bulk of what is valuable in them. This style is, I dare say, no easy thing to characterize succinctly, but for all its peculiarities, two things, in particular, stand out to me: the creative and the aesthetic. The former, we might say, consists in the hypothetical postulate 'what if,' whereas the latter sets aside the speculative in favor of the declarative 'as if.' What sets Wittgenstein apart in this respect is his immense capacity to move between these disparate poles so as to be able to conceive of every 'what if' as a potential 'as if,' and vice versa. It is through this back and forth between the creative and the aesthetic that we become capable of moving from the mere envisaging of the possibility of alternative forms of life to actually abiding by them as truths for which no further justification is required. This is not to say, of course, that adopting a form of life amounts to a proof in any ultimate sense; it is merely a declaration of acquiescence to a way of life that is, in many respects, arbitrarily selected. In a sense, it constitutes a form of 'world-making,' one that consists not only in the ability to see every possibility as commensurable with every other, but also, and just as importantly, in the willing acceptance of all their concomitant ramifications.

While I would be the first to admit that the views described above are not ones explicitly espoused by Wittgenstein in the *Investigations*, I do believe we can read him as coming very close to saying as much in §367. "Compare a concept with a style of painting. For is even our style of painting arbitrary? Can we choose one at pleasure? (The Egyptian, for instance.) Or is it just a matter of pretty and ugly?" The answer, as with many of Wittgenstein's open-ended questions, could be both yes and no. Can we choose to paint like the Egyptians? Well, yes, but one might have difficulty in justifying it according to contemporary notions of art-making. At any rate, if one did choose to paint in the style of the Egyptians, it would not—and perhaps could not—be for any of the reasons that the Egyptians did. Nevertheless, this is no categorical imperative that either requires or prevents us from choosing any style of painting. Similarly, can we choose our concepts at will? Could we choose to believe that the world was flat, for instance? Again, the answer is both yes and no. Some concepts (such as the shape of the world) are so ensconced in collectively shared worldviews that they become difficult to deny without having to endure the rebuke of so called 'common sense.' There is, however, a world of difference between 'difficult' and 'impossible,' and the concept 'the world is flat' is still one that remains open to us, no matter how far-fetched it may seem.

As Wittgenstein himself realized, there is a fundamental connection between beliefs of this kind and the concepts we derive from them.

> If anyone believes that certain concepts are absolutely the correct ones, and that having different ones would mean not realizing something that we realize – then let him imagine certain very general facts of nature to be different from what we are used to, and the formation of concepts different from the usual ones will become intelligible to him.[108]

How we decide such matters, whether they be styles of paintings, concepts, forms of life, or metaphysical axioms, is, to a large extent, a matter of 'pretty and ugly,' but only if we mean by this 'accepted or rejected.' Yes, we can choose these things at will, but in so choosing we are, in a certain sense, determining what our idea of 'existence' shall consist in.

# Notes

1  Note that Wittgenstein is not the topic of Mackie's essay, nor is he even mentioned in it. The article is referenced only for the sake of drawing attention to some of the problems that are associated with the concept of metaphysical neutrality.

2  Peter van Inwagen, *Material Beings* (Ithaca, NY: Cornell University Press, 1990).

3  Penelope Mackie, "Ordinary Language and Metaphysical Commitment," *Analysis* 53, no. 4 (October 1993): 243.

4  Ibid., 250.

5  Ibid., 250.

6  Gordon Baker, "Wittgenstein on Metaphysical/Everyday Use," *The Philosophical Quarterly* 52, no. 208 (July 2002): 289.

7  Ibid., 302.

8  Marjorie Perloff, "From Theory to Grammar: Wittgenstein and the Aesthetic of the Ordinary," *New Literary History* 25, no. 4 (Autumn 1994): 902.

9  George Leonard, *Into the Light of Things: Art of the Commonplace from Wordsworth to John Cage* (Chicago: University of Chicago Press, 1995), 19.

10  Ibid., 12.

11  "Natural Supernaturalism" is the title of Chapter VIII of Carlyle's *Sartor Resartus* in which Diogenes Teufelsdröckh "finally subdues under his feet this refractory Clothes-Philosophy, and takes victorious possession thereof." See *Sartor Resartus: The Life and Opinions of Herr Teufelsdröckh* (London: Chapman & Hall, 1831), 203.

12  Ibid., 206.

13  Wittgenstein, *Philosophical Investigations*, sec. 201.

14  Ibid.

15  Ibid., sec. 200.

16  Ibid..

17  Ibid. sec. 201.

18  Ibid., sec. 202.

19  John McDowell, "Wittgenstein on Following a Rule," *Synthese* 58, no. 3 (1984): 340.

20  Ibid., 342.

21  Saul Kripke, *Wittgenstein on Rules and Private Language: An Elementary Exposition* (Cambridge, MA: Harvard University Press, 1984), 7.

22  Ibid. 60.

23  Ibid,. 55.

24  Ibid. 60.

25  Ibid. 87.

26  Ibid., 101.

27  Kripke, *Wittgenstein on Rules and Private Language*, 105.

28  See, e.g., Warren Goldfarb, "Kripke on Wittgenstein on Rules," *The Journal of Philosophy* 82, no. 9 (September 1985): 471–88; Paul Hoffman, "Kripke on Private Language," *Philosophical Studies: An International Journal for Philosophy in the Analytic Tradition* 47, no. 1 (January 1985): 23–28; Donna M. Summerfield, "Philosophical Investigations 201: A Wittgensteinian Reply to Kripke," *Journal of the History of Philosophy* 28, no. 3 (July 1990): 417–38; Patricia H. Werhane, "Some Paradoxes in Kripke's Interpretation of Wittgenstein," *Synthese* 73, no. 2 (November 1987): 253–73; Crispin Wright, "Kripke's Account of the Argument Against Private Language," *The Journal of Philosophy* 81, no. 12 (December 1984): 759–78.

29  For two such examples see Alex Byrne, "On Misinterpreting Kripke's Wittgenstein," *Philosophy and Phenomenological Research* 56, no. 2 (June 1996): 339–43; George Wilson, "Semantic Realism and Kripke's Wittgenstein," *Philosophy and Phenomenological Research* 58, no. 1 (March 1998): 99–122.

30  Gordon Baker and P. M. S. Hacker, "On Misunderstanding Wittgenstein: Kripke's Private Language Argument," *Synthese* 58, no. 3 (March 1984): 408.

31  Ibid., 408.

The Humble Origin of Words 115

32 Jacques Derrida, *Of Grammatology* (Baltimore, MD: Johns Hopkins University Press, 1997), 159.

33 Ibid., 158.

34 Baker and Hacker, "On Misunderstanding Wittgenstein," 421.

35 Kripke, *Wittgenstein on Rules and Private Language*, 3.

36 Baker and Hacker, "On Misunderstanding Wittgenstein," 422.

37 Wittgenstein, *Philosophical Investigations*, sec. 66.

38 Baker and Hacker, "On Misunderstanding Wittgenstein," 422.

39 Ibid., 423.

40 Wittgenstein, *On Certainty* (Oxford: Blackwell, 1977), sec. 18.

41 Baker and Hacker, "On Misunderstanding Wittgenstein," 423.

42 Kant, *Critique of the Power of Judgment*, §18, 5: 237.

43 Immanuel Kant, *Kant's Theory of Taste: A Reading of the Critique of Aesthetic Judgment*, Modern European Philosophy (Cambridge: Cambridge University Press, 2001), 4.

44 Kant, *Critique of the Power of Judgment*, §22 5: 239.

45 Freud, *Civilization and Its Discontents*, 42.

46 It is for precisely this reason that societies have a vested interest in policing the actions of its members: What one person does is an open invitation for someone else to do likewise. According to Althusser, there are two principal ways by which a populace may be coerced: the Repressive and Ideological State Apparatuses. Whereas the former functions via repression, the latter operates by altering the ideas we have about the real effect of our actions within a society. Thus a state is ideologically successful when it can convince its members that their "actions are inserted into *practices*" that are themselves "governed" by rituals "within the *material existence of an ideological apparatus*." That is to say, in other words, that the most effective state is the one that can convince people to unhesitatingly act according to ideologies that are not their own. See *On Ideology* (New York; London: Verso, 2008), 42.

47 Jean-Paul Sartre, *Existentialism Is a Humanism* (New Haven, CT: Yale University Press, 2007), 24.

48 Jean-Paul Sartre, *Being and Nothingness*, trans. Hazel Barnes (New York: Washington Square Press, 1992), 583.

49 Ibid., 584.

50 Wittgenstein, *Philosophical Investigations*, sec. 77.

51 The constant back and forth between descent and assent is indeed a persistent feature of the style Wittgenstein employs throughout the *Investigations*. As Kripke notes, the book "is written as a perpetual dialectic, where persisting worries, expressed by the voice of the imaginary interlocutor, are never definitely silenced" (*Wittgenstein on Rules and Private Language*, 3). This is also one of the *Investigations'* enduring strengths, and in this respect it is reminiscent of the Platonic dialogues in

which Socrates is usually the victor but doubts are nevertheless left unresolved. The dialectic form of the *Investigations*, like the crystalline structure of the *Tractatus*, is thus treated by Wittgenstein with a bent that is undeniably artistic. The style in which the *Investigations* is written—and the aesthetic force of its prose—is even enhanced by the fact that there is often no clear distinction between Wittgenstein and his interlocutor. One might even say that the Wittgenstein of the *Investigations* is the best opponent of his former philosophical persona—which despite being handily refuted by his later self, was always in some sense willing and able to critique all his revamped considerations.

52 Ludwig Wittgenstein, *Philosophical Occasions, 1912–1951*, ed. James Klagge and Alfred Nordmann (Indianapolis, IN: Hackett Publishing, 1993), 235.

53 Ludwig Wittgenstein, *Philosophical Remarks* (Chicago: University of Chicago Press, 1980), sec. 92.

54 Wittgenstein, *Philosophical Grammar*, 77.

55 Ludwig Wittgenstein, *Preliminary Studies for the "Philosophical Investigations": Generally Known As the Blue and Brown Books* (New York: Harper Torchbooks, 1960), 17.

56 Ibid., 17.

57 Wittgenstein, *Philosophical Investigations*, sec. 1.

58 Ibid., sec. 3.

59 Ibid., sec. 7.

60 Ibid., sec. 90.

61 Ibid., sec. 66.

62 David Finkelstein, "Wittgenstein on Rules and Platonism," in *The New Wittgenstein*, ed. Alice Crary and Rupert Read (London: Routledge, 2000), 68.

63 Ibid., 68.

64 Alice Crary, "Wittgenstein and Political Thought," in *The New Wittgenstein*, ed. Alice Crary and Rupert Read (London: Routledge, 2000), 130.

65 Stanley Cavell, "Excursus on Wittgenstein's Vision of Language," in *The New Wittgenstein*, ed. Alice Crary and Rupert Read (London: Routledge, 2000), 35.

66 Ibid., 35.

67 Wittgenstein, *Philosophical Investigations*, sec. 65.

68 Cavell, "Excursus on Wittgenstein's Vision of Language," 35.

69 Ibid.

70 Ibid.

71 Friedrich Nietzsche, "Twilight of the Idols," in *Twilight of the Idols; and, The Anti-Christ* (London: Penguin, 1990), 40.

72 Hans-Johann Glock, *A Wittgenstein Dictionary* (Oxford: Blackwell, 1996), 124.

73 "Man is naturally a political animal. Proof that man is a political animal in a higher sense than a bee or any other gregarious creature: Nature creates nothing without

The Humble Origin of Words 117

purpose. Man is the only animal possessing articulate speech as distinguished from mere sounds." See *The Politics of Aristotle*, trans. J. E. C. Welldon (London: Macmillan and Co., 1883), x.

74 Wittgenstein, *Philosophical Investigations*, sec. 327.

75 Newton Garver, *This Complicated Form of Life: Essays on Wittgenstein* (Chicago: Open Court, 1994), 242–43.

76 The only occurrence of *Lebensformen* occurs in §345 of *Philosophy of Psychology – A Fragment* (previously known as Part II of the *Investigations*). "What has to be accepted, the given, is – one might say – *forms of life*." Though this passage is important in regards to Wittgenstein's conception of certainty, Garver, on page 251 of *This Complicated Form of Life*, seems to treat the use of the plural as an aberration. "Wittgenstein's wording suggests that he may be presenting the idea tentatively rather than with conviction." This is a convenient account as far as Garver's argument is concerned, but there is little textual evidence, one way or the other, that would indicate whether Wittgenstein was hesitantly using *Lebensformen* or not. There is therefore no reason to consider it as a deviation from his more regular use of *Lebensform*.

77 Garver, *This Complicated Form of Life*, 246.

78 Ibid., 248.

79 Ibid., 246.

80 Wittgenstein, *Philosophical Investigations*, sec. 100.

81 Garver, *This Complicated Form of Life*, 240.

82 It is precisely this model which held sway over Wittgenstein in the *Tractatus*, and no doubt part of the paradoxical difficulties he encounters therein stems from the doctrine that names must designate absolutely simple elements of being. But as Wittgenstein would later realize in the *Investigations*, "The paradox disappears only if we make a radical break with the idea that language always functions in one way, always serves the same purpose: to convey thoughts." *Philosophical Investigations*, 109.

83 The same problem applies equally as much to the naming of sensations: The grammar of object and name can very easily produce a distorted picture of the relationship between a sensation and the word for that sensation. This does not show, however, as John W. Cook has pointed out, "That sensations cannot have names, it shows that since the view that sensations are private allows sensations to have 'no place in the language-game' and thereby makes it impossible to give any account of the actual (that is, the 'public') use of sensation words, we must, if we are to give an account of that language game, reject the view that sensations are private." See "Wittgenstein on Privacy," *The Philosophical Review* 74, no. 3 (July 1965): 312.

84 Wittgenstein, *Philosophical Investigations*, sec. 58.

85 Nietzsche, *The Will to Power*, sec. 568.

86  Ibid., sec. 522.

87  Ibid., sec. 479.

88  Linda L. Williams, *Nietzsche's Mirror: The World as Will to Power* (Lanham, MD: Rowman & Littlefield, 2001), 3.

89  Friedrich Nietzsche, "The Genealogy of Morals: An Attack," in *The Birth of Tragedy & The Genealogy of Morals* (New York: Anchor Books, 1990), sec. 13.

90  Nietzsche, *Beyond Good and Evil*, sec. 23.

91  Robert Pippin, *Nietzsche, Psychology, and First Philosophy* (Chicago: University of Chicago Press, 2010), 85. Pippin here seems to be using the term "metaphysics" synonymously with "ontology," which is certainly within the realm of its traditional use. It does not, however, encompass the broader sense of "first philosophy" as a set of "axiomatic" principles.

92  Wittgenstein, *Philosophical Investigations*, sec. 121.

93  Ibid., sec. 122.

94  Ibid., sec. 120.

95  Ibid., sec. 122.

96  Ibid., sec. 123.

97  Ibid., sec. 125.

98  Ibid., sec. 126.

99  Michael Forster, *Wittgenstein on the Arbitrariness of Grammar* (Princeton, NJ: Princeton University Press, 2004), 7.

100  Wittgenstein, *Philosophical Investigations*, sec. 89.

101  Gordon P. Baker and P. M. S. Hacker, *Wittgenstein – Rules, Grammar, and Necessity: Essays and Exegesis of 185–242*, 2nd ed. (Chichester, UK: Wiley-Blackwell, 2009), 46.

102  Ibid.

103  Immanuel Kant, *Critique of Pure Reason*, trans. Paul Guyer and Allen W. Wood (Cambridge: Cambridge University Press, 1998), A 24/B 39.

104  Wittgenstein, *Philosophical Investigations*, sec. 309.

105  Ludwig Wittgenstein, *Zettel* (Berkeley, CA: University of California Press, 2007), sec. 416.

106  Think, for example, of some of the biggest influences on Wittgenstein's philosophical development: Schopenhauer, Weininger, Spengler, Tolstoy, and Frazer—amongst others—each of whom either grappled with problematic ideas that were nevertheless worthy of consideration in their own right or otherwise concerned themselves with the problems of life in general.

107  In much the same way as Kant had "deny knowledge in order to make room for faith." *Critique of Pure Reason*, 1998, Bxxx.

108  Wittgenstein, *Philosophical Investigations*, sec. 366.

# 4

# At the Foundation of Well-Founded Belief

The problems that have thus far been outlined in the previous chapters have all been centered around the claim that there can be no 'escape from metaphysics' or a metaphysics that is somehow 'neutral,' 'incorrigible,' or 'necessarily the case.' I have also argued that at least part of Wittgenstein's philosophical career is bound up with this difficulty and the hopeless struggle to overcome it. In the *Tractatus*, he thinks the problem of metaphysics can be solved by basing language on a properly constructed logical foundation. By the time of the *Investigations*, it is the return to the ordinary usage of language that would seem to remedy our habitual backsliding into metaphysical rumination. But both of these tactics, as we have seen, fail for various reasons, many of which stem from self-referential inconsistencies involved in the general denial of metaphysics via suppositions that claim a special non-metaphysical status that they, in fact, do not have. This problem of metaphysics is, so my contention goes, primarily a result of Wittgenstein's dual abhorrence of and fascination with questions of a deeply metaphysical nature—a characteristic that inevitably makes its way into his first two books.

This is not the case, however, where *On Certainty* is concerned—the last of Wittgenstein's three great works and, to my mind, his greatest. It is a text that occasionally strikes remarkably similar chords as those that belong more properly to the earlier stages of his philosophical development while at the same time extending those lines of inquiry into entirely novel territory. Chief among these, of course, is a prolonged engagement with the concept of certainty, which, to be sure, is not one that Wittgenstein had previously ignored but was never front and center in his considerations. In addition to the new philosophical paths onto which it embarks, there is also a completely different stylistic flavor to the book. At times it reads almost conversationally, as if one were debating these points with Wittgenstein face-to-face instead of reading them some six decades hence. No doubt this is due, in part, to the fact that the notes which comprise *On Certainty* were written in relative haste as compared to the *Tractatus* and the

*Investigations*, both of which Wittgenstein labored on for extended periods of time. It therefore lacks the high degree of polish that is the hallmark of his writings eventually intended for publication.

But beyond this more casual tone, there is something else—something of an air of resignation—even though to term it thus is perhaps a bit of a misnomer, and I should hasten to add that I do not here use it in a pejorative sense. If we are to call it that, we must understand it as the sort that empowers one to reappraise even the most basic of one's assumptions, no matter how difficult the task. "The *edifice of your pride* has to be dismantled," Wittgenstein himself realized, "And that is terribly hard work."[1] *On Certainty* is just such a work of edifice dismantling. While this may be in part due to his cognizance of his impending death at the hands of prostate cancer, there also seems to be a subtle shift in the expectations he has for the task of philosophy. There can be no 'overcoming' of metaphysics, no 'demonstration' of its impossibility, no 'special set' of nonsensical utterances that somehow avoid running afoul of their own dictates. Nor can there be any ultimately solid foundation of knowledge; no indubitable, incorrigible, self-apparent or primary truths; no simple element of being or thing-in-itself. There are only the assumptions with which we proceed *as if* they were certain but are unable to prove. At the foundation of well-founded belief lies belief that is not founded.[2] We must willingly accept philosophy as a project onto itself, one taken up without preconceived expectations as to what it ought to accomplish *a priori*, or we must not do it at all. The intent of this chapter is, therefore, not to demonstrate that Wittgenstein managed to solve the problem of metaphysics as he seemed to think he did in the *Tractatus* and the *Investigations*, but that he comes to terms with and makes a strong case for its insolubility.

The problem of metaphysics is not, of course, one that is unique to Wittgenstein. Indeed, many of those who were influenced by his early philosophy often exhibit strains of it as well. This is especially the case where some of the more positivist leaning philosophers are concerned, such as we see, for instance, in the work of A. J. Ayer. Many of the *a priori* propositions have, he tells us, tended to attract the notice of philosophers precisely "on account of their certainty," even though they invariably derive this quality from "the fact that they are tautologies." All too often, however, philosophers are wont to confuse such tautological statements with metaphysical sentences. The problem with this, according to Ayer, is that a metaphysical sentence is not "a genuine proposition" in the sense that it expresses "neither a tautology nor an empirical hypothesis," both of which taken together "form the entire class of significant propositions." The conclusion that Ayer would thus have us reach based on this supposition is "that all metaphysical assertions are nonsensical."[3]

*At the Foundation of Well-Founded Belief*            121

The degree to which Ayer's views on metaphysics can be attributed to Wittgenstein is a matter of some difficulty, and I will not here undertake an exhaustive analysis of that relationship. One of the main differences I would like to draw attention to, however, concerns the question of whether tautologies can be considered amongst the class of 'significant propositions.' The Wittgenstein of the *Tractatus* differs notably from Ayer in one key respect in this regard: Tautologies cannot be included within the realm of so-called meaningful language. As he puts it in 5.5303, "Roughly speaking, to say of two things that they are identical is nonsense, and to say of *one* thing that it is identical with itself is to say nothing at all." A tautology, according to Wittgenstein's view on the matter, is not a 'significant proposition'—that designation belongs only to hypotheses of an empirical nature. While it is true that they may not be nonsensical in the same way that statements of a metaphysical ilk are, they are nevertheless senseless in that they do not signify anything that is contingently true. Tautologies, as it were, stand at the border between sense and nonsense, and it is for this reason, as I have argued in Chapter 2, that they are more akin to metaphysical statements than they are to the propositions of natural science. They are neither a part of the world nor properly speaking external to it; they are rather what makes possible the existence of every state of affairs that happens to be the case at any given point in time, the sum of which constitutes the 'world.'

Regardless of whatever other differences might exist between Wittgenstein's definition of tautology and the one proffered by Ayer, let us set them aside for the time being and provisionally assume, for the sake of argument, that Ayer's definition of metaphysics is correct: What distinguishes a metaphysical sentence from other kinds that we can construct is that the former makes no claim to logical validity or empirical verifiability. In acquiescing to this definition, however, we have not, as of yet, proven that the formulation of metaphysical sentences is unnecessary or even avoidable in the construction of any philosophical system. In fact, just this kind of unverifiable metaphysical assumption underpins Ayer's belief in the ability of significant propositions to "anticipate the course of our sensations."[4] The hypothesis 'empirical hypotheses are significant only if they have predictive power' is itself not a significant proposition for the simple reason that it does not predict future sensations. But the point here is not so much to show that Ayer's definition of metaphysics is inadequate; it is rather to show that his criterion for significant propositions is dependent on the sort of non-significant propositions which he is attempting to repudiate. In all actuality, metaphysics, which according to Ayer is exemplified by its nonsensicality—by which he means that they cannot be substantiated by any

122          *Wittgenstein and the Problem of Metaphysics*

sort of proof—suffices as a passable characterization of the term. All that we are required to admit is that metaphysics is essentially definitional, and strictly speaking a definition is itself nonsense inasmuch as it cannot be given any ultimate foundation.

Part of Ayer's problem is that his method tends towards regression—it must give a series of justifications for justifications. His verification criterion—itself an attempt at a justification—simply begs the question of its own justification without answering the question as to why our axioms require a justification in the first place. Why does knowledge—if it is true—necessitate a foundation of absolute certainty, or at least the highest degree attainable in a world marred by perpetual uncertainty? In answering this question, the first step is to begin by identifying the source of the regress and, to a large extent, this lies in a phenomenon that Nietzsche had already noted in Book 1, §2 of *The Gay Science*: the "desire for certainty." Indeed, one of the goals of his philosophy, in general, was to "show that the question concerning certainty is already in itself a *dependent* question, a question of the second rank."[5] Certainty, as far as Nietzsche was concerned, is a psychological state only and does not distinguish between things as 'they appear to be' and 'things as they really are.' "Being and appearance, regarded psychologically, yield no 'Being-in-itself,' no criterion for 'reality,' but only degrees of appearance, measured according to the strength of the sympathy which we feel for appearance."[6]

Nietzsche, no doubt, is drawing our attention to the confusion between the psychological state of being certain and certainty itself. The question is, of course, how are we to tell the difference between feeling certain and actually being certain? The psychological feeling of being certain is surely something very much like 'being unable to be convinced otherwise.' When this feeling occurs, one finds one's self incapable of being swayed from a conviction that is steadfastly held. When in such a state, no amount of evidence, rhetoric, or persuasion can alter one's beliefs to the contrary. The feeling of being absolutely certain is, in other words, generally typified by either an inability or unwillingness to see things differently. This is not to say that a whole host of reasons may not be produced in support of beliefs, but they do not require them in order to be indefatigably held. The psychological state of being certain can occur whether there is proof to support it or not—which is also why no amount of evidence is sufficient to alter it. In part, this is why Nietzsche dismisses this state of psychological certainty as a "criterion of reality." Being certain is based merely on the "strength of the sympathy" which we feel for the way things appear to us. It is thus an aesthetic inclination and an inclination that cannot in any sense be a justification for knowledge prior to the "question of values,"[7] which is, as Nietzsche claimed, "More *fundamental* than the question of certainty."[8]

The argument of this chapter is, therefore, in much the same vein as the one Nietzsche makes above, but it will also go further in arguing that Wittgenstein comes to something of a similar conclusion in *On Certainty*. Though not as polemical as Nietzsche, Wittgenstein's critique of certainty as a criterion of knowledge in the grand philosophical style is no less poignant. Wittgenstein's terminology is also significantly different from Nietzsche's, but there are nevertheless many similarities between the points being made by both. Although there is nothing in *On Certainty* which is similar in form to Nietzsche's 'metaphysics of art,' I will argue that something very close to it can be inferred from many of his writings. A conclusion of this sort is reinforced by the fact that art, and especially music, were central components of Wittgenstein's life—a biographical fact remarkably similar to Nietzsche's. Both are well known to have been musical virtuosos. Nietzsche, though not gifted at composition, was astonishingly able at improvising on the piano. Carl von Gersdorff, a friend from Nietzsche's youth, noted that he "would have no difficulty in believing that even Beethoven did not improvise in a more moving manner than Nietzsche."[9] Wittgenstein was also well endowed with a keen musical sensibility and was able to "whistle whole movements of symphonies, his showpiece being Brahms's *St Anthony Variations*, and that when other people whistle something wrong, Wittgenstein would stop them and firmly tell them how it should go."[10] Wittgenstein's views on art, music, and aesthetics are, however, not the topic of this chapter (these topics will be addressed in more depth in the following one). This chapter will focus on the exegesis of *On Certainty* along with the claim that from its basic tenets, we can derive an aesthetic conception of the nature of metaphysics that dispenses with the problem of metaphysics in general.

*On Certainty* consists largely of a running commentary on two essays by G. E. Moore: "A Defense of Common Sense" published in 1925 and "Proof of an External World" published in 1939. In the former article, Moore details a list of propositions that he claims to "*know*, with certainty, to be true,"[11] which are too numerous to repeat in full, but include such assertions as "I have a human body," "my body has never been far from the surface of the earth," "the earth has existed for many years before my birth," "many other bodies exist now and have existed in the past, many of which have ceased to exist before I was born," etc.[12] Moore goes on to claim that "such an expression as 'the earth has existed for many years past' is the very type of unambiguous expression, the meaning of which we all understand."[13]

In "Proof of an External World" Moore begins by noting the "scandal of philosophy" to which Kant refers in the preface of the *Critique of Pure Reason*: that the existence of external things must be taken on faith, a problem that Kant had thought he had solved by showing "the objective reality of outer intuition."[14] This is a solution that Moore is by no means satisfied with. In order that we may devise a proof that will remedy this malady, he first sets about rephrasing the question "Are there things outside of us?" as "Are there things external to our minds which can be met with in space?"[15] With this question in mind, Moore claims that "I can prove now, for instance, that two human hands exist. How? By holding up my two hands, and saying, as I make a certain gesture with the right hand, 'Here is one hand', and adding, as I make a certain gesture with the left, 'and here is another.'"[16]

Wittgenstein, of course, begins *On Certainty* by making reference to Moore's proof, "If you do know that *here is one hand*, we'll grant you all the rest."[17] Right from the outset, we see what will be a vital component of Wittgenstein's critique. It is not that Moore fails to give a valid proof that there are such things that are 'separate from the mind' and 'can be met with in space'—he does just that by way of a *modus ponens*. If this is a hand, then external things exist. This is a hand. Therefore, external things exist. *Definition*: a hand is an external object (i.e., it is separate from the mind and can be met with in space). It is exactly with this definition that our suspicions lie, however, as Wittgenstein rightfully points out. It should be noted, however, that Moore only claims that his proof is valid if we are willing to accept his propositions as true. As he acknowledges, some will find this proof unsatisfactory. "They will say that I have not given what they mean by a proof of the existence of external things. In other words, they want a proof of what I assert *now* when I hold up my hands and say 'Here's one hand and here's another'.... This, of course, I haven't given; and I do not believe it can be given."[18] On this point, Wittgenstein agrees with Moore. No proof of the sort that Moore alludes to (and which his critics, including Wittgenstein, ask for) can be given.

Although there are many interrelated topics of which Wittgenstein treats in *On Certainty*, one of the most central of them is concerned with enumerating the various ways in which the phrase 'I know . . .' can be used and misused within the language-game. "Now, can one enumerate what one knows (like Moore)? Straight off like that, I believe not.—For otherwise, the expression 'I know' gets misused."[19] The misapplication of this phrase stems from what Wittgenstein calls the "preeminently philosophical"[20] use. As the phrase is utilized in this sense, it is meant to exemplify a state of unflappable metaphysical certainty that its speaker is claiming to possess—the kind of "immovable point" from which one could

# At the Foundation of Well-Founded Belief

"shift the entire earth"[21] that Descartes so longed for. Declarations of the sort 'I know ...' do not constitute such an Archimedean point. "Even if the most trustworthy of men assures me that he knows things are thus and so, this by itself cannot satisfy me that he does know. Only that he believes he knows. That is why Moore's assurance that he knows ... does not interest us."[22] This applies equally to cases where "*very many* (I do not say *all*) ... of *us*" can be said to know all the same things "with regard to *himself* or *his* body" which "each of us has frequently known."[23] For as Wittgenstein retorts, "From its *seeming* to me—or to everyone—to be so, it doesn't follow that it *is* so."[24] Such an instance where we know something in common is by no means a guarantor of its truthfulness or a marker of its certainty. Besides this, the claim to know something that everyone else also presumably knows (in the metaphysical, preeminently philosophical sense) is not expressed, nor can it be expressed, by the phrase 'I know ...' or 'we know....' Wittgenstein directs our attention to this point when he asks, "Why doesn't Moore produce as one of the things that he knows, for example, that in such-and-such a part of England there is a village called so-and-so? In other words: why doesn't he mention a fact that is known to him and not to every one of us?"[25]

The answer, it would seem, is because by so doing, Moore believes himself to be demonstrating the sort of thing we can be metaphysically certain about. Empirical propositions of the sort 'in such-and-such a part of England there is a village called so-and-so' do not seem to qualify as 'preeminently philosophical' in the same way that Moore's use of the phrase 'I have a human body' does. This is not to say, however, that these apparently 'self-evident truisms' are not things that one can legitimately have knowledge about. When we attempt to claim certainty about the kind of propositions that Moore gives as examples, we are not saying, in effect, 'I cannot be mistaken.' Rather, what we are acknowledging is the common foundation of the language-game, the rules of which we all collectively agree to. The rules themselves are not properly an object of knowledge in the way that empirical propositions are. This is because 'knowing' (and likewise doubting) are not concepts that exist outside of the language-game.

It is for this reason that the kinds of statements that Moore claims to know seem so puzzling. "'I know that I am a human being.' In order to see how unclear the sense of this proposition is, consider its negation."[26] When one makes statements of this kind, so Wittgenstein thinks, it seems as if we "have known something the whole time, and yet there is no meaning in saying so, in uttering this truth."[27] On the other hand, when someone says I know that "there are over ... species of insects,"[28] we are liable to ask how it is that the knowledge in question was arrived at. To which one could respond, 'I read it in a reputable book,' or 'I have it on authority from an entomologist who makes a careful study of the subject,' etc. For Wittgenstein, then, "If someone says he knows something, it must be something that, by general consent, he is in a position to know."[29] Under normal circumstances, of course, general consent suffices to assuage any doubt as to the legitimacy of a knowledge claim. We would not expect, for example, that a scholar of medieval European history would need to provide evidence for making certain generalized claims about the Hundred Years' War. We assume, and rightly so, that to be a scholar means having done a sufficient amount of research into a topic to warrant a kind of expertise that we do not habitually question. We may, to be sure, come to find out that our trust had been misplaced, but this too would be open to the possibility of being proven one way or the other.

All of this is to say, in other words, that knowledge is only ever possible where there is also the possibility of providing a justification for it, and this is done by making an appeal to various commonly held standards of validation that will differ according to the kind of language-game being played at any given time. The same, however, cannot be said for the standards of validation themselves. Propositions of these kinds play a much more foundational role in the language-game. While it is true that they constitute the prerequisites of knowledge, they are themselves not an object of knowledge. In a manner of speaking, they do not belong to the language-game of knowing because they form the basis on which it operates. This is why when we say we 'know with absolute certainty' something as foundational as 'I have a human body,' we are misusing the phrase 'I know.' We are, in effect, attempting to know without a foundation for knowing.

Within a language-game, some propositions play a more fundamental role than others, but this fact does not confer upon them the status of philosophical preeminence. This is to say, in other words, that there is no absolutely necessary or certain basis for the language-game. It is, as Wittgenstein puts it, "Something unpredictable. I mean: it is not based on grounds. It is not reasonable (or unreasonable). It is there—like our life."[30] Now, if this is the case—if this 'thereness' underlies the whole edifice of the language-game—then we would seem to have no choice but to admit that language is nothing if not an arbitrarily pieced together construct, one that depends on whatever conditions or forms of life happen to exist here and now. No doubt these can and do change over time, but in order for the language-game to function at all, some of the propositions on which it depends would have to remain provisionally unassailable. "If I want the door to turn, the hinges must stay put."[31] This does not mean, of course, that the pin that holds the hinge in place may not be removed. Language works perfectly well even if we are unable to give an ultimate and unshakable grounds for its

At the Foundation of Well-Founded Belief     127

foundation, just as a door functions without the benefit of permanently affixed hinges. We are quite mistaken, however, if we take the necessary immobility of foundational propositions as a demonstration of their indubitability. At a certain point in the language-game of justification, the possibility of going any further is denied to us. "At the end of reason comes *persuasion*,"[32] and persuasion is, as any good rhetorician knows, a matter of aesthetics as anything else. Convincing someone else to assent to the legitimacy of a justification necessitates a universal expectation of agreement, and this comes, as we have already seen, via the normativity implicit within judgments of taste.

The worry over the misuse of the phrase 'I know' was one that had also expressed itself in much of Wittgenstein's earlier work. In the *Tractatus*, for example, Wittgenstein remarks of skepticism that it "is *not* irrefutable, but obviously nonsensical, when it tries to raise doubts where no questions can be asked. For doubt can exist only where a question exists, a question only where an answer exists, and an answer only where something *can be said*."[33] Accordingly, one cannot raise skeptical doubts about a tautology because, strictly speaking, it says nothing. One cannot, therefore, say that 'I know' that 'A = A' because one cannot also say 'I doubt' that 'A = A.' Much the same point—albeit for somewhat divergent motives—is similarly made in the *Investigations*. One of the things that the argument against private language is meant to show us, after all, is that the proposition, 'Only I know with absolute certainty what sensations I am experiencing,' fails to accomplish what it purports to do, and that is to give us at least one instance of a necessarily true and certain fact about which we cannot be mistaken. But the irony of this argument is, of course, that the *a priori* exclusion of doubt from the language-game also precludes the inclusion of knowledge. It is, Wittgenstein concludes, therefore "correct to say 'I know what you are thinking', and wrong to say 'I know what I am thinking'. (A whole cloud of philosophy condenses into a drop of grammar.)"[34] It is this same 'cloud of philosophy,' Wittgenstein contends, that surrounds Moore's proof of an external world. 'I know that I have a hand' amounts to a misuse of the phrase 'I know' because we do not have any clear sense of what it would be like to doubt this fact, and if the possibility of doubt does not exist, then neither does the possibility of knowledge. This is why I can rightly claim to 'know' what someone else is thinking because I can just as easily imagine what it would be like to doubt it. In other words, 'I know what you are thinking' means I have a fairly cohesive idea of what's 'in' your mind, although my estimation, of course, might turn out to be wrong.

It is remarkable to note that Wittgenstein employs an epistemological theory that remains virtually unchanged through nearly every phase of his work, especially when considering the otherwise significant transformations that it would undergo. This theory is, roughly stated, that one can only know something where one can also doubt it. It makes no sense according to this conception to say 'I know that …' if one cannot also say 'I doubt that …' of the same thing. Under usual circumstances, for instance, attempting to doubt the existence of one's hand would not be taken as a demonstration of the infallibility of one's knowledge. Rather, it would quite possibly be taken as a sign of psychosis, as Wittgenstein seems to suggest in §467 of *On Certainty*. "I am sitting with a philosopher in the garden; he says again and again 'I know that that's a tree', pointing to a tree that is near us. Someone else arrives and hears this, and I tell him: 'This fellow isn't insane. We are only doing philosophy.'" What purpose, then, could such a statement as 'I know that that's a tree' serve in a language-game? We might imagine, as Wittgenstein does, that the phrase 'I know' might be used in situations where "no one could doubt it, [it] might be a kind of joke and as such have meaning."[35] Another example of a meaningful use of the expression 'I know' would be when "someone with bad sight asks me: 'do you believe that the thing we can see there is a tree?' I reply, "I *know* it is; I can see it clearly and am familiar with it."[36] The collective lesson to be learned from each of these examples is a simple one: Whenever "one says 'I know'" one also "mentions how one knows, or at least one can do so."[37] As a philosophical expression of certainty, though, or a demonstration of the existence of things external to the mind, it makes no contextual sense within the language-game to say 'I know that that's a tree' because there is no way to demonstrate the grounds from which one is basing one's claim.

This is why, as Moore is willing to admit that the premises on which his demonstration of an external world are predicated cannot themselves be proven true—we either accept them or we do not, and if we do, the proof is valid, and if not then it is not. The problem that arises from this concession, however, is quite a formidable one. If nothing compels us with the universally binding force of a categorical imperative, why ought we to act one way and not another? What reason could there be for anyone to assent or dissent to these premises or any other? Unsurprisingly, Moore is ultimately unable to answer these questions and is thus forced to reject those "who are dissatisfied with these proofs merely on the ground that I did not know the premises."[38] On this point, no doubt, Wittgenstein is in agreement with Moore: All proofs rest on one or more premises that cannot, when all is said and done, be known beyond any shadow of a doubt. This does not, however, deprive all proofs in general of their efficacy, which is why Moore insists that we can persist in speaking about such things that we "cannot prove" but can nonetheless know with certainty, among which are "the premises of [the] two proofs"[39] that he offers us. It is this point, as we have seen, that bears the brunt of Wittgenstein's criticism. If Moore cannot first provide a proof for the premise that 'this is a hand,' then the whole evidentiary structure for the assertion that 'there are objects separate from the mind and that may be met with in space' falls apart.

In his book *Moore and Wittgenstein on Certainty*, Avrum Stroll suggests that one of the problems with Moore's approach is that he was, "Like most traditional epistemologists, ... working under the spell of a powerful philosophical model deriving from Descartes."[40] "This model," he continues, "Made the need to give a proof of the external world virtually irresistible."[41] To be sure, one of the primary targets of Moore's proof is the skeptics and idealists who call the existence of the self-subsisting corporeal world into question. The problem with this attempted refutation, however, is that rather than disproving his adversaries, Moore only invites the very skeptical objections it is meant to overcome. At most, all that Moore is able to demonstrate is that the doubts raised by the idealist and the skeptic are *also* based on 'unproved premises' and therefore, in the absence of any such proof, we ought to err on the side of 'common sense.' But for all its supposed universality, common sense has an unusually high susceptibility to deviation. This helps explain, I think, why Moore feels it incumbent upon himself to offer us all kinds of reasons for why we ought to favor his particular brand of 'common sense' premises over those of the skeptic or idealist, none of which, I imagine, would ultimately be convincing to someone who was already predisposed to that way of thinking. Even the seemingly contradictory way in which idealist philosophers allude "to the existence of other philosophers ... [or] the human race"[42] while simultaneously denying that there are "*very many other human beings, who have had bodies and lived upon the earth*"[43] can be met with the retort of the solipsist: The apparent existence of other people is merely a phantasmal construct of my own self-consciousness. The only thing that I can know with any degree of certainty is the existence of my mind, and therefore there is no contradiction in making reference to other human beings while also disavowing the existence of their corporeal bodies or their proximity to an equally non-corporeal planet. But even if we were to assuage the metaphysically fantastical objections of the solipsist, we would still need to face those of the irrationalist. We could simply refuse to accept the idea of consistency outright as merely one amongst many unprovable premises, none of which have any special claim to self-evidence.

Why, then, did Moore place such an unusually high degree of value on common sense? Certainly, he is not the first philosopher to do so, nor has he been the last. While we may not be inclined to accept his proof of an external world as valid, there is still something undeniably appealing to it in its own right. There is a finality about the sorts of things Moore enumerates that can perhaps only be adequately described as 'intuitively self-evident.' Perhaps this is why the mere declaration of their truth *seems* to suffice as a demonstration of it. For Wittgenstein, however, the mere assurance on Moore's part that he does know "can't accomplish anything here"[44] precisely because they are the kinds of things that, "Roughly speaking, all of us know, if he knows them."[45] This is not to say, of course, that these kinds of pronouncements are philosophically insignificant, but what value they do possess is not as a result of their being absolutely irrefutable. In order to see why the premises of Moore's proof are so compelling, we must first forgo the question of their certitude and instead ask ourselves what it would be "like to discover that it was a mistake."[46] What would it be like, in other words, to realize that the statement, 'I know this is a hand,' was wrong? An explanation for a mistake here would, more than likely, be along the lines of 'you were suffering a hallucination' or possibly, 'you need to have your eyes checked; they are obviously poor.' In either case, we would have no difficulty in showing that the error in question occurred as a result of some clearly identifiable cause and, as such, would be perfectly explainable. Suppose, however, that no cause of this sort could be discovered, and the person who made the mistake was deemed to be of sound mind and body in every appreciable respect. What would a mistake look like under these kinds of circumstances? Would it even be possible to speak of 'knowing' and 'not-knowing' where the possibility of these kinds of mistakes was not ruled out from the very beginning?

The fact that we find it difficult to imagine a world in which people regularly make such totally erroneous judgments reveals a crucial fact for Wittgenstein: What we are pointing towards—however unintentionally—when we say a phrase like 'I know that this is a hand' is not some self-evident truism about which there is no possibility of error but rather a grammatical proposition whose place at the foundation of the language-game ensures its status as incontrovertible. Anyone who is acquainted with how the language-game is played will also be acquainted with the propositions on which it is founded. This familiarity may not come by way of conscious recognition, but the fact that we can get on with the game at all shows just how much we readily assimilate its most basic assumptions—so much so that they virtually disappear into the background of our ordinary language usage. That is why Moore's propositions seem as though they are unconditionally true—he would appear to be giving a testable hypothesis when, in fact, he is giving the conditions under which a hypothesis can be tested. As Wittgenstein puts it, "All testing, all confirmation and disconfirmation of a hypothesis takes place already within a system ... [it is] the element in which arguments have their life."[47] The propositions that Moore draws our attention to, however, lack this kind of contextualization and are therefore purely vacuous. Although they may be stated in the form of a hypothesis, in reality, they constitute part of the very structure that we use to confirm or disconfirm hypotheses in general. Consequently, Moore's propositions are not apposite to uses like 'I know ...' because they are the grounds for knowing in general. "And isn't that what Moore wants to say, when he says he *knows* all these things?—But is his knowing it really what is in question, and not rather that some of these propositions must be solid for us?"[48]

The lesson to be learned here, to put it in the words of Rush Rhees, is that "there are certain experiential propositions such that the opposite is never considered; where anything like doubt or any alternative is simply ruled out. And without this there could not be language-games at all."[49] This essential revelation into the nature of language-games was, as far as Wittgenstein was concerned, the only thing worthy of being lauded in Moore's essays of 1925 and 1939. The irony here, of course, is that Moore did not seem to appreciate the full extent of his own discovery. While Wittgenstein duly appreciated the "*logical* insight" that Moore's use of the phrase 'I know' provided, he adamantly denied that anything like a metaphysical doctrine of realism could "be proved by means of it."[50] What, if anything, is convincingly demonstrated by these kinds of declarations is that certain propositions in the language-game must, of necessity, not come into question. This does not, however, equate to 'knowing' in the sense that Moore thinks it does, i.e., in the preeminent philosophical sense.

It is worth mentioning here that Moore—unlike Wittgenstein—was not hostile to metaphysics in general. He was, to be sure, disdainful of nearly every variety of idealist metaphysics, a rebellious attitude that no doubt stems from the fact that Neo-Hegelianism was "the predominant ontological view"[51] which he would have encountered in his intellectual youth. He did, however, have a very specific sense of what the term metaphysics meant, as can be gleaned from the text of *Some Main Problems of Philosophy*. "The first and most important problem of philosophy is: To give a general description of the *whole* Universe."[52] What is notable about this conception is, of course, the realistic spirit that undergirds it. This spirit, no doubt shaped in part by the physical sciences, is most distinctly typified by the belief that the first problem with which philosophy has got to deal with before it can even begin to address any others is the development of a methodology to determine what sorts of things there are in the Universe. Not in the sense of an exhaustive list which inventories the whole of existence, but

132      *Wittgenstein and the Problem of Metaphysics*

rather in the sense of a schematic that distinguishes what is real from what is not. In this sense, Moore was an ontological realist, as E. D. Klemke has noted in his detailed analysis of Moore's metaphysics. Although he certainly could be associated with other kinds of realism, including the epistemological, transcendental, and axiological sorts, Moore's "defense of other forms of realism stem from his adherence to and defense of ontological realism."[53]

While Wittgenstein's critique of Moore is, by and large, focused on the misleading epistemological implications involved in the attempt to provide proofs for the existence of the external world, it also implies, as we have seen, a denial of the kind of ontological realism generally favored by Moore. This does not mean, of course, that by rejecting realism that Wittgenstein is thereby offering some sort of negative endorsement of idealism. Rather, what Wittgenstein is objecting to is the idea that there can be such a thing as a proof for any metaphysical premise, be it realist, idealist, or otherwise. This is because, Wittgenstein insists, the phrase "'A is a physical object' . . . is a logical concept. . . . And that is why no such proposition as 'There are physical objects' can be formulated."[54] Roughly speaking, the designation of a corporeal object as 'physical' is part of its definition; to then assert that there are such things as physical objects is only to assume the initial point. 'There are physical objects' is thus nonsense according to the *Tractarian* definition because it attempts to say something that can only be shown. Whether or not we accept this definition, one thing is for certain: It hardly seems fair to answer "the scepticism of the idealist" with the assurance that the concept 'physical object' is a logical one that must be accepted if we are to proceed in the use of the language-game.[55] Likewise, for the realist: To simply insist that the proposition 'there are physical objects' is nonsensical will probably not convince anyone philosophically committed to the tenets of realism. "For them after all it is not nonsense."[56]

One of the ways we might begin to address this issue is, as Wittgenstein suggests, to simply say that "this assertion, or its opposite is a misfiring attempt to express what can't be expressed like that. And that it does misfire can be shown."[57] The question left unanswered here, of course, is whether such a demonstration would suffice as an effective tool for winning over the realist or the idealist. Is it enough to simply tell them that their metaphysical doctrines are predicated on the misapplication of certain propositions in the language-game? In some cases, no doubt, this could be a contributing factor, but as a general rhetorical tactic, it hardly qualifies as bulletproof. As I have argued earlier, the problem of how to go about affecting such a radical shift in one's world view belongs principally to the realm of creativity. It challenges us to see things from the multitude of possible

At the Foundation of Well-Founded Belief                    133

perspectives or otherwise find some justification for the refusal—an operation that I call aesthetic. While it is true that Wittgenstein does not overtly deal with either of these subjects in *On Certainty*, he does devote a significant amount of time to the problem of justification, both in terms of its function within the language-game and its limitations. Wittgenstein realized, quite rightly, that where disagreements of a metaphysical variety are concerned, proofs are of little avail. What is needed is not a demonstration of validity but rather a seismic shift in the kinds of foundational propositions we are willing to accept *without* proof. In order to accomplish this, Wittgenstein remarks in §37 of *On Certainty*, "An *investigation* is needed in order to find the right point of attack for the critic." Finding the 'right point of attack' does not consist so much in any one particular method—it is a systematic endeavor that must occur within the broader scope of an investigation if it is to have the desired effect of changing someone's mind. A momentous shift in world view requires an equally momentous shift of metaphysical footing, and this sort of metaphysical sea change is more often precipitated by a conglomerate of minor definitional or axiomatic alterations rather than one that occurs cataclysmically out of the blue. Though such ground-shaking incidents that radically modify one's metaphysical footing can and probably do happen, they are likely the exception and not the rule.

Although the lines of thinking developed by Wittgenstein throughout the course of his later work were long in gestation, the influence they exerted over a diverse set of scholarly fields is somewhat unusual. One of the most notable examples of this can be found in Thomas Kuhn's 1962 book *The Structure of Scientific Revolutions*, published only nine years after the original release of the *Philosophical Investigations*. In fact, the final stages of *Structure* were, as Baker, Chen, and Anderson point out, "Begun only five years after" the initial appearance of the *Investigations* when "interest in Wittgenstein's later work" was at its peak.[58] It was during this time that Kuhn's own interest in Wittgenstein would have been sparked through many conversations with Stanley Cavell, a colleague of Kuhn's at Berkeley in the late 1950s. There is little doubt, as John Gunnell points out, that these discussions were of vital importance to the development of "Kuhn's final version of the manuscript," even though the basic argument "had been formulated before [he] arrived in Berkeley."[59] Nevertheless, the debt that Kuhn owed to Wittgenstein's work in the *Investigations* is obvious throughout *Structure*, despite the fact that it may not have been instrumental in the formulation of the book's basic premise.

For all their similarities, the relationship between Wittgenstein and Kuhn has not been one that has garnished a tremendous amount of attention in the secondary literature. What little there is has tended to focus, as Hanne Andersen notes, on "paradigms, language games, and the role of examples or exemplars (Barker 1986, 1989; Cederbaum 1983; Kindi 1995; Maudgil 1989), or with the empirical vindication of Kuhn's and Wittgenstein's accounts provided by cognitive psychology (Andersen et al. 1996; Chen et al. 1998)."[60] Where the topic of family resemblance is concerned, however, much less has been said, which is somewhat perplexing given just how important the idea was for Kuhn.[61] This general oversight is one that Andersen purports to remedy, especially as it relates to the controversy in Wittgenstein studies known as the problem of wide-open texture. This problem stems, as David Bloor puts it, from the way in which Wittgenstein's theory of family resemblance allows us to "exploit all kinds of crisscrossing similarities" in such a way that the criterion for how we judge a thing to be similar can eventually be expanded to include theoretically everything.[62]

In many respects, the difficulties outlined by the open-texture interpretation of family resemblance reiterate many of those presented by the rule-following paradox: Anything can be made to accord with a rule in much the same way that similarities can be strung together in an all-encompassing totality. Indeed, in many respects, one could argue, the open-texture problem is an offshoot of the rule-following paradox. The way in which one thing is judged as similar to another depends, after all, on the kinds of rules we employ for making this determination. We might, for instance, adopt the vaguely Russellian method proposed by Eileen Cornell Way and limit the applicability of family resemblance according to a hierarchy of super and subtypes. According to this theory, "A subtype would [entail] a supertype," but not the other way around.[63] While a solution along these lines would seem, at first glance, to avoid the pitfalls of the wide-open texture problem, it most certainly is open to criticism from the perspective of the rule-following paradox. If the members of any set—be they of the sub or super variety—are determined by the application of a rule, then the problem of wide-open texture will inevitably find a way to seep back into the notion of family resemblance. This is why, as Andersen argues, any workable solution must avoid recourse to relevant features. Turning to Kuhn, she suggests, allows us to see that "dissimilarity between instances of contrasting concepts" must be considered "on a par with similarity among instances of a single concept."[64]

Whether Andersen's analysis of the wide-open texture problem manages to avoid the same difficulties encountered by Cornell Way is not a matter that I will here weigh in on. The only point we need to take away from this admittedly brief commentary is that most interpreters of the Kuhn–Wittgenstein connection

At the Foundation of Well-Founded Belief 135

have tended to rely principally on the *Investigations* as their point of reference. Relatively few have looked to the text of *On Certainty* as a source for further elucidating the implications of *Structure*. In many respects, this is hardly surprising. While the *Investigations* were on the cutting edge of philosophy at the time, Kuhn completed his now famous and much-debated book. *On Certainty* would have to wait another seven years to see the light of day. Kuhn, therefore, would not have been privy to this work at the time he penned *Structure*, but the depth of his insight into the later work of Wittgenstein is perhaps best demonstrated by the degree to which he anticipated many of the arguments that would later appear in the last of Wittgenstein's three greatest works. What I would therefore like to accomplish here is to attempt a reading of *Structure* using *On Certainty* as the basis for analysis. Such a reading would, I think, not only shed light on the content of each text, but it would also begin to open up the dialogue between Kuhn and Wittgenstein into territories that it has hitherto shied away from.

A paradigm, as Kuhn defined it, consists in "universally recognized scientific achievements that for a time provide model problems and solutions to a community of practitioners."[65] Paradigms can include "law, theory, application, and instrumentation together,"[66] all of which form the basis on which a community of practitioners is trained to understand. They thus are "committed to the same rules and standards for scientific practice. That commitment and the apparent consensus it produces are prerequisites for normal science, i.e., for the genesis and continuation of a particular research tradition."[67] Although paradigms consist primarily in the maintenance and continuation of such traditions, they are also, by their very nature, subject to change over the course of history. These changes need not be precipitated by any one cataclysmic, world-altering scientific discovery. Generally speaking, the shifts are much more gradual, and they are often commenced when a paradigm begins "failing in application to its own traditional problems."[68] When this occurs, there is a recognition on the part of the community of practitioners that the standards that sustain and perpetuate the current paradigm are no longer applicable. A recognition of this sort, Kuhn says, "was the prerequisite to Copernicus' rejection of the Ptolemaic paradigm and his search for a new one."[69] With this alteration in paradigms, there is also a subsequent alteration in world view, so much so that we may "be tempted to exclaim that when paradigms change, the world itself changes with them."[70]

Scientific revolutions of the sort brought about by Copernicus are, to be sure, the exception rather than the rule. Normal scientific activity—i.e., science that operates according to the accepted standards of a given paradigm—could not proceed at all if it was constantly bombarded by drastic overhauls of its fundamental operating principles. This is why, generally speaking, there are revolutions only when incommensurable paradigms make competing claims about the nature of the world. "To be accepted as a paradigm," Kuhn writes, "a theory must seem better than its competitors, but it need not, and in fact never does, explain all the facts with which it can be confronted."[71] As such, no one paradigm is ever capable of accounting for the totality of possible future experimental data. Even the much sought-after holy grail of theoretical physics—the so-called theory of everything— would really only consist of a general outline of the physical universe. Even if something like it is ever discovered, there will no doubt be much work for science yet to do (and of course, the paradigm in which the theory of everything is housed might someday be rendered obsolete by a future paradigm shift).

It is at this point, however, that we encounter difficulty with Kuhn's theory of paradigms, not unlike what I have earlier described as the problem of metaphysics. Indeed, Kuhn himself seemed to have an inkling of it: "Like the choice between competing political institutions," he writes, the choice "between competing paradigms proves to be a choice between incompatible modes of community life." This choice is one that is "not and cannot be determined merely by the evaluative procedures characteristic of normal science" precisely because they depend upon the particular paradigm which "is at issue." When one paradigm enters "into a debate about paradigm choice," as surely it must, its role in that debate "is necessarily circular."[72]

In cases where coextensive paradigms do not necessarily produce any obvious discord with one another, however, the problem of circularity would seem to be less of an issue. The standard model of physics, for example, is by no means incompatible with the evolutionary model of biology. Although each is part and parcel of a larger scientific paradigm, we could also think of them as paradigms in their own right. While it is true that all organic compounds are ultimately governed by the physical laws of the universe, it is, nevertheless unnecessary and even facetious to reduce one to the terms of the other. Biology and physics, at least in a limited sense, are predicated on incommensurable paradigms. They each have their own aims, scopes, standards, and methodologies, which are simply not interchangeable with one another.

This fact alone, of course, does not necessarily imply the existence of some sort of insoluble disagreement between the physical and life sciences. That there should exist a hierarchy in the multitude of disciplines and sub-disciplines which make up the collective enterprise we call science is hardly surprising. While these may, at

At the Foundation of Well-Founded Belief            137

times, be at odds with each other in terms of aims and methods, this need not, and rarely does, result in the kind of crisis that would force us to choose between two completely different paradigms. Even in those cases where a paradigm fails to address its traditional problems adequately, the result is not always one of revolution. It is, after all, possible to imagine that the practitioners of any one particular paradigm may dogmatically refuse to alter the fundamental tenets under which they operate despite the brevity of any proof that might be leveraged against them. To be sure, most scientists are usually persuaded by the evidence when it is sufficiently convincing. One of the ideals to which all scientists—if they are good scientists—must strive to attain is, after all, that of disinterestedness. As with every ideal, however, the reality of the situation does not always live up to the best-case scenario. Part of the reason for this is, as I am attempting to show, because all paradigms involve an element of choice. Even the question of how to interpret the facts and to determine how they fit into the scope of a broader paradigm is not one that has an easily identifiable answer. At some point, we are faced with a question that cannot be decided objectively, and when this happens the problem of circularity will inevitably insert itself into the justifications of paradigm choice.

While there is, in the end, no clear-cut way to entirely eliminate a certain degree of circular reasoning from each and every decision involved in the selection of and assent to the various theories, tools, and techniques that help make up a paradigm, this does not mean, as Kuhn notes, that a group of practitioners cannot use "its own paradigm to argue in that paradigm's defense." Even though this may be tantamount to begging the question, it does not, as he goes on to say,

> Make the arguments wrong or even ineffectual. The man who premises a paradigm when arguing in its defense can nonetheless provide a clear exhibit of what scientific practice will be like for those who adopt the new view of nature. That exhibit can be immensely persuasive, often compellingly so. Yet, whatever its force, the status of the circular argument is only that of persuasion. It cannot be made logically or even probabilistically compelling for those who refuse to step into the circle.[73]

One cannot be convinced then by logic or evidence alone, no matter the degree of probability involved. When all is said and done, a paradigm shift is a matter of rhetoric, of persuading others to see things differently than they already do— which is, to a considerable extent—a matter of aesthetic manipulation. The importance of aesthetics in paradigm formation is a point that Kuhn takes note of several times throughout *Structure*. Apart from reasons that are either logically or probabilistically compelling, "There are the arguments, rarely made entirely explicit, that appeal to the individual's sense of the appropriate or the aesthetic—the new theory is said to be 'neater,' 'more suitable,' or 'simpler' than the old."[74] The information that such adjectives are meant to convey in relation to the theories which they describe is, not surprisingly, that of value judgments. There is, of course, nothing that logically mandates a principle such as Occam's razor. The belief that all other things being equal, the simpler explanation is preferable to the complex one is as much an aesthetic maxim as anything else. Though they may not be the only thing that figures into a paradigm choice, "Nevertheless, the importance of aesthetic considerations can sometimes be decisive."[75] When new paradigms are proposed, so Kuhn suggests, "Something must make at least a few scientists feel that the new proposal is on the right track, and sometimes it is only personal and inarticulate aesthetic consideration that can do that."[76]

Despite his recognition of the importance of aesthetics in paradigm formation, Kuhn does temper his ruminations by suggesting that new paradigms do not "triumph ultimately through some mystical aesthetic. On the contrary, very few men desert a tradition for these reasons alone."[77] This point, as it seems to me, is a prudent one. To say that aesthetics is the sole or even primary mover behind the shift in scientific world views would be a gross simplification of a multifaceted phenomenon. Nevertheless, it is important for us not to forget just how much the general scientific ethos is itself a kind of aesthetic system whose most basic principles cannot be proven. The idea that empirical evidence offers us some insight into the basic structure of the physical universe is something that science is simply incapable of substantiating. This is not to say that because science lacks an ultimate foundation for one of its most basic premises that it is therefore rendered inept. The business of science gets on quite well even though it takes a whole host of assumptions as givens. From a pragmatic vantage point, the utility of science is undeniable, and in an everyday sense, it gives us the closest thing to truth that we are ever likely to approximate, but a method for divining the ultimate and irrefragable Truth it is not. When I say, therefore, that science is predicated on an aesthetic footing, I do not simply have in mind those purely formal aspects of beauty identified by Khun, such as 'neatness,' 'suitability,' and 'simplicity.' Rather, what I am attempting to draw our attention to is the way in which science is dependent on an array of axiomatic principles whose primary function is normative. To be sure, the concept of 'reasoned arguments based on evidence and predictive power' is as much a value judgment as is the evaluation of a painting or a poem, but on a more basic level, it helps us to distinguish the activities that can properly be called scientific from those that are not.

*At the Foundation of Well-Founded Belief*                    139

Unfortunately, there are no hard and fast rules for making this delimitation. Like all aesthetic judgments, in science, there can be no such thing as a rule that necessitates assent to the precepts that make it possible in the first place. One either accepts or rejects the criteria on which the scientific endeavor is premised—attempting to prove them only leads to the circular reasoning that science was supposed to help free us from.

The problem of justification is one, of course, that Kuhn does not take up in any explicitly prolonged fashion, but it is, I might suggest, a good place to begin looking for some parallels between his work in *Structure* and that of Wittgenstein in *On Certainty*. The first similarity that we might therefore point to would be the important role context plays in any justification, whether in paradigms or in language-games. What each of these provides, in a certain sense, are the basic structures in which normative scientific and linguistic practices can occur. Understood as such, paradigms and language-games could also be thought of as partly 'metaphysical'—if we take that oft-maligned term to mean 'basis for judgment' rather than the more traditional definition of the investigation into 'reality qua reality.' For Wittgenstein, however, the basis for judgment was something we are both born into and which is never set in stone. Indeed, 'learning how to judge' is an important aspect of how we learn to use language in the first place, and the same might well be said of activities that make up the normal scientific endeavor. If scientists are to do meaningful work, they must be 'brought up' in the tradition to which they will contribute. They are taught the various skills which they will need in order to correctly identify the problems with which a paradigm is concerned and also how to address those concerns in a manner that is recognized as valid by the community of practitioners. Within the current paradigm of chemistry, for instance, students are not instructed in the techniques for the transmutation of base metals into gold because this is a problem that has become incompatible with current practices. As Wittgenstein recognized, however, the activity of learning "what is to be investigated and what not"[78] was one that had consequences far beyond the purview of science: It was, as he saw it, an integral component of learning how to use language in the first place.

This is especially the case where the seemingly perennial questions of ontology and epistemology are concerned. When children embark down the path of language acquisition, they do not begin by learning "that books exist, that armchairs exist, etc. etc.,—they learn to fetch books, sit in chairs, etc. etc." This is not to say that "questions about the existence of things" will not arise in time. Sooner or later, just about every child is bound to ask a question like, "Is there such a thing as a unicorn?"[79] The point Wittgenstein is drawing our attention to here is that language and practice are, from the very outset, intimately tied up with one another. If you are to obey an order such as "bring me a book,"[80] you will have to be familiar with what a book is, and your understanding will be reflected in the fact that you carried out the instruction. If you do not know or are in doubt as to what a book is, that information is something which you can discover. "Therefore," Wittgenstein concludes, "in order for you to be able to carry out an order there must be some empirical fact about which you are not in doubt. Doubt itself rests only on what is beyond doubt."[81] This fact does not imply, however, that there must be any one particular thing that must be beyond doubt in the context of all language-games. There is, in other words, no Cartesian foundation which is at the bottom of all language-games. Nor is it necessarily possible to say, as Wittgenstein hastens to add, "That in any *individual* case that such-and-such must be beyond doubt if there is to be a language-game—though it is right enough to say that *as a rule* some empirical judgment or another must be beyond doubt."[82] If there were no such empirical judgment that was beyond doubt, then there would be, as far as Wittgenstein is concerned, no such thing as doubt at all. "A doubt without an end is not even a doubt."[83]

Language-games are, in this sense, the context in which doubting must take place, and if there is going to be a language-game at all, then there must be something that cannot be doubted. This 'something which cannot be doubted' is precisely what is metaphysical in any given form of life. It is the basis for all judging, and without it, no judgment would be possible at all, least of all a judgment of doubt. We must learn to first believe in something that is not doubted, and only then can we learn to doubt. This does not mean, we should hasten to add, that this amounts to some sort of proof of the veracity of the beliefs that make up the bedrock of the language-game. From the fact that "doubt comes *after* belief"[84] it does not follow that foundational beliefs are not subject to doubt. There are, according to Wittgenstein, "Certain events [that] would put me into a position in which I could not go on with the old language-game any further. In which I was torn away from the *sureness* of the game."[85] Many things might have this effect, but in general they all run contrary to what we have come to expect in the ordinary sequence of events. Thus, Wittgenstein poses the question, "What if something *really unheard-of* happened?—If I, say, saw houses gradually turning into steam without any obvious cause, if the cattle in the fields stood on their heads and laughed and spoke comprehensible words; if trees gradually changed into men and men into trees."[86] If such things really did happen, they would, Wittgenstein suggests, threaten to undermine the very foundation of the language-game itself. It might even do so to the point that we

At the Foundation of Well-Founded Belief 141

could no longer use the language-game as we had done before. In such instances, we would quite likely have to construct a new language-game that was based on a new foundation that took account of our new experiences. This new language-game, however, would most certainly be incommensurable with the previous one such that the old world-view would become, once the paradigm shift had been made, unrecognizable (just as we do not today understand what it is like to truly believe in a solar system that is anything but heliocentric).

There is no doubt that Wittgenstein viewed some elements of the language-game as serving a foundational role. These elements are, as I have already intimated, simply 'beliefs' in the sense that they are not the sort of thing that philosophers would traditionally categorize as 'true' knowledge. "The difficulty," Wittgenstein says, "is to realize the groundlessness of our believing."[87] While our beliefs are the ground on which the entire language-game rests, they are themselves not grounded on anything else. This means, in effect, that there is no ultimate and eternal foundation that serves as the basis of all our knowledge. Rather, the certainty of the language-game shows itself in our actions, in the assumptions we make, the way we use language, and the form of life that we live. "My life shows that I know or am certain that there is a chair over there, or a door, and so on. – I tell a friend e.g. 'Take that chair over there', 'Shut the door', etc. etc."[88]

The idea that Wittgenstein develops here in *On Certainty*—that the foundation of the language-game is predicated on a series of baseless suppositions that must be accepted on what amounts to faith—is also one that bears some resemblance to the *Tractarian* concept of 'showing'. Such a similarity has also been noted by Jerry H. Gill in "Saying and Showing: Radical Themes in Wittgenstein's 'On Certainty'." "Wittgenstein's main contention in *On Certainty* is," he claims, "That the character of epistemological bedrock can only be *displayed* or allowed to *show itself*; every attempt to doubt it or justify it become entangled in self-stultifying confusion."[89] Part of what Wittgenstein accomplishes in *On Certainty* is a way of viewing epistemology that allows us to escape this 'self-stultification' that renders obsolete the necessity of justifying knowledge in an absolute sense. If we 'know' something (in Wittgenstein's sense of the word), we are always capable of saying how we know. In situations where we claim to know something that is fundamental (i.e., metaphysical), we are always placed in a position where we are forced to give a justification of a belief that was itself formerly used as a justification. Thus we are stuck in a regress of justification where nothing is allowed to be taken as foundational. Without this framework in which to operate, there would be no such thing as knowing or doubting, truth or falsehood. Although our epistemological framework is, in part, an inherited component of the cultural and biological form of life one lives, there is nothing logically necessary, self-evident, indubitable, or incorrigible about it. It is, in some sense, "Misleading to speak as if we choose or *assume* the various aspects of our epistemological framework,"[90] as Gill states. "This way of putting it makes it sound arbitrary and self-conscious when in fact it is not."[91] It is no doubt true, as Wittgenstein writes, that the whole activity of making judgments is one that must, to a certain degree, be "in conformity with mankind."[92] Gill is thus quite right if he means that the individual cannot choose to be indoctrinated in one epistemological framework instead of another. This does not mean, however, that the epistemological framework is itself necessary. Although a certain form of life might be predicated on a certain kind of epistemological framework—and necessarily so—there is no reason to suppose that it might be rejected outright. This, of course, would imply a new form of life that may be incommensurable with the old one. Whether it is accepted or rejected, whether by a group or an individual, the act of accepting it unquestioningly or rejecting it outright is a decision that cannot be made according to a predetermined rule. Nothing forces us to the assent of one form of life over another, but the assent itself is always one that takes the form of a judgment of taste. Choosing to reject this subjectively universal call for acquiescence is likewise something not mandated. As I have earlier written, envisaging alternative possibilities is an essentially creative capacity, one that is predicated on the maxim: Everything can be otherwise than it is.

Wittgenstein's critique of the 'preeminent philosophical' quest for certainty is one that has important implications for the problem of metaphysics as it has been variously described thus far. Metaphysics, inasmuch as it has been characterized by the search for the immutable, has found itself caught in a vicious circle of justification. This circle has implicitly or explicitly dogged nearly every metaphysical doctrine in the history of Western philosophy. Whatever first principles that metaphysics might concern itself with, whether it be ontology— as has been its traditional trajectory—or something other besides, there has always been the problem of justifying the axioms with which one begins a philosophical inquiry. Thus, no matter the sort of metaphysical system that we begin with, it seems as if we are always led back to the question, 'How do we know?' This is, as Wittgenstein recognized, precisely where the problem lies. "It is as if 'I know' did not tolerate a metaphysical emphasis,"[93] for as soon as we claim to know something metaphysical, we are always placed in a position in which we must give a justification for our knowledge. Where the axioms of metaphysics are concerned, there is nothing to base them on, for metaphysics *is* the basis of knowledge. With this line of thinking, we have already been lured into the epistemological circle at the center of the problem of metaphysics.

In order to know anything, we must have a basis for our knowledge, but in order to have such a basis, we must allow ourselves the opportunity to cease giving justifications *ad infinitum*. We must also resist the temptation to resort to the tired old refrain of "immediate certainties" which naïvely presumes, as Nietzsche once noted, that cognition could get "hold of its object purely and simply as 'the thing in itself,' without any falsification taking place either on the part of the subject or the object."[94] The problem with this line of thinking, as Nietzsche well knew, is that there are no criteria that would allow us to separate the feeling of being certain from actual certainty in itself. All judgments of certainty are judgments made within the context of a particular psychological state. The fact that something *seems* certain is, to be sure, no proof that it *is* certain. This is not to say that what is believed to be an 'immediately certain intuition' might not be correctly applied to something which is actually certain in itself. If there are such things that are, properly speaking, 'true in themselves,' it might happen that our cognition might get a hold of them simply by chance alone. Whether we do or whether we do not, however, will not be something which we will ever be privy to. In either case, the feeling of being 'absolutely correct' is always the same: It tells us nothing of whether we might actually be correct or not.

How, then, do we escape this problem of metaphysics? If we require metaphysics in order to have knowledge but can give no meta-epistemological basis that justifies the use of one metaphysical schematic over another, how is knowledge possible at all? For starters, we might begin by taking a cue from the work of John Dewey. He notes that "modern philosophies, in spite of their great diversity," have retained "the conception of the relation of knowledge to reality formulated in Greek thought."[95]

> The notion of a separation between knowledge and action, theory and practice, has been perpetuated, and that the beliefs connected with action are taken to be uncertain and inferior to value compared with those inherently connected with objects of knowledge, so that the former are securely established only as they derived from the latter.[96]

Part of the esteem with which theory is held over practice is due in part, Dewey contends, to a biological necessity. "Man who lives in a world of hazards is compelled to seek for certainty."[97] This drive, which is necessitated by the demands of life, became a value in its own right apart from its function in securing even a modest amount of "control over nature."[98] For Dewey, this is the source of the privileging of knowledge over action. This is simply because pure, *a priori* knowledge is, in all instances, certain knowledge in comparison to

144    *Wittgenstein and the Problem of Metaphysics*

practical knowledge. "There is nothing outside ourselves," as Nietzsche would put it, "About which we are allowed to conclude that it will become thus and so, must be thus and so: we ourselves are what is more or less certain, calculable. Man is the rule, nature without rule."[99]

Part of the problem of metaphysics, then, lies in this artificial separation of what is often referred to in philosophy as the difference between 'knowing that' and 'knowing how.' For Wittgenstein, there is no getting beyond the sort of certainty that is provided to us by the form of life we live and the actions that are associated with it. This is, so to speak, the 'foundation' of the very possibility of being certain about anything. So, in a very real sense, we are quite content to act as if we had the sort of absolute certainty that philosophers have endeavored to discover without actually having it. What is important are the choices that we make and not their ultimate foundation. Indeed, the ultimate foundations of our certainty are the choices that we make. There can be no self-sufficient and ultimately certain metaphysical theory that accounts for our actions apart from the actions themselves. We must choose to use one explanation of things amongst an untold number of them. Our selection, although it cannot be given any ultimate justification, is simply constituted in our aesthetic sensibilities. For us, metaphysics will always be constituted by this sentiment in particular. When our ability to give justification runs dry, and we have reached the bedrock of our knowledge, the only explanation left for us to give is 'this seems better than that.' There is no other justification possible. There is nothing that is self-evident, indubitable, incorrigible, or ultimately certain about it. There is only aesthetic preference.

# Notes

1    Wittgenstein, *Culture and Value*, 26.

2    Wittgenstein, *On Certainty*, sec. 253.

3    A. J. Ayer, *Language, Truth, and Logic* (New York: Dover Publications, 1952), 41.

4    Ibid., 97.

5    Friedrich Nietzsche, *The Will to Power (Volumes I and II)*, trans. Anthony Ludovici (Lawrence, KS: Digireads, 2010), sec. 587.

6    Ibid., sec. 588.

7    Ibid.

8    Ibid.

9    Quoted in Julian Young, *Friedrich Nietzsche: A Philosophical Biography* (Cambridge: Cambridge University Press, 2010), 31.

# At the Foundation of Well-Founded Belief 145

10 Monk, *Ludwig Wittgenstein*, 443.

11 G. E. Moore, "A Defense of Common Sense," in *Selected Writings*, ed. Thomas Baldwin (New York: Routledge, 1993), 106.

12 Ibid., 107–8.

13 Ibid., 111.

14 G. E. Moore, "Proof of an External World," in *Selected Writings*, ed. Thomas Baldwin (New York: Routledge, 1993), 148.

15 Moore, "A Defense of Common Sense," 149–50.

16 Ibid., 166.

17 Wittgenstein, *On Certainty*, sec. 1.

18 Moore, "Proof of an External World," 169.

19 Wittgenstein, *On Certainty*, sec. 6.

20 Ibid., sec. 415.

21 Descartes, *Meditations on First Philosophy*, 16.

22 Wittgenstein, *On Certainty*, sec. 137.

23 Moore, "A Defense of Common Sense," 108–9.

24 Wittgenstein, *On Certainty*, sec. 2.

25 Ibid., sec. 462.

26 Ibid., sec. 4.

27 Ibid., sec. 466.

28 Ibid., sec. 465.

29 Ibid., sec. 555.

30 Ibid., sec. 559.

31 Ibid., sec. 343.

32 Ibid., sec. 611.

33 Wittgenstein, *Tractatus Logico-Philosophicus*, 2001, sec. 6.51.

34 Wittgenstein, *Philosophical Investigations*, sec. 315.

35 Wittgenstein, *On Certainty*, sec. 463.

36 Ibid., sec. 483.

37 Ibid., sec. 484.

38 Moore, "Proof of an External World," 170.

39 Ibid.

40 Avrum Stroll, *Moore and Wittgenstein on Certainty* (New York: Oxford University Press, 1994), 98.

41 Ibid.

42 Moore, "A Defense of Common Sense," 115.

43 Ibid.

44 Wittgenstein, *On Certainty*, sec. 390.

45 Ibid., sec. 100.

46 Ibid., sec. 32.

47 Ibid., sec. 105.

48 Ibid., sec. 112.

49 This does not mean, I would only add, that the kinds of experiential propositions Rheese is referring to here are ultimately immune from any form of doubt. The lesson of the skeptic, if there is such a thing, is that nothing, no matter how much it may be taken for granted, is beyond the hermeneutics of suspicion. What it does mean is that if we are going to carry on with one kind of language-game than there must be certain moves within it that need to be ruled out right from the first. See *Wittgenstein's "On Certainty": There – Like Our Life* (Oxford: Blackwell, 2006), 57.

50 Wittgenstein, *On Certainty*, sec. 59.

51 E. D. Klemke, *A Defense of Realism: Reflections on the Metaphysics of G. E. Moore* (Amherst, NY: Humanity Books, 2000), 33.

52 G. E. Moore, *Some Main Problems of Philosophy* (New York: Collier, 1966), 14.

53 Klemke, *A Defense of Realism*, 33.

54 Wittgenstein, *On Certainty*, sec. 36.

55 Moore's tactic of holding up his hands in front of the idealist and insisting that 'here are two hands' is even less effective in this regard.

56 Wittgenstein, *On Certainty*, sec. 37.

57 Ibid.

58 Peter Baker, Xiang Chen, and Hanne Anderson, "Kuhn on Concepts and Categorization," in *Thomas Kuhn*, ed. Thomas Nickles (Cambridge: Cambridge University Press, 2003), 239.

59 Gunnell's suggestion here runs contrary to "the common assumption" in the secondary literature that "Wittgenstein's work, mediated through Cavell, played a major role in the formulation of Kuhn's basic thesis." See *Social Inquiry After Wittgenstein and Kuhn: Leaving Everything as It Is* (New York: Columbia University Press, 2014), 21.

60 Hanne Andersen, "Kuhn's Account of Family Resemblance: A Solution to the Problem of Wide-Open Texture," *Erkenntnis* 52, no. 3 (2000): 315.

61 At one point in *Structure* Kuhn suggests that Wittgenstein's idea of a "network of overlapping and crisscross resemblances" might also "very well hold for the various research problems and techniques that arise within a single normal-scientific tradition" (45).

62 David Bloor, *Wittgenstein: A Social Theory of Knowledge* (London: Macmillan, 1983), 31.

63 Eileen Cornell Way, *Knowledge, Representation and Metaphor* (Oxford: Intellect, 1994), 216.

64 Andersen, "Kuhn's Account of Family Resemblance: A Solution to the Problem of Wide-Open Texture," 315.

65 Thomas S. Kuhn, *The Structure of Scientific Revolutions* (Chicago: University of Chicago Press, 1996), x.

66 Ibid., 10.

67 Ibid., 11.

68 Ibid, 69.

69 Ibid.

70 Ibid., 111.

71 Ibid. 17.

72 Ibid., 94.

73 Ibid.

74 Ibid., 155.

75 Ibid., 156.

76 Ibid. 158.

77 Ibid.

78 Wittgenstein, *On Certainty*, sec. 472.

79 Ibid., sec. 476.

80 Ibid., sec. 519.

81 Ibid.

82 Ibid.

83 Ibid., sec. 625.

84 Ibid., sec. 160.

85 Ibid., sec. 617.

86 Ibid. sec. 513.

87 Ibid., sec. 166.

88 Ibid., sec. 7.

89 Jerry H. Gill, "Saying and Showing: Radical Themes in Wittgenstein's 'On Certainty,'" *Religious Studies* 10, no. 03 (September 1974): 282.

90 Ibid., 284.

91 Ibid.

92 Wittgenstein, *On Certainty*, sec. 156.

93 Ibid., sec. 482.

94 Nietzsche, *Beyond Good and Evil*, sec. 16.

95 John Dewey, *The Quest for Certainty: A Study of the Relation of Knowledge and Action* (New York: Putnam, 1960), 29.

96 Ibid., 29.

97 Ibid., 3.

98 Ibid.

99 Friedrich Nietzsche, *Human, All Too Human: A Book for Free Spirits* (Lincoln, NE: University of Nebraska Press, 1996), sec. 111.

# 5

# To Tell a Riddle

From the very beginning, metaphysics has been a project that has endeavored to formulate so-called 'first principles' which would, if successful, elucidate the nature of reality qua reality in such a way as to leave no doubt about how things stand in and of themselves. The difficulty with this undertaking, however, has always been that every description we might devise seems to necessitate a justification for why we *choose* one way of characterizing things as opposed to any other. In this respect, metaphysics is continually dogged by those perennial epistemological questions of "What do we know?" and "How do we know it?"[1] Two possible answers present themselves here: Either we are forced to make the assertion that the first principles we are advancing are in some respect self-evident, or we must admit that a regress is unavoidable, in which case knowledge—in any meaningful sense—is impossible. As anyone who is familiar with the problem of the criterion will no doubt recognize, both of these responses are less than satisfactory, and the primary reason for this is, as I have already argued, that our criterion for what counts as knowledge is itself fundamentally flawed. If we indulge in the assumption that true knowledge must also be certain knowledge, the only result we can expect to attain is a vicious circle. Being free of this circle means, amongst other things, putting aside the need for any ultimate, god's eye perspective in favor of a justification that is, in the end, purely aesthetic. Whatever reality is in itself, for us, it is always a mode of description before it is anything else, complete with all our various biases that turn out to be nothing more than the manifestation of our need to make existence accord with our desires. "*If* there were gods, how could I stand not to be a god! *Therefore* there are no gods."[2]

Surely, the astute reader might say, aesthetics cannot be reduced to a mere epistemological function whose sole purpose is to guard against the threat of either regress or circularity. Does this not reenact the same reductive gesture we were attempting to be rid of in the first place? What of that venerable tradition which encompasses the science of the beautiful and the exaltation of the sublime? Do these have nothing of value to add to a consideration of Wittgenstein's philosophical output? To the concerns raised by these questions, I readily admit no small amount of negligence, which is why, in what follows, we will aim to bring them more fully into focus as they relate to the problem of metaphysics within the corpus of Wittgenstein's work. In part, I will attempt to demonstrate that a metaphysics of art is at work in virtually every stage of his philosophy, albeit in a latent form that is not always readily apparent. As we will see, for Wittgenstein—much like Nietzsche—the world was justifiable only as an aesthetic phenomenon, one that was beyond the purviews of logical necessity or linguistic analysis. But in addition to this, we will also see the degree to which the mystical nature of aesthetics—especially as it concerns the problems of poetics and style—are central features of Wittgenstein's thought that have too often been ignored.

There are few philosophers who were more endowed with such a keen aesthetic sense of the poetic *possibility* of philosophical language as Wittgenstein was. Plato would, of course, be counted chief amongst them, with Nietzsche and Kierkegaard trailing close behind. Subjective rankings aside, it is safe to say that for Wittgenstein, philosophy was, first and foremost, an artful undertaking, and any approach to his work that forgoes this realization will inevitably miss what is most significant about it. Some of Wittgenstein's commentators, unfortunately, have regarded this feature of his philosophy as more or less superfluous. One such author is Peter Carruthers. Anyone can see, he notes, that the *Tractatus*

> is a work of extraordinary beauty; yet what makes it attractive is partially responsible for its obscurity. Firstly, because it is written in the style of pithy aphorism, without properly developed explanations of its own doctrines. And secondly, because it is mostly presented in the form of oracular statements, without supporting arguments.... Such a mode of writing serves no one well. In attempting to ride two horses at once (truth and beauty), it risks falling between them. In philosophy it is clarity and explicitness that matter above all. For only what is plainly stated can be reliably assessed for truth.[3]

This assessment of the *Tractatus* is unfortunately all too common of overly analytic interpretations, many of which, by and large, fail to grasp the essential importance that aesthetics plays in the communication of ideas. Carruthers, in an apparent dismissal of the 'obscurity' of the *Tractatus*, attempts to do what Wittgenstein was perhaps incapable of doing. "In my own writing," Carruthers says, "I will try to be as open and straightforward as possible."[4] Such a stylistic methodology might indeed be well suited to the general scope and purpose of exegetical writing, but this cannot be used as a justification for dismissing the

*To Tell a Riddle*

importance of aesthetics in Wittgenstein's work. This includes not only his genuine stylistic concerns about writing—which he repeatedly expressed in his notebooks—but also the conceptual apparatus of aesthetic explanation. "Writing in the right style is setting the carriage straight on the rails,"[5] Wittgenstein remarks, and sometimes the right style is more pertinent to the presentation of an idea than any other means of communication. One such example for Wittgenstein is Biblical Scripture, which is not always clear and is often full of historical inaccuracies. This, however, is completely beside the point for Wittgenstein. "Isn't it possible," he asks, "that it was essential in this case to 'tell a riddle'?"[6] What is important about Scripture for Wittgenstein is not the historical narrative that it tells. In fact, the narrative need

> not be more than quite averagely historically plausible *just so that* this should not be taken as the essential, decisive thing. . . . What you are supposed to see cannot be communicated even by the best and most accurate historian; and *therefore* a mediocre account suffices, is even to be preferred.[7]

It is precisely this preference that is, I would suggest, one of the enduring features of Wittgenstein's own work, which is not to say that it is in any sense 'mediocre.' What I mean here is that the precise formulation of question and answer, riddle and solution, was never one that was central to his philosophical project at any phase. Despite the rigorous logical criterion of the *Tractatus*, or the more sober treatment of language in the *Investigations*, for Wittgenstein the way something was said was just as important as what was being said, if not more so. Naturally, this led him to develop a distinctive style that can be unusually hard to pin down. This is due in part, no doubt, to the sort of philosophical inquiry that he is attempting to conduct. "I find it important in philosophizing to keep changing my posture, not to stand for too long on *one* leg, so as not to get stiff."[8] It is no wonder, then, that Wittgenstein would favor an aphoristic style of writing which, more often than not, forgoes explanation or demonstration, because they tend to make one philosophically stiff and 'systematic.' "The will to a system is a lack of integrity,"[9] Nietzsche once wrote, and one can surmise that much the same ethical dictum holds for Wittgenstein as well. Besides avoiding the stagnation of a systematic doctrine, an aphoristic form of writing can also give voice to ideas that could not otherwise be expressed by alternative means. This was also, so it would seem, simply the only way in which Wittgenstein could structure his thoughts without artificiality.

> If I am thinking about a topic just for myself and not with a view to writing a book, I jump about all around it; that is the only way of thinking that comes

naturally to me.... I *squander* an unspeakable amount of effort making an arrangement of my thoughts which may have no value at all.[10]

With the above considerations in mind, there is still at least one undeniable difficulty when taking up an examination of Wittgenstein's aesthetics: He published nothing on the subject during his lifetime aside from two somewhat cryptic remarks in the *Tractatus*. One of these appears in 4.003:

> Most of the propositions and questions to be found in philosophical works are not false but nonsensical. Consequently we cannot give any answer to questions of this kind, but can only point out that they are nonsensical. Most of the propositions of philosophers arise from our failure to understand the logic of our language. (They belong to the same class as the question whether the good is more or less identical than the beautiful.) And it is not surprising that the deepest problems are in fact *not* problems at all.

Though it should come as no surprise that Wittgenstein thought that statements like "the Good is more or less identical than the Beautiful" are nonsense, what is odd is that he later asserts in 6.421 of the *Tractatus* that "Ethics and aesthetics are one and the same," which, by the light of his own philosophy, would seem to be a statement without sense. This is the paradoxical nature of Wittgenstein's philosophy, however, and is not only indicative of his attitude towards metaphysics but aesthetics as well. He searched for a language devoid of metaphysical utterances, but in so doing, he could not refrain from speaking metaphysically. He wants to say that it is senseless to ask whether the Good is more or less identical to the Beautiful but cannot stop himself from asserting that indeed they are. So, is the realm of the aesthetic for Wittgenstein limited only to senseless statements such as 6.421? Is the point to 'tell a riddle?' Or, are we more successful in reaching the unsayable, and thereby the aesthetic and the ethical, when we abstain from speaking about them altogether?

These questions would be more problematic if this were all that Wittgenstein gave us on the above topics. However, remarks on ethics, beauty, art, music, poetry, literature, etc. are scattered throughout his *Nachlass*. Many, which do not belong to any sustained work, are collected in English under the title of *Culture and Value*. These comments give us further insight into Wittgenstein's thoughts on aesthetics. By themselves, they lack a cohesiveness that more prolonged treatment would produce. We, therefore, must read these aggregated comments in light of his more robust philosophical works. In so doing, one begins to see the importance of the aesthetic and ethical in all aspects of Wittgenstein's work. The *Tractatus*, which on a cursory reading may seem to be solely on the subject matter of logic, takes on a completely different air. His later work also takes on an added dimension when seen as a book that is, at least in part, about the ethical and the aesthetic.

In his pre-*Tractatus* notebooks, Wittgenstein makes several entries of interest concerning art and aesthetics. In the vein of the mystical, around which much of his early thinking centers, he writes, "Aesthetically, the miracle is that the world exists. That there is what there is."[11] It would be misguided to see this statement as merely an avowal of aesthetic pleasure alone. The wonderment *at* existence, so indicative of the *Tractatus*, is for Wittgenstein the only possible metaphysical explanation *for* existence—and aesthetic experience is indicative of this. In the next entry, Wittgenstein goes on to ask, "Is it the essence of the artistic way of looking at things, that it looks at the world with a happy eye?"[12] In the *Tractatus*, he remarks, "The world of the happy man is a different one from that of the unhappy man."[13] And again, in the *Notebooks*, he says, "For there is certainly something in the conception that the end of art is the beautiful. And the beautiful *is* what makes happy."[14] How one looks at the world, whether it is with a happy or an unhappy eye, does not "alter the world, it can alter only the limits of the world, not the facts—not what can be expressed by means of language. In short, the effect must be that it becomes an altogether different world. It must, so to speak, wax and wane as a whole."[15]

It is without a doubt that aesthetic contemplation for Wittgenstein is typified by viewing the world in a particular way. In a clarification of what he means by "ethics and aesthetics are one," he writes,

> The work of art is the object seen *sub specie aeternitatis*; and the good life is the world seen *sub specie aeternitatis*. This is the connexion between art and ethics. The usual way of looking at things sees objects as it were from the midst of them, the view *sub specie aeternitatis* from outside. In such a way that they have the world as background.... The thing seen *sub specie aeternitatis* is the thing seen together with the whole logical space.[16]

To see an object aesthetically, one must see it in the entirety of its context—that is, the entirety of its *metaphysical* context. "Good art is," Wittgenstein says, "A complete expression,"[17] which is exactly the reason why the propositions of aesthetics cannot properly be expressed in language. The logic of our language is incapable of a higher order; it cannot explain why it is, but only that it is. It cannot give a complete metaphysical picture of an object (and hence an aesthetic one), for it would have to be capable of showing itself as though it were from the outside, which is exactly what Wittgenstein thinks language is incapable of doing. His aim, as he explains in the preface of the *Tractatus*,

154 *Wittgenstein and the Problem of Metaphysics*

> Is to draw a limit to thought, or rather—not to thought, but to the expression of thoughts: for in order to be able to draw a limit to thought, we should have to find both sides of the limit thinkable (i.e. we should have to be able to think what cannot be thought). It will therefore only be in language that the limit can be drawn, and what lies on the other side of the limit will simply be nonsense.[18]

Though we may not be able to 'think the other side' of a limit, the fact that we can draw a limit at all to language would also denote—by way of a negative definition—what may not be spoken of in language. This, of course, does not mean that aesthetics becomes any less nonsensical as a result. It only means that we are capable of telling the difference between what can be said from what cannot. Even though a judgment of value will not find adequate expression in language, nevertheless its sense will show itself in the fact that its sense may not be expressed in language.

For Wittgenstein, it is our subjective vantage point within the world that renders us incapable of thinking the other side of a limit. For a subjective viewer immersed in the world, it will appear as if there are no limits to the world, just as "our visual field has no limits."[19] To see the limit would require that we see the other side of the limit, but language does not allow us to do this, which is why "*the limits of my language* mean the limits of my world."[20] Again, as with his attitude towards metaphysics, Wittgenstein's reasoning becomes seemingly paradoxical with regards to aesthetics. For he not only states that in order to think a limit, we would have to think the unthinkable, but also that "to view the world sub specie aeterni is to view it as a whole—a limited whole."[21] What is this sort of contemplation if it is not thinking the other side of a limit or at least thinking *from* the other side? If the work of art is the object seen *sub specie aeternitatis*, how is it that we can contemplate it at all if by so doing, we should have to think what cannot be thought? Part of the answer, no doubt, stems from the fact that aesthetic experience is typified by its mystical quality. A good work of art is also a 'complete' work of art. Thus, when we view any given object as a work of art, we are doing so as if it were from an eternal vantage point outside of the limits of the world. This is despite the fact that such a vantage is, strictly speaking, not one which we may occupy. "Feeling the world as a limited whole— it is this that is mystical."[22]

Not surprisingly, Wittgenstein's claim that 'ethics and aesthetics are one and the same' has been the source of a good deal of disagreement in the secondary literature. Kathrin Stengel has noted that this dictum "has often been misunderstood as stating the ontological identity of ethics and aesthetics. To be blunt: this reading is simply wrong, both logically and grammatically."[23] Part of her reasoning centers on the translation that Pears and McGuinness made of Wittgenstein's original German phrase "Ethik und Aesthetik sind Eins." A more literal rendition of this final parenthetical statement of 6.421 is rendered by C. K. Ogden as "Ethics and aesthetics are one."[24] Stengel, in conjunction with Ogden's translation, suggests that the relationship between ethics and aesthetics for Wittgenstein is "rather one of interdependence than of identity."[25] There is, according to Stengel, an ethical component to the aesthetic point of view in Wittgenstein's work, and vice versa. They are not 'one and the same' ontologically, logically, or grammatically speaking, but the one does presuppose the other. "The interdependence of ethics and aesthetics," Stengel says, "is rooted in the fact that the ethical, as a way of understanding life in its absolute value, expresses itself in aesthetic form, while aesthetic form (i.e., style) expresses the ethical as an individual, yet universal, aspect of the artistic act."[26]

Michael Hodges has said that what Wittgenstein meant by "ethics and aesthetics are one" is that "the good life—the happy life—consists of an aesthetic apprehension and appreciation of the world in which will and idea are an essential unity. The metaphysical subject and the willing ethical subject are one and the same."[27] There seems to be some credibility to this interpretation, despite the fact that Hodges waffles between implying that ethics and aesthetics are separate but unified and that they are also ontologically indistinguishable. A strong case could be made that the 'good life' for Wittgenstein is also the 'happy life.' "The happy life is good," he says, "The unhappy bad."[28] When we see the world with a 'happy eye' we also see it beautifully. Therefore a happy life is also both good and beautiful, and an unhappy life is neither. What lesson are we meant to learn from such dictums if, strictly speaking, they are nonsense? What does it mean to be happy, and why is a happy life also an ethical and aesthetic life? Wittgenstein himself has no definitive answer to offer us. When he asks himself, "why should I live *happily*," his only response is that it "seems to me to be a tautological question; the happy life seems to be justified, of itself, it seems that it *is* the only right life."[29] Thus there is really only one sort of ethical maxim that Wittgenstein can offer us. "It seems one can't say anything more than: Live happily!"[30] What this happy life consists of, however, is "in some sense deeply mysterious!"[31] For if we attempt to answer the question "What is the objective mark of the happy, harmonious life?" the only answer we might give is "that there cannot be any such mark, that can be *described*. This mark cannot be a physical one but only a metaphysical one, a transcendental one."[32]

156 *Wittgenstein and the Problem of Metaphysics*

This final remark is an important one. The correct life, which is the good and the happy life, is not one that can be described in propositional language. It is, therefore, 'transcendental' according to Wittgenstein's use. This means, as he states in the *Notebooks*, that "ethics does not treat of the world. Ethics must be a condition of the world, like logic."[33] It is important to take note of Schopenhauer's influence on Wittgenstein here because ethics, like logic or aesthetics, "can only enter through the subject."[34] It is this 'willing subject,' which Wittgenstein sometimes refers to as the 'metaphysical subject,' that is the basis not only for the happy or unhappy world but for the world in general. "As the subject is not a part of the world but a presupposition of its existence, so good and evil are predicates of the subject, not properties in the world."[35] Logic, ethics, and aesthetics, then, all collapse into the metaphysical subject. Not only does this seem to suggest that there could be no such thing as a world without a prerequisite subject, but it also suggests that the world must also necessarily be an ethical and aesthetic concern for the metaphysical subject. "Can there be a world that is neither happy nor unhappy?"[36] Wittgenstein asks himself, albeit rhetorically. For as far as he is concerned, the existence of the world is based on the existence of a metaphysical subject which transcends it. This subject is also the 'willing subject' in Schopenhauer's sense, and it is this willing that makes the world either 'happy' or 'unhappy.' There can ultimately be no such thing as a subject that stands in a value-neutral relationship to the world, for there would then be nothing 'transcendent' about the metaphysical subject. A subject that stood in a value-neutral relationship to the rest of the world would cease to be a subject altogether, in which case it would become completely objective. In other words, what differentiates the subject from the object is that the latter can be described via propositional language, the former cannot. The metaphysical subject resists this sort of description precisely because it stands in an ethical and aesthetic relationship with the world. If we subtract this from the subject, then there is nothing left to distinguish it from any other object.

The transcendent nature of ethics and aesthetics for Wittgenstein was a result of the intertwined relationship of logic, thought, and metaphysics. What is not logical cannot exist. Nor can we think or speak meaningfully about what is not logical. From this metaphysical position, we are led to the inevitable conclusion that all ethical or aesthetic propositions—or any propositions that attempt to express any kind of value, for that matter—are senseless. Wittgenstein's point in all of this is not to deride such value propositions, however—far from it. For Wittgenstein, they were of the utmost importance, and there can be no denying that we are quite capable of the sort of contemplation that can and does assign value to a world that is utterly devoid of it. A value proposition, strictly speaking, refers to nothing insofar as there is nothing in the world which it shares the logical structure of. Therefore, if there is to be such a thing as the 'contemplation of values,' it must be a mystical sort of experience that transcends the world of non-values. This sort of contemplation, then, is possible only because we are capable of viewing the world as if from the vantage point of eternity.

The fact that we might not actually do so when we contemplate the meaning or value of life and existence is completely beside the point. What matters is that we are capable of imagining what it would be like to occupy a universal vantage— what Thomas Nagel has characterized as "the view from nowhere," or at least nowhere in particular. "While transcendence of one's own point of view in action," he says, "Is the most important creative force in ethics ... its results cannot completely subordinate the personal standpoint and its prereflective motives. The good, like the true, includes irreducibly subjective elements."[37] The problem of how to combine a subjective viewpoint with that of an objective one, without giving priority to one over the other, is one that Nagel ascribes a key importance to. This problem, as it relates to ethics, has an analogous problem in metaphysics. The difficulty there lies in "combining into some conception of a single world those features of reality that are revealed to different perspectives at different levels of subjectivity or objectivity."[38] The gist of Nagel's point is that although the subjective and objective can sometimes conflict, we need not adopt one to the exclusion of the other. Nor are the terms of one necessarily reducible to terms of the other. It is something of a metaphysical prejudice that the subjective is considered antithetical to the objective and vice versa. Varying modes of inquiry might require varying degrees of each, and there is no reason why we cannot assume that the subjective and objective can coexist.

These difficulties perhaps find no better expression than in the work of Kant, for whom the beautiful was that "which pleases universally without a concept."[39] Although in practice we might disagree quite strongly about what we deem to be beautiful, when we do make this judgment, we do so *as if* it were universally valid for everyone. Indeed, when one is truly convinced that something is beautiful, one is usually quite incapable of understanding how anyone could disagree. Kant suggests something similar when he states that when someone "pronounces that something is beautiful, then he expects the very same satisfaction of others."[40] The validity of a universal judgment is thus characterized by a certain kind of 'ought.' It has the form 'everyone ought to find this beautiful' and not 'everyone does find this beautiful.' Any particular disagreement that we might have concerning what we deem to be beautiful is immaterial. The only qualification that a disinterested judgment of taste requires is that it be made as if it were universally the case. There is, Kant says, "A claim to validity for everyone without the universality that pertains to objects, i.e., it must be combined with a claim to subjective universality."[41] Unlike an objective universal judgment—which is universal, logically speaking—a subjective universal judgment "does not rest on any concept."[42] There can therefore be no "inference at all to logical universal validity."[43] This is because aesthetic universal validity "does not pertain to the object at all ... in its entire logical sphere, and yet it extends it over the whole sphere of those who judge."[44] Categorically speaking, then, there can be no such thing as an objectively universal aesthetic judgment. "If one judges objects merely in accordance with concepts, then all representation of beauty is lost. Thus there can also be no rule in accordance with which someone could be compelled to acknowledge something as beautiful."[45] This subjective universality, which pertains to determinations of beauty, cannot be governed by rules simply because it would, by definition, no longer be concerned with beauty.

There is much in Wittgenstein's portrayal of aesthetic and ethical contemplation that is reminiscent of Kant, even if Wittgenstein arrived at his position by a somewhat different route. One of the most prominent similarities between the two is their insistence that aesthetic contemplation is transcendent. For Kant, a judgment of taste was universal and, as such, transcended all empirical experience. One does not need to verify that the judgment of others conforms with one's own because a judgment of taste calls for the universal conformity of everyone. It is not concerned with whether this conformity is empirically verifiable. It is also, in this sense, both pure and *a priori*. In other words, transcendence in Kant's sense lays the ground for the possibility of all judgments of taste in general. Wittgenstein's sense of transcendence is related but slightly different. In the first place, Wittgenstein seems to hold the position that an aesthetic judgment is not universal in the sense that 'everyone ought to find this beautiful.' However, it is universal in the sense that the beautiful is what is seen from the viewpoint of eternity. Kant's transcendental philosophy, on the other hand, sought to demonstrate that all of our experience was already predicated on our *a priori* faculties. Wittgenstein, too, ascribed logic to this kind of metaphysical place in his early philosophical system (see 6.13 of the *Tractatus*). The propositions of logic for Wittgenstein were not transcendental, but the fact that they were capable of mirroring the world was. This is to say that no proposition of logic is capable of representing how it is capable of representing anything in the first place. Logic in this sense is transcendental because it is prior to the possibility of there being a world at all and also because it is incapable of expressing its priority. Thus, for Wittgenstein, there can be no 'objective' conception of beauty in the sense that logic is utterly incapable of expressing any proposition of value. There is, in other words, no 'hierarchy' of logic. This is, in some respects, remarkably similar to Kant, inasmuch as the universal validity of a judgment of taste is not at all dependent on the logical sphere of an object. If it was, it would cease to be subjectively universal and would become objectively so. A judgment of taste, therefore, cannot be logical for Kant either.

The similarities between Kant and Wittgenstein have been noted by other scholars as well. Newton Garver has suggested that "there are striking differences between Kant and Wittgenstein in terminology, but when these are discounted it is difficult to discern any differences of doctrine."[46] In particular, Garver regards both Kant and Wittgenstein as critical philosophers, both of whom "disparage speculative philosophy,"[47] and therefore apply various metaphysical constraints on what philosophy can meaningfully accomplish. Broadly speaking, this is undoubtedly true; and though Garver details the various epistemological "schemata" and "criteria" that Kant and Wittgenstein employ respectively, the critical methodologies of each have important implications for their ethical doctrines as well. Kant famously stated in the preface of the second edition of the *Critique of Pure Reason* that he must "abolish *knowledge*, to make room for *belief*."[48] We might similarly say that Wittgenstein had to limit logic in order to make room for value. Although Wittgenstein held no maxim directly comparable to that of the categorical imperative if he were to give us one, it might be something along the lines of 'act according to a universal good will,' which is of course not very far removed from the categorical imperative. After all, one of the primary aims of Kantian philosophy is to show that the categorical imperative is predicated on the *a priori* concept of an autonomous will. In the *Groundwork of the Metaphysics of Morals*, Kant suggests "that a good will seems to constitute the indispensable condition even of worthiness to be happy,"[49] a sentiment that Wittgenstein would likely have no objection to.

Wittgenstein, it will be recalled, saw a fundamental connection between what was good and what was happy. This is also, in a certain sense, the connection between the ethical and the aesthetic. This should come as no surprise, insofar as Kant's conception of the categorical imperative and disinterested judgments of taste are both predicated on a universal ought. In a similar way, the ethical and the aesthetic for Wittgenstein are predicated on a universal vantage. Life, as seen from the eternal, is good, and the existence of the world—from the same point of view—is also beautiful. Just as Kant thought that "a good will is not good because of what it effects ... it is good in itself,"[50] the argument could be made that Wittgenstein considered the good and happy life to be the only justifiable one to live and that such a life was possible only through the good-will of the metaphysical subject. There is also no reason why one ought to choose the good and beautiful life over one that is not. It can only be metaphysically justified by the imperative 'one ought to choose it.' Wittgenstein's sense of ethical obligation is thus, like Kant's, undeniably deontological. "Everything seems to turn, so to speak, on *how* one wants."[51] Accordingly, the will must be "first and foremost the bearer of good and evil."[52] Thus it is through the will that both the ethical and the aesthetic come into a world that is otherwise devoid of value. If we were incapable of willing, we would also be incapable of seeing the world as either good or bad, beautiful or ugly, happy or unhappy. To illustrate the point, Wittgenstein asks, "Can we conceive a being that isn't capable of Will at all, but only of Idea (of seeing, for example)? In some sense this seems impossible. But if it were possible then there could also be a world without ethics."[53]

Wittgenstein's views on ethics are further explicated in a popular lecture he gave on the topic on November 17, 1929, to the Heretics Society in Cambridge. The various contentions that he makes as regards the subject have much in common with those to be found in the *Notebooks* and the *Tractatus*. A few statements, however, bear a mark more indicative of the *Investigations*. This is not at all surprising given the fact that this was something of a transitional period for Wittgenstein. *The Blue and Brown Books*, which were produced from lectures Wittgenstein gave between 1933 and 1935, already contain many of the central tenets of the *Investigations*. There are also a few instances in this lecture where Wittgenstein's view of ethics seems to further overlap with that of Kant's.

Wittgenstein begins the lecture by adopting the definition of ethics that Moore used in *Principia Ethica*: ethics is "the general enquiry into what is good."[54] There is more than just this superficial similarity between Wittgenstein's "Lecture on Ethics" and Moore's *Principia*. This is despite the fact that Wittgenstein did not seem to think very highly of *Principia*, as he expressed to Russell in a letter from 1912.

> I have just been reading a part of Moore's Principia Ethica: ... I do not like it at all. (Mind you, quite *apart* from disagreeing with most of it.) ... Moore repeats himself dozens of times, what he says in 3 pages could – I believe – easily be expressed in half a page. *Unclear* statements don't get a bit clearer by being repeated!![55]

Despite the negative opinion of Moore's philosophy, it does seem to have acted as something of a catalyst for Wittgenstein's thinking, just as it later would with

*On Certainty.* This assessment, by and large, would appear to be in tune with how Wittgenstein himself viewed his own ability to develop ideas. "I believe that my originality (if that is the right word) is an originality belonging to the soil rather than to the seed. (Perhaps I have no seed of my own.) Sow a seed in my soil and it will grow differently than it would in any other soil."[56]

Despite his dislike for *Principia*, much of what Wittgenstein says about the senselessness of ethics is reminiscent of the 'naturalistic fallacy' that Moore took so much care to detail in *Principia*. Moore's contention there is that the term 'good' is a simple one, meaning that it cannot be defined. This is unlike a term such as 'horse,' which comprises a great many simple qualities which, when taken together, constitute its definition. The naturalistic fallacy occurs when we mistakenly confuse a simple term with a complex one. In the case of the good, the fallacy occurs when we assign it all sorts of various qualities, such as John Stuart Mill does when he says "that pleasure, and freedom from pain, are the only things desirable as ends."[57] Moore contends that Mill falls into the naturalistic fallacy by "using the words ... 'desirable as an end' as absolutely and precisely equivalent to the words 'good as an end.'"[58] And according to Mill, the only thing desirable as an end is pleasure. Therefore, the only thing good for Mill is pleasure and pleasure alone. There is no doubt that Moore agrees that pleasure is good, but he categorically rejects the possibility that we can specifically define what good is.

This, it would seem, is something that accords with much of Wittgenstein's early philosophy. Just as logic will not allow us to define what a 'simple' is, it will not allow us to define what the 'good' consists of either. Like Moore, Wittgenstein sees it as something that cannot be meaningfully explicated in language. Every attempt in so doing is only capable of giving us what Wittgenstein calls the "trivial" or "relative" sense of the term. A trivial judgment of this sort is one that uses 'good' in relation to a specific end. That is to say, as Wittgenstein puts it, that "the word good in the relative sense simply means coming up to a certain predetermined standard."[59] For example: "This is the right way you have to go if you want to get to Granchester in the shortest time."[60] Thus, if one's goal is to get to Granchester as quickly as possible, the shortest route will also be the one that is 'good' and the longest will be the one that is 'bad.' When the words 'good' and 'bad' are used thusly, they are not in any conceivable sense 'ethical,' they only make an assertion about the way things are. Thus Wittgenstein asserts,

> Every judgment of relative value is a mere statement of facts and can therefore be put in such a form that it loses all the appearance of a judgment of value....

> Although all judgments of relative value can be shown to be mere statements of facts, no statement of fact can ever be, or imply, a judgment of absolute value.[61]

Like Kant, there is nothing about the mere logic of any given state of affairs that has the compelling force of an absolute judgment. "The *absolute good*, if it is a describable state of affairs, would be one which everybody, independent of his tastes and inclinations, would *necessarily* bring about or feel guilty for not bringing about."[62] But, Wittgenstein hastens to add, there is not, nor could there be, such a state of affairs that has "the coercive power of an absolute judge,"[63] as he calls it. No such state of affairs has the characteristic 'ought' that is necessary of such an absolute judgment of value or a categorical imperative.

This is not to say, however, that we cannot have experiences of the absolute. Wittgenstein gives us two examples. The first of these is the wonderment at existence. When we have an experience of this sort, we are "inclined to use such phrases as 'how extraordinary that anything should exist' or 'how extraordinary that the world should exist.'"[64] The second of these experiences is what Wittgenstein calls "the experience of feeling *absolutely* safe. I mean the state of mind in which one is inclined to say 'I am safe, nothing can injure me whatever happens.'"[65] One of the first things that one notices in the examples that Wittgenstein produces is a methodological procedure indicative of the *Investigations* in which various uses of a phrase or phrases are compared in order to draw out the family resemblances. When applied to an experience of the absolute, it becomes readily apparent "that the verbal expression which we give to these experiences is nonsense!"[66] Taking the example of 'wondering at existence' again, Wittgenstein suggests that it only makes sense to wonder at something when it is possible that one could imagine it otherwise. This does not apply to the wonderment at existence because we have no idea what it would look like for there to be nothing instead of something. We are left to wonder over what essentially amounts to a tautology—even though it is "just nonsense to say that one is wondering at a tautology."[67] Thus Wittgenstein is led inevitably to the conclusion that these verbal expressions, which "*seem*, prima facie, to be just *similes*,"[68] are all related to one another by way of a shared nonsensicalness. "I see now," Wittgenstein says, "That these nonsensical expressions were not nonsensical because I had not yet found the correct expressions, but that their nonsensicality was their very essence."[69]

This gives us further insight into what Wittgenstein might have possibly meant by 'ethics and aesthetics are one.' What is common to both the aesthetic and the ethical is their nonsensicality. This, of course, does not reduce the two to ontological equivalency; it only suggests that they share a similar characteristic.

Both the ethical and the aesthetic are thus joined by the same sort of 'ought' in Wittgenstein's thought. There is, as B. R. Tilghman has noted, "An absolute and logically necessary character"[70] to Wittgenstein's sense of ethical and aesthetic judgments—a sentiment that is similarly noted by Roland Barthes in *S/Z*: "Beauty (unlike ugliness) cannot really be explained.... Like a god (and as empty), it can only say: *I am what I am*."[71] This, of course, tells us nothing of what beauty is. It is, as Barthes says, simply empty, and that is all we can say about it. "Every direct predicate is denied it," he goes on. "The only feasible predicates are either tautology ... or simile."[72] Wittgenstein, too, likened statements of value to similes, but the problem with a simile is that it either leads us into an infinite regress, or it brings us back to a tautology. "Thus, beauty is referred to an infinity of codes: *lovely as Venus?* But Venus lovely as what? As herself?"[73] This, it would seem, is the only way to halt the series of similes: "Hide it, return it to silence, to the ineffable, to aphasia."[74] In other words, similes must come to an end somewhere, and when they do, they must end in tautological silence.

Although Wittgenstein wrote relatively little on the topics of ethics and aesthetics, he did, nevertheless, manage to arrive at a fairly cohesive theory of how ethical and aesthetic judgments are possible given the constraints that his logic demands. When he altered his views about language in his later work, his views on aesthetics also seem to have changed accordingly—although the remarks about ethics and aesthetics are perhaps even sparser in the *Investigations* than they are in the *Tractatus*. Thankfully, Wittgenstein gave a series of lectures on aesthetics at Cambridge during the summer of 1938, which are characterized by a methodology much more akin to the *Investigations* than the *Tractatus*. It is also important to note that nothing which now comprises the record of these lectures was written by Wittgenstein himself. It was collected from the notes of students in attendance. These collected notes, however, are significantly similar to one another and to the general thrust of Wittgenstein's philosophy to warrant the belief that they more or less reliably reflect a good deal of what Wittgenstein had to say in his lectures. Short of a verbatim dictation, it is as close to an accurate record as one could want.

Wittgenstein begins these lectures by claiming "the subject (Aesthetics) is very big and entirely misunderstood as far as I can see."[75] Part of Wittgenstein's reasoning behind this assertion is that the word "'beautiful' ... is an adjective, so you are inclined to say: 'This has a certain quality, that of being beautiful.'"[76] This is as a result of the grammatical function of adjectives in general, which can give us the erroneous impression that a particular quality is 'possessed' by a particular thing. The problem with this assumption, as Wittgenstein points out, is that it runs contrary to the way we actually learn to use words like 'beautiful' in the first place. "If you ask yourself how a child learns 'beautiful', 'fine', etc., you find it learns them roughly as interjections."[77] We are lured into the concept of subject and predicate when thinking about expressions such as 'this is beautiful' when in reality they occur in an "enormously complex situation . . . in which the expression itself has almost a negligible place."[78] We are thus accustomed to thinking about aesthetic expressions in terms of a primitive language-game instead of a complex one. Furthermore, interjections of approval, according to Wittgenstein, are of very little importance where aesthetic appreciation is concerned. "When aesthetic judgments are made, aesthetic adjectives such as 'beautiful' 'fine', etc., play hardly any role at all."[79] Take, for example, the critique of music. When discussing a musical piece, we might be inclined to say "'Look at this transition', or . . . 'The passage here is incoherent'. . . . The words you use are more akin to 'right and 'correct' . . . than to 'beautiful' and 'lovely'."[80] This is not to say that interjections do not enter into aesthetic appreciation at all. One can certainly be awestruck by the beauty of something, but very often, this expression by itself is not enough to distinguish between someone who is in a position to make an aesthetic judgment from someone who cannot. "When we make an aesthetic judgment about a thing, we do not just gape at it and say 'Oh! How marvelous!' We distinguish between a person who knows what he is talking about and a person who doesn't."[81]

There are many ways in which we make this distinction, but the use of aesthetic interjections alone is not one of them. If one were to listen to Bach's *Brandenburg Concertos*, one might certainly take note of their beauty. One might even be struck dumb with wonder upon hearing them, but if the only thing one was able to say about them were 'how wonderful', then we would not consider the person who said such a thing to have a well-informed sense of 'taste'. If, however, one were to mention their historical prominence in the repertoire of Baroque music, for example, or to point out the degree of technical virtuosity involved in their performance, then we would certainly be more inclined to treat such a person as someone who was in a position to make aesthetic judgments. It is interesting to note here that Wittgenstein's conception of aesthetic appreciation is strangely akin to his epistemological doctrine. Just as one must be in a position to demonstrate that one has a good basis for saying 'I know such and such', one must also be in a similar position to demonstrate the ability to make an aesthetic judgment. In the former case, simply saying 'I know' does not suffice for showing that it is true, just as in the latter case, the statement 'this is beautiful' is not a sufficient demonstration that one has the kind of authority required to make an aesthetic judgment. Aesthetic appreciation is, in other words, part of a way of life and only has meaning within that context. It is, therefore, "not only difficult to describe what appreciation consists in, but impossible. To describe what it consists in we would have to describe the whole environment."[82] The idea of giving such an all-encompassing description is something that Wittgenstein continually rejected throughout his work. One can never depict the whole environment because the depiction—which is, in a certain sense, as much a part of the environment as that which it depicts—is incapable of depicting itself as though from the outside. That would, of course, require a second-order metaphysics, and if we start down that path, it will not be long before we begin to encounter the infinite regress that is so indicative of the problem of metaphysics.

The inability to precisely state what it is aesthetic appreciation consists in is one of the main themes of Wittgenstein's lectures on aesthetics. A second but equally important theme Wittgenstein addresses is what he refers to as a 'science of aesthetics.' The use of the term 'science' in this phrase, it should be stressed, does not appear to coincide in any sense with the German word *Wissenschaft*, which of course translates into English as 'science.' The German word has a much broader sense than its English equivalent often connotes. In German, the term *Wissenschaft* can refer to a systematic study of any topic, whereas in English, the word 'science' has come to be almost inseparable from its association with the natural sciences—which is the epitome of the 'scientific methodology' in the majority of the English speaking world. It is this conception of science in the English sense that Wittgenstein seems to have in mind when he refers to a 'science of aesthetics,' especially as this notion is related to psychology. This idea is one that Wittgenstein flat out rejects. "People often say that aesthetics is a branch of psychology. The idea is that once we are more advanced, everything— all the mysteries of Art—will be understood by psychological experiments. Exceedingly stupid as the idea is, that is roughly it."[83] Wittgenstein's hostility to this notion is essentially bound up with what he sees as a confusion between the problems of science as compared to those of aesthetics. "Aesthetic questions have nothing to do with psychological experiments, but are answered in an entirely different way."[84]

The issue at the heart of this confusion is the belief that a causal explanation suffices as an answer to an aesthetic puzzle. We might suppose, for instance, that, given enough time, neuropsychology might be able to identify the particular parts of the brain that are involved when making aesthetic judgments of certain kinds. An explanation of this sort might hold that the feeling of puzzlement we sometimes have when considering a work of art is something which is caused by certain chains of neurons firing, such that when they are strung along in the correct sequence, the experience of 'aesthetic puzzlement' is produced in our minds. To be sure, it would be naïve to suggest that there is not something along these lines going on in the brain, but it would be equally naïve to suggest that a causal explanation of this sort is going to be of any use to us whatsoever when we are discussing the problems of aesthetics. The causal explanation that this interpretation offers us is simply not very well suited to this sort of application. Of course, because it is a causal explanation, we might even

> dream of predicting the reactions of human beings, say to works of art. If we imagine the dream realized, we'd not thereby have solved what we feel to be aesthetic puzzlements, although we may be able to predict that a certain line of poetry will, on a certain person, act in such and such a way. What we really want, to solve aesthetic puzzlements, is certain comparisons—grouping together of certain cases.[85]

David Novitz, in an article appearing in the collection of essays *Wittgenstein, Aesthetics, and Philosophy*, has taken note of the apparent tensions that exist in Wittgenstein's lectures on aesthetics. "On the one hand," Novitz says of Wittgenstein,

> he emphasizes the role played by rules in our aesthetic response to a work of art; on the other, he contests the view that our aesthetic impressions and judgments can be explained in a law-like way.... And yet, if rules do figure prominently in our aesthetic responses, it is difficult to see why there should not be law-like, perhaps scientific, explanations of aesthetic judgment.[86]

Part of the difficulty that arises from this apparent conflict is bound up with what Wittgenstein means by 'aesthetic appreciation,' which is impossible to describe without also describing the culture within which an aesthetic judgment takes place. "The words we call expressions of aesthetic judgment play a very complicated rôle, but a very definite rôle, in what we call a culture of a period. To describe their use or to describe what you mean by a cultured taste, you have to describe a culture."[87] This implies that if aesthetic appreciation is bound up with a culture, then what it means to appreciate may have more or less circumscribed boundaries, depending on how it was used during a given period. One culture may have a more exacting use of appreciation, another a more nebulous one. In some sense, then, a culture determines the rules by which aesthetic judgments are made. There is certainly no clear boundary between breaking the rule and following it, but in describing a culture, we are also, in some sense, describing a form of life, part of which is composed by the game of aesthetic appreciation. Thus, "What we now call a cultured taste perhaps didn't exist in the Middle Ages.

An entirely different game is played in different ages."[88] This, of course, does not mean that it is impossible to transgress the boundaries of a particular cultural epoch, for if it did, the rules would never change, and there would be no such thing as development in the arts. As Wittgenstein points out, for example, "You can say that every composer changed the rules, but the variation was very slight; not all the rules were changed. The music was still good by a great many of the old rules."[89]

Novitz's question thus deserves some attention. If aesthetic appreciation is in some sense governed by rules, and, if there can be such a thing as following or not following the rules, then why does scientific explanation—which is an explanatory system as much predicated on rules as is the taste of a particular culture—give us an unsatisfactory account of aesthetic appreciation? The answer to this question, so Novitz argues, lies in what people desire in a work of art.

> The rules that reflect what people want have a certain social significance, and it is our grasp of this significance that gives us a socially informed understanding of the ways in which rules can be tweaked or transformed to good or bad aesthetic effect. It is this knowledge, this 'feeling for the rules', that informs aesthetic judgment. It is something that is learned by becoming acquainted with tradition and conventions that inform the culture of a period; not something that is natural to us.[90]

Novitz seems to be suggesting that just because both aesthetic appreciation and scientific explanation are in some sense rule-governed does not mean that the latter can supplant the former. Each is, so to speak, a kind of language-game, and each has its own standards that may or may not be applicable in other contexts. We do not, nor should we, expect that the rules of one game are of any use in another. If we use the rules of chess to play checkers, no one would be under any pretense that we were still in some sense playing checkers. A similar analogy may be made about psychology's relationship to aesthetics. If we apply the rules of psychological inquiry to aesthetic questions, we are not thereby doing aesthetics. It should thus come as no surprise that the questions of aesthetics remain unanswered by causal explanations. Psychology cannot solve the problems of aesthetics any more than aesthetics can do likewise for psychology. A problem has a place in a particular game to which it belongs, and if we try to transplant it into a different one, it becomes an entirely different problem.

The above example brings up an important point. It is no doubt obvious that language-games of varying sorts often come into conflict with one another. Part of the objection to a psychological explanation of aesthetics is that the former

168          *Wittgenstein and the Problem of Metaphysics*

seeks to circumvent the latter, thus making the language-game of aesthetics superfluous. There is thus an essential disagreement involved in the question as to what sort of explanation suffices where an aesthetic puzzle is concerned. Settling these conflicts is rarely a task which admits of an easy solution if it admits of one at all. This is, as we know, the basic task which Jean-François Lyotard sets out to undertake in *The Differend*. "A case of differend between two parties takes place when the 'regulation' of the conflict that opposes them is done in the idiom of one of the parties while the wrong suffered by the other is not signified in that idiom."[91] In philosophical discourse, the object of the game is to discover the rule by which the investigation will be conducted, and when an aesthetic question is considered against the backdrop of psychology, it is hardly surprising that it should cease to be intelligible when the conflict has already presupposed the regulation of a scientific idiom. When we say that an aesthetic question feels out of place when considered in the context of psychology, we are in part suggesting that the question itself no longer has an aesthetic charm. It loses its luster, so to speak. The very thing that made the question interesting in the first place was the context in which it was posed, and remembering this fact can help us to avoid the disagreements that are caused by a confusion between language-games before they even get started.

This is not to say, we must caution, that every dispute between idioms can be brought to a satisfactory resolution. Some are, as Wittgenstein would point out in *On Certainty*, simply irreconcilable. "Where two principles really do meet which cannot be reconciled with one another, then each man declares the other a fool and heretic."[92] This seems to be the only possible outcome that a dispute over fundamental principles can come to. If one refuses to see the world in a particular way, then no amount of 'evidence' will prevail in convincing one to a contrary point of view. Indeed, where metaphysics is concerned, there is no such thing as being 'convinced by the evidence.' To see an axiom of metaphysics as correct is simply to see it as aesthetically preferable as compared to other possible axioms. While there is nothing that necessitates the adoption of any given metaphysical axiom, we must not forget that this freedom of choice all but ensures that disputes about which axioms to accept will occur.

As I already mentioned, the problem of conflicts raised in Wittgenstein's critique of certainty is dealt with in a much more extensive fashion in *The Differend*. In many important respects, it is a book that overlaps with a good deal of Wittgenstein's own writing. This is especially true as regards what Lyotard refers to as 'phrases' and 'regimens.' A 'phrase' for Lyotard is something akin to a basic 'unit' of language but, unlike the notion of Wittgenstein's 'simples' in the

*Tractatus*, which has an 'absolute' value in itself, Lyotard's phrases have more in common with Wittgenstein's later conception of meaning. A phrase, according to Lyotard, "Is constituted according to a set of rules (its regimen),"[93] and it is this regimen—which is similar in its scope to Wittgenstein's concept of the language-game—that gives a phrase its meaning. There is also no such thing as one single-phrase regimen. Regimens can take on any number of given characteristics and can be governed by any number of different rules. Thus there can be a regimen of "reasoning, knowing, describing, recounting, questioning, showing, ordering, etc.,"[94] each of which may not necessarily be "translated from one into the other."[95] They can, however, be "linked one onto another in accordance with an end fixed by a genre of discourse."[96]

Another key feature of Lyotard's phrases is their multiplicity. "There are as many universes as there are phrases. And as many situations of instance as there are universes,"[97] he tells us. Of course, this multitude of possible phrases can come into conflict with one another, and when they do, it is because there is no "rule of judgment applicable to both arguments."[98] The resulting *differend* is distinguished from what Lyotard refers to as "litigation," which is a conflict that may be settled via recourse to a commonly accepted rule. Where a *differend* is concerned, on the other hand, it is important to note that "one side's legitimacy does not imply the other's lack of legitimacy. However, applying a single rule of judgment to both in order to settle their differend as though it were merely litigation would wrong (at least) one of them (and both of them if neither side admits this rule)."[99]

There is thus a definite ethical dilemma involved in a dispute amongst phrases, one that is not easily solved without doing harm to one party or another. Each party may hold to any given number of irreconcilable phrases with no clear way of bridging the gap between them. Thus, we must endeavor to discover a method that allows us to link regimens without resorting to the subjectification involved in translating one regimen into another. Such a method "denies itself the possibility of settling, on the basis of its own rules, the differends it examines."[100] In so doing, Lyotard can no doubt be read as offering us a very poignant defense of our right to disagree, much as William James did for our "right to believe at our own risk any hypothesis that is live enough to tempt our will."[101] If it were not for this assumed right—that various parties can hold irreconcilable beliefs—then there really could be no such thing as the *differend* at all. Likewise, implicit within the sense of James's 'right to believe'—which, in a manner of speaking, is the aesthetic capacity to accept without proof—there is also an ethical imperative that accompanies this right which demands that we afford the same right to others. This is exactly the imperative the *differend* places on us. It denies the

170       *Wittgenstein and the Problem of Metaphysics*

assumption that disputes must necessarily be settled, which is itself a way of settling disputes.

There is also a definite metaphysical implication within Lyotard's concept of the *differend*; for although he allows the possibility of irreconcilable difference between phrases, he does not allow for the possibility of there being no phrase at all. "What escapes doubt," he says, "is that there is at least one phase, no matter what it is. This cannot be denied without verifying it *ideo facto*. *There is no phrase is a phrase. . . . The phrase currently phrased as a phrase does not exist* is a phrase."[102] The very same line of reasoning could just as easily be extended to metaphysics as well. To deny metaphysics is to do metaphysics, and, as a result, the denial ends up contradicting itself. This is a point that Lyotard also acknowledges, but his solution to the difficulty is to suggest that "the phrase considered as occurrence escapes the logical paradoxes that self-referential propositions give rise to."[103] A phrase is not subject to self-reference because it is not a proposition within a regimen. A phrase simply is; it is not subject to a truth calculus like a proposition is. Rather, propositions are, according to Lyotard, "Phrases under the logical regimen and the cognitive regimen."[104] It is these regimens that set the condition by which a proposition might either be true or false. Phrases cannot be either true or false apart from this regimen, but the regimen itself is predicated on any number of given phrases, which themselves can never be subject to the rules of the regimen. A phrase must stand outside the regimen, which means that it cannot be subject to the regimen. A phrase, therefore, "Cannot be its own argument,"[105] for this would be to apply the propositional function outside of the context of the regimen in which it has any sense.

The problem of metaphysics, which has been variously described throughout this text, has been typified by two main tendencies. The first of these is the desire to do away with metaphysics and the resulting self-referential incoherence that follows from this position. The second of these tendencies is the desire for the indubitable, which, if it could be discovered, would rid us of the need for metaphysics altogether and thus the inconsistency in denying it. Reasons for thinking that both of these tendencies are untenable have been given throughout. Lyotard, however, seems to put it especially well:

> The self-referentiality of a negative phrase prohibits a decision concerning its truth or falsehood . . . ; and the self-referentiality of an affirmative phrase allows any statement to be demonstrated. . . . But phrases can obey regimens other than the logical and the cognitive. They can have stakes other than the true. What prohibits a phrase from being a proposition does not prohibit it from being a

phrase. That there are propositions presupposes that there are phrases. When we are surprised that there is something rather than nothing, we are surprised that there is a phrase or that there are phrases rather than no phrases.[106]

Lyotard's last remark here, as we have seen, is very much in keeping with Wittgenstein's own aesthetically inclined mysticism. The wonderment at existence that is typified by this aesthetic-mystical tendency is first and foremost the expression of a metaphysical principle. The question 'Why is there something rather than nothing?' can only be answered because we can give it an aesthetic justification. Whatever existence is, it is inseparable from how we set out to describe it, and we can give no justification as to why we ought to choose one mode of description as opposed to another other than the aesthetic one.

There is a "queer resemblance," Wittgenstein once wrote in 1936, "between a philosophical investigation (perhaps especially in mathematics) and an aesthetic one."[107] The mathematician is, after all, "always inventing new forms of description. Some, stimulated by practical needs, others, from aesthetic needs,—and yet others in a variety of ways.... The mathematician is an inventor, not a discoverer."[108] The forms of description that a mathematician chooses are very much predicated on the needs that they fulfill. One of these, no doubt, is an aesthetic one, and mathematicians can be as much lured by the beauty of a proof as any other factor. This, of course, does not imply that the axioms around which a proof is constructed are themselves self-evidently true. They are only true insofar as they serve to accomplish some other end. Wittgenstein would also come to criticize the belief that arithmetic could be reduced to logic—which was a central tenet of Russell's philosophical work—on similar grounds. "But who says that arithmetic is logic, or what has to be done with logic to make it in some sense into a substructure for arithmetic? If we had, e.g., been led to attempt this by aesthetic considerations, who says it can succeed?"[109] There is, of course, no guarantee that our aesthetic considerations will lead us to success, but then again, what counts as success depends partly on how we differentiate it from failure. In other words, the rule for determining this difference will inevitably depend on an aesthetic consideration because what counts as a 'success' and a 'failure' will be predicated on the criteria which we are willing to accept and abide by. And thus, "'Anything – and nothing – is right.' – And this is the position in which, for example, someone finds himself in ethics or aesthetics when he looks for definitions that correspond to our concepts."[110]

What then can we learn from Wittgenstein's philosophy? The first lesson that we might heed is that metaphysics is simply unavoidable in philosophical inquiry. His attempts in the *Tractatus* and the *Investigations* to rid his analysis of metaphysical implications entirely always met with a self-referential incoherence. *On Certainty* frees us from this inconsistency by acknowledging that inquiry must come to an end somewhere—and where it does, we must simply accept our beliefs as true without being able to prove that they are. The second lesson that we might learn seems to have been implicit in Wittgenstein's philosophical writings since the very beginning. It is, broadly speaking, the mystical sentiment that is strikingly present in his earlier philosophical works. In a certain sense, this gives us a way of resolving the problem of metaphysics. When we are faced with the decision of how we ought to describe existence, we are always put in the position of 'viewing it from afar.' It is as if how we describe set the whole parameter of what there can be, and in so doing we are delimiting the whole of existence. Given that we can produce no ultimate justification for how we describe, we are always forced to admit that the only thing that stands at the bottom of all our estimations is a simple and indefinable aesthetic preference.

# Notes

1  Roderick M. Chisholm, *The Problem of the Criterion* (Milwaukee, WI: Marquette University Press, 1973), 12.
2  Nietzsche, *Thus Spoke Zarathustra*, 2006, 65.
3  Carruthers, *The Metaphysics of the Tractatus*, xiii.
4  Ibid., xiii–xiv.
5  Wittgenstein, *Culture and Value*, 39.
6  Ibid. 31.
7  Ibid. 31.
8  Ibid. 27.
9  Nietzsche, "Twilight of the Idols," sec. 26.
10  Wittgenstein, *Culture and Value*, 28.
11  Wittgenstein, *Notebooks*, 86.
12  Ibid.
13  Wittgenstein, *Tractatus Logico-Philosophicus*, 2001, sec. 6.43.
14  Wittgenstein, *Notebooks*, 86.
15  Wittgenstein, *Tractatus Logico-Philosophicus*, 2001, sec. 6.43.
16  Wittgenstein, *Notebooks*, 83.
17  Ibid.
18  Wittgenstein, *Tractatus Logico-Philosophicus*, 2001, 3–4.
19  Ibid., sec. 6.4311.

20 Ibid., sec. 5.6.

21 Ibid., sec. 6.45.

22 Ibid., sec. 6.45.

23 Kathrin Stengel, "Ethics as Style: Wittgenstein's Aesthetic Ethics and Ethical Aesthetics," *Poetics Today* 25, no. 4 (Winter 2004): 611.

24 Wittgenstein, *Tractatus Logico-Philosophicus*, trans. C. K. Ogden (New York: Barnes & Noble, 2004).

25 Stengel, "Ethics as Style," 612.

26 Ibid., 617.

27 Hodges, *Transcendence and Wittgenstein's Tractatus*, 149.

28 Wittgenstein, *Notebooks*, 78.

29 Ibid.

30 Ibid.

31 Ibid.

32 Ibid.

33 Ibid., 77.

34 Ibid., 79.

35 Ibid.

36 Ibid. 78.

37 Thomas Nagel, *The View from Nowhere* (New York: Oxford University Press, 1989), 8.

38 Ibid., 8.

39 Kant, *Critique of the Power of Judgment*, 5: 219.

40 Ibid. 5: 212.

41 Ibid.

42 Ibid., 5: 215.

43 Ibid.

44 Ibid.

45 Ibid.

46 Garver, *This Complicated Form of Life*, 57.

47 Ibid., 51.

48 Immanuel Kant, *Critique of Pure Reason* (London: Henry G. Bohn, 1855), xxxv.

49 Immanuel Kant, *Groundwork of the Metaphysics of Morals* (Cambridge: Cambridge University Press, 1998), IV 393.

50 Ibid., IV 394.

51 Wittgenstein, *Notebooks*, 78.

52 Ibid., 76.

53 Ibid, 77.

54 Moore, *Principia Ethica*, 2.

55 McGuinness and Wright, *Ludwig Wittgenstein, Cambridge Letters*, 13.

56 Wittgenstein, *Culture and Value*, 36.

57 John Stuart Mill, *Utilitarianism* (London: Parker, Son and Bourn, 1863), 10.

58 Moore, *Principia Ethica*, 65.

59 Wittgenstein, "A Lecture on Ethics," 5.

60 Ibid., 6.

61 Ibid., 5–6.

62 Ibid., 7.

63 Ibid., 7.

64 Ibid., 8.

65 Ibid. 8.

66 Ibid.

67 Ibid., 9.

68 Ibid.

69 Ibid., 11.

70 B. R. Tilghman, *Wittgenstein, Ethics, and Aesthetics: The View from Eternity* (Albany, NY: State University of New York Press, 1991), 55.

71 *S/Z* (New York: Hill & Wang, 1974), 33.

72 Ibid., 33.

73 Ibid., 34.

74 Ibid.

75 Ludwig Wittgenstein, *Lectures and Conversations on Aesthetics, Psychology, and Religious Belief*, ed. Cyril Barrett (Berkeley, CA: University of California Press, 2007), 1.

76 Ibid.

77 Ibid., 1–2.

78 Ibid., 2.

79 Ibid., 3.

80 Ibid.

81 Ibid., 6.

82 Ibid., 7.

83 Ibid., 17.

84 Ibid.

85 Ibid., 29.

86 David Novitz, "Rules, Creativity and Pictures: Wittgenstein's Lectures on Aesthetics," in *Wittgenstein, Aesthetics, and Philosophy*, ed. Peter Lewis (Burlington, VT: Ashgate Publishing, 2004), 55.

87 Wittgenstein, *Lectures and Conversations on Aesthetics, Psychology, and Religious Belief*, 8.

88 Ibid., 8.

89 Ibid., 6.

90 Novitz, "Rules, Creativity and Pictures: Wittgenstein's Lectures on Aesthetics," 69.

91 Jean-François Lyotard, *The Differend: Phrases in Dispute* (Minneapolis, MN: University of Minnesota Press, 1988), 9.

92 Wittgenstein, *On Certainty*, sec. 611.

93 Lyotard, *The Differend*, xii.

94 Ibid.

95 Ibid.

96 Ibid.

97 Ibid., sec. 122.

98 Ibid., xi.

99 Ibid.

100 Ibid., xiv.

101 James, *The Will to Believe*, 29.

102 Lyotard, *The Differend*, sec. 99.

103 Ibid.

104 Ibid.

105 Ibid.

106 Ibid.

107 Wittgenstein, *Culture and Value*, 25.

108 Ludwig Wittgenstein, *Remarks on the Foundations of Mathematics*, ed. G. H. von Wright, R. Rhees, and G. E. M. Anscombe (Cambridge, MA: The MIT Press, 1983), sec. 168.

109 Ibid., III—85.

110 Wittgenstein, *Philosophical Investigations*, sec. 77.

# 6

# Always an Elsewhere

If, as I have suggested, metaphysics is the branch of philosophy that postulates axioms of truth and devises definitions based on those truths, it can do so only by way of the subject that postulates them as universal. That is to say, in other words, that all axiomatic truths are true only insofar as the metaphysical subject is willing to believe that they are true. This willingness to believe, however, is one that cannot be predicated on any conceivable self-evident or indubitable principle. In order to advance an axiom of truth from which we can derive definitions, we must be willing to forgo proof. Indeed, it is through such an act of 'faith' that the ability to provide proof becomes possible in the first place. By nominating an axiom as 'true,' the metaphysical subject expects the acquiescence of everyone else. It is thus a judgment of taste, in Kant's sense, and takes the form of subjective universality. Consequently, we find that the metaphysical subject—through its claim to universality—finds that it too must possess the form of finality inherent to its judgment. Without this form, there would be no possibility of making aesthetic judgments of the sort required for establishing any axiom of truth. When we reflect, however, on what this metaphysical subject must truly be, we find that it is nothing: A Being-for-itself, to borrow Sartre's term. It does not exist inside the world because it is the limit of the world—the form of its finality.

Thus, the argument of this chapter will be threefold: One, all metaphysical axioms of truth are judgments of taste and hence possess the finality of form indicative of such judgments; two, because the metaphysical subject is the limit of the world, it does not exist in the world (and is consequently a kind of nothingness); and three, works of art provide us with the possibility of mystical experience by exhibiting the limit of the world from within the world. These assertions, however, bring up what is perhaps a larger issue for subjectivity. In suggesting that the metaphysical axioms possess a finality of form and that the metaphysical subject substantiates such axioms based on the aesthetics of choice, it would appear that we are making a case for a metaphysics of being while denying the metaphysics of becoming any legitimacy. This inference we will explicitly deny. Instead, we will suggest that the metaphysical subject has the quality of being 'ethico-aesthetic.' That is to say, in other words, that the metaphysical subject maintains both an aesthetic and ethical component: The former is concerned with the aesthetics of being and the latter is concerned with the creativity of becoming. These two features of the ethico-aesthetic subject are, as we will maintain, irreducible to one another. In aesthetics, we discover a 'faith in being,' and in ethics we discover the 'spirituality of becoming.' When combined, we arrive at a sense of religion that upholds the necessity of both being and becoming. We will conclude by suggesting that works of art are also 'religious' in this sense, insofar as they are constituted in the hybridity of being and becoming.

In fleshing these arguments out, we must first be careful to distinguish between the metaphysical subject—the philosophical 'I'—and the 'I' of the natural sciences, i.e., the human body, which is, according to Wittgenstein, "A part of the world among others, among animals, plants, stones etc., etc."[1] This, of course, seems to inevitably lead Wittgenstein to a quasi-Cartesian dualism in which the metaphysical subject is housed in the fragment of nature, which is the human body. Wittgenstein, however, arrived at this dualism, not through a process of eliminating doubt in order to arrive at a bedrock of certainty. His approach is rather more Kantian in nature and produces a division more reminiscent of that between the noumenal and phenomenal. This split in Wittgenstein's conception of subjectivity, for instance, does not lead to any skepticism as to the existence of things outside the mind. There is, however, a clear delineation in Wittgenstein between what is and what is not intelligible. That is to say, in other words, that the human body can be explicated in natural terms according to various definitions that the metaphysical subject postulates as given. It is for this reason that the human body (as a subject of the natural sciences) is thinkable. The metaphysical subject itself, however, is subject to no such explication—it is the basis for explication and hence must be entirely unintelligible and therefore 'nonexistent' in naturalistic terms.

This point leads us to an equivalent problem regarding art. If art is to be thinkable in the Wittgensteinian sense, it would have to be possible to provide a definition of art that would precisely mirror the state of affairs under which it exists in the world. While doing so would provide the necessary construct in which art can be thought, it would also be unable to avoid the same dualistic divide between the 'natural' human body and the 'supernatural' metaphysical subject that plagued Wittgenstein's own mystically inclined logical theory of language. On one level, the work of art is but an object amongst others in the world, and when it comes to providing a theory of art on this level, there is no

*Always an Elsewhere*

real difficulty to be encountered in describing all the formal and ideological components that go into making it what it is. The only result to be attained is the enumeration of facts, and this is the province of art history, not of philosophy. The real problem, therefore, is not to be discovered in the gathering and interpretation of various truths. What is significant about the work of art is the way in which its meaning perpetually slips beyond the facts, and this necessitates that we distinguish between the metaphysical work of art and its physical manifestation. Without this distinction, there is no way to conceive of the possibility of art as an exemplar of mystical experience, which was, for Wittgenstein, its most important feature.

This is not without some rather peculiar consequences, however. First, we must be willing to admit that there is an aspect of art that categorically resists definition and consequently the possibility of intelligibility. In fact, we must go so far as to argue that even the sum total of every conceivable definition does not exhaust the possibility of art. Second, if there is some feature of art that does not lend itself to intelligibility, we seem forced to the conclusion that in some sense, it does not exist—a point that is bolstered by the fact that Wittgenstein considered existence and thought to be essentially one and the same. The work of art is thus a kind of nothingness. It exhibits for us the possibility of finality and hence intelligibility without which thought would be impossible. Art, as a 'form' of non-intelligibility, presents the world to us as a limited, intelligible whole. Such a presentation, however, is not possible, strictly speaking, from within the boundaries of the world. Art, like the metaphysical subject, does not 'exist' in the proper sense of the word. We cannot, therefore, apply any metaphysical limitation on either. Both are 'absolutely free', which amounts to the same as 'absolutely nothing.'

Throughout the preceding chapters, we have paid a great deal of attention to the problem of metaphysics and its implications for Wittgenstein's philosophy, the main point of which has been to call attention to several key features of metaphysical inquiry. The first of these is that metaphysical propositions are primarily definitional in an *a priori* sense. They cannot be deduced from experience and are therefore not justified by experience. *A priori* principles "are the indispensable basis of the possibility of experience itself,"[2] as Kant tells us. This brings up the second feature of metaphysical inquiry, which we must again take note of. One of the fundamental convictions that underlie Kant's metaphysics is the belief that

> in the judgments of pure reason, opinion has no place. For as they do not rest on empirical grounds, and as the sphere of pure reason is that of necessary truth

and *a priori* cognition, the principle of connection in it requires universality and necessity, and consequently perfect certainty,—otherwise we should have no guide to the truth at all.[3]

The difficulty here, as I have already tried to demonstrate, stems primarily from the problem of the criterion. In order to confer certitude on any piece of knowledge, we must have some standard by which to judge it, and ultimately we do so by predicating our claim on some foundational set of axioms that we take to be givens. We cannot prove the truth of these axioms without begging the question, which is why, in the end, all claims to certainty are, at best, statements about the psychological condition of the person who holds them. Roughly speaking, the only fact conveyed by such a claim is that we are either unable or unwilling to imagine things otherwise than we do. It is a creative failure, one wrought by the over-extension of aesthetic judgments from the realm of subjective universality into that of the objective.

Metaphysics can therefore not be about 'knowledge.' It is what makes knowledge possible. As Wittgenstein tells us in *On Certainty*: "'I know' often means: I have the proper grounds for my statement,"[4] and it is, as I maintain, metaphysics which supplies such a ground. It thus makes no sense to say that one can know that an axiom of metaphysics is true without giving further metaphysical grounds on which to base the claim. One must simply abide by the realization that our knowledge cannot be ultimately and universally justified. It is for this reason that we can no more escape metaphysics than we can escape the inevitability of death. "That the human spirit will ever give up metaphysical research is," Kant tells us, "as little to be expected as that we should prefer to give up breathing altogether, in order to avoid inhaling impure air."[5] Metaphysical speculation is at the very heart of human nature, and even the most unreflective of individuals will have reason to engage in it from time to time. The problem for Kant, therefore, was not the question of how to escape metaphysics, but rather of how to divine "a recognized standard" that would prevent people from shaping it "after [their] own pattern."[6] To what extent this can be done, however, is a matter of some debate. If by 'recognized standard' we merely mean 'commonly agreed upon,' then there is no real difficulty in at least hypothetically arriving at some set of principles that are generally applicable to a sub-set of individuals who choose to cede to them. If, however, we use the phrase 'recognized standard' as approximately equivalent in meaning to the phrase 'objectively universal,' then there is not—nor can there be—such a standard. The axioms of metaphysics can only be subjectively universal and, like judgments of taste, they do "not rest on any concept."[7] There can thus be no such thing as "any inference at all to logical universal validity"[8] where aesthetic judgments are concerned. The recognized standards of metaphysics, however, belong as much to the realm of aesthetics as do judgments of taste. Even the laws of logic—which are themselves the paradigmatic exemplar of objective universality—are only apparently universal. Even the nearly universal assent of everyone that the principles of logic enjoy is not a demonstration of their objective universality.

What, then, is the link between this conception of metaphysics and the work of art? The first step in answering this question is to recall a different yet not unrelated question which Kant poses in the *Prolegomena*: "*How is nature itself possible?*"[9] The importance of this question for Kant cannot be overstated. It is, as he writes, "The highest possible point that a transcendental philosophy can ever reach."[10] There are two possible senses of 'nature' this question addresses according to Kant: the material and the formal. Nature in the material sense is predicated on "the constitution of our sensibility, according to which it is in its special way affected by objects which are in themselves unknown to it and totally distinct from it."[11] Nature in the formal sense, which is to say, "The totality of the rules under which all appearances must come in order to be thought as connected in an experience,"[12] consists in those apparatuses *of* the understanding which make nature in the material sense legible *to* the understanding. The conclusion that Kant is forced to make from this is that the 'laws of experience' amount to the same thing as the 'laws of nature.'

Even today, it must be admitted that metaphysics can scarcely attain any higher question than the one Kant has already posed for us. 'How is nature itself possible?' is still the problem with which metaphysics has got to grapple. For the majority of philosophers in the Western canon, the inclination in answering this question has always been to make an appeal to the self-evidence of first principles, but when pressed, there is seemingly not a one amongst them that can escape the withering reproaches of the skeptic unscathed. We thus seemed forced to admit that there is no objectively universal standard that demands that we adopt one metaphysical supposition to the exclusion of all others. Objectivity, despite Kant's claim otherwise, cannot both be the methodology and the aim of metaphysics without begging the question, a point which Karl Jaspers has made so excellently that it deserves to be quoted at length.

> The fundamental difficulty is that Kant, in striving to disclose the conditions of all objectivity, is compelled to operate within objective thinking itself, hence in a realm of objects which must not be treated as objects. He tries to understand the

subject–object relationship in which we live as though it were possible to be outside it. He strives towards the limits of the existence of all being for us; standing at the limit, he endeavors to perceive the origin of the whole, but he must always remain within the limit. With his transcendental method he strives to transcend while remaining within the world. He thinks about thought. Yet he cannot do so from outside of thought, but only by thinking.[13]

The circularity involved in Kant's methodology that Jaspers draws our attention to is also indicative of certain aspects of Wittgenstein's philosophy. It is, in short, one of the most difficult problems with which metaphysics has got to contend. How do we justify a principle of metaphysics without assuming the very principle that we are attempting to give credence to?

One of the ways we might achieve this end is by coming to the realization that metaphysical reasoning can never be all-encompassing. While metaphysics is capable of dictating the boundaries of philosophical inquiry, it cannot do likewise for metaphysics itself. In other words, metaphysics cannot be used as a justification for metaphysics without falling into circular reasoning. What is beyond metaphysics—that is, the justification for metaphysics—is, and must forever be, a thing-in-itself. That is why, as Jaspers points out, "The 'thing in itself' is not a thing but a symbol at the limit of cognition, signifying the phenomenality of all knowing being."[14] The signification at the limit of cognition—which finds its terminus precisely where metaphysical justification cedes its claim of legitimacy to the unknowable—will never be an object of cognition. The realm of the noumenal, though it cannot be accessed by cognition, nevertheless, "is present in our freedom, in the Ideas, in the contemplation of the beautiful."[15] Even though the noumenal does not present itself to cognition as a phenomenal object, it still exhibits itself as the necessary ground on which the phenomenal is predicated. Put in Wittgenstein's terms, "What expresses *itself* in language, *we* cannot express by means of language. Propositions *show* the logical form of reality. They display it."[16]

In part, this is why Kant's third critique is the lynchpin of his metaphysics, inasmuch as the "purposiveness of nature" is "a special concept of the reflecting power of judgment, not of reason; for the end is not posited in the object at all, but strictly in the subject and indeed in its mere capacity for reflecting."[17] The concept of purposiveness, which is made possible by the reflecting power of judgment, is what presents us with the possibility of a universal ground. This is precisely why a judgment of taste—which is both subjective and universal—is indispensable to metaphysics: The satisfaction inherent "in the beautiful must depend upon reflection on an object that leads to some sort of concept"[18] and therefore "must contain a ground of satisfaction for everyone."[19] It is the mechanism that allows us to bridge the gap between the subjective and the objective. Reflective judgments of taste not only contain the possibility of universal satisfaction, they also demand it. This, in turn, explains how it is possible to disagree about judgments of taste. In the first place, there must be some claim on which a disagreement can pivot. The claim must call for universal agreement but not enforce it. It must embody "lawfulness without law and a subjective correspondence of the imagination to the understanding without an objective one."[20] If such a claim had the weight of law, it would not tolerate descent and would thus necessitate objective universality. This is why disagreement is not possible as regards judgments of universal objectivity; likewise, in the case of the subjectively agreeable, but for the opposite reason. Because the subjectively agreeable makes no claim to universality of any kind, there can be no disagreement about it. In order for there to be such a thing as disagreement where judgments of taste are concerned, three components are necessary: it must be based on pleasure; it must be subjective, and it must be universal.

This puts us in a position to make an analogy between judgments of taste and the axioms of metaphysics. To begin with, it must be admitted, *prima facie*, that disagreements abound in metaphysics just as they do in aesthetics. There can thus be no such thing as a universally objective standard in metaphysics as long as the possibility of disagreement exists about what that standard ought to be. The very fact that disagreement is possible is already an indication that metaphysics does not extend beyond the validity of subjective universality. This is to say, in other words, that we adhere to metaphysical axioms only insofar as we derive aesthetic pleasure from the act of *supposing* them to be true, and it is this pleasure—for all intents and purposes—that *makes* those axioms true *for us*. Beauty is, therefore, an inseparable component of any metaphysics. It is what allows for the possibility of truth and falsehood in the first place. "In beauty we behold a radiant truth, but not the knowledge of any object,"[21] as Jaspers puts it. This radiant truth that beauty reveals is the condition of truth itself. That anything can be true is the truth of beauty; it is the supersensible condition on which judging is grounded. This is why, as Jaspers goes on, "Kant stresses the uncertainty of correct subsumption in judgments of taste. Here, where derivation ceases, where the feeling of pleasure is the only predicate of judgment, a new and fundamental responsibility arises: to perceive the supersensible through participation in the universally valid."[22] Derivation must terminate at some juncture, and when it does, there is no further justification to be given any judgment save an aesthetic one.

184 *Wittgenstein and the Problem of Metaphysics*

The benefit in subsuming metaphysics under the subjectively universal claim of aesthetics is that it allows us to escape the circularity inherent to the problem of metaphysics. It does, however, leave a particularly insidious problem untouched: essentialism, which can occur all too easily when we misconstrue a subjectively universal judgment as universally objective. This is not an altogether easy trap to avoid falling into, however. Once one has become convinced of the truth of a subjective universal judgment, it can be nigh on impossible to be convinced otherwise. Worse still, it can be extraordinarily difficult to resist the temptation to universalize based on one's subjective convictions. This is, one could argue, what allowed Kant to make the leap from the rationality of the self to the rationality of humanity. It also invites the conclusion, whether expressly stated or tacitly implied, that there is some essence in which humanity partakes. The assumption is, as Sartre explains in *Existentialism and Humanism*, that:

> Man possesses a human nature; that 'human nature,' which is the conception of human being, is found in every conception of Man. In Kant, the universality goes so far that the wild man of the woods, man in the state of nature, and the bourgeois are all contained in the same definition and have the same fundamental qualities.[23]

The objectifying implications of this are all but obvious. 'Human,' according to this conception, means 'coming up to some predetermined standard.' "The essence of man precedes that historic existence which we confront in experience,"[24] as Sartre puts it. The trouble is, of course, that by insisting on a human essence with which one has got to conform in order to qualify as human, we must seemingly disavow ourselves of our individual subjectivity—and more importantly, our *responsibility* for the act of self-creation which is at the very foundation of subjectivity. In order for there to be such a thing as a subjective universal judgment at all, there must first be a subject from which it can originate, and in order for there to be a subject, our existence must precede our essence. There can be no *a priori* definition of human essence.

> Man first of all exists, encounters himself, surges up in the world – and defines himself afterwards. If man ... is not definable, it is because to begin with he is nothing. He will not be anything until later, and then he will be what he makes of himself.[25]

Subjectivity, as Sartre conceived of it, implies two things primarily. "On the one hand, the freedom of the individual subject and, on the other hand, that man cannot pass beyond human subjectivity."[26] In *Being and Nothingness*, Sartre makes it clear that the term 'subjectivity' "does not mean here the belonging to a subject;... That is subjective which can not get out of itself."[27] This conception of subjectivity has two primary consequences. Firstly, it denies the possibility of an objectively universal judgment precisely because it would constitute a "passing beyond human subjectivity." Secondly, by so denying this possibility, we affirm the irreducible freedom that subjectivity embodies. When we attempt to apply an objectively universal judgment to the 'reality' of individual subjectivity, we are not only decreeing that things could not be otherwise for the self but, in fact, that they could not be different for anyone at all. Thus, the inherent implication involved in the idea of *a singular* human nature (as expressed by an objective universal judgment) is always in effect a denial of our fundamental freedom. When we advance the claim that there is a human reality in which we all commonly participate, and necessarily so, we have resorted to a kind of despotism—both of the self and of the other.

This, of course, raises a whole set of issues surrounding the nature of the self and subjectivity in general. Sartre is keen on rejecting any notion of subjectivity that would have the effect of fixing the self permanently in place (thus objectifying it). Whatever else the self is (or is not), it is first and foremost radically free. This freedom is something denied to the self of Descartes' *res cogitans*: Whatever else the self is, it must first and foremost be a thinking thing which reflects on its own thought as the very condition of its being. As Sartre observed in "The Transcendence of the Ego," however, this

> reflecting consciousness does not take itself for an object when I effect the *Cogito*. What it affirms concerns the reflected consciousness.... The consciousness which says *I Think* is precisely not the consciousness which thinks. Or rather it is not *its own* thought which it posits by this thetic act.[28]

Thus, as Sartre puts it in *Being and Nothingness*, "The first condition of all reflection is a pre-reflective *cogito*," which, as he maintains, "Does not posit an object."[29] One might say in this sense that the ultimate effect, if not the ultimate aim, of Descartes' *Cogito* is to objectify subjectivity, to make it an object of knowledge or, more precisely stated, the foundation of knowledge. The subjectivity that the *Cogito* is meant to substantiate is one of absolute certitude. In fact, it never achieves this certitude because the act of reflection that revealed it is never 'thought-in-itself' but only a mimetic approximation of it. "My *I*, in effect, is *no more certain for consciousness than the I of other men*. It is only more intimate."[30]

Sartre's point in all of this is relatively simple if somewhat cumbersomely put. "What the for-itself lacks is the self—or itself as in-itself."[31] Put in slightly more prosaic language, the 'self' in Sartre's terms is never a thing that has any fixed being. It is for-itself alone and is never in-itself. It never is anything save for what it might become, and thus it is never really anything at all. Because it belongs to the 'that which might be but has not yet come to be,' it is a perpetual nothingness—the forever non-realized potential of the future.[32] It is neither determined by past events nor present conditions. A being-in-itself, on the other hand, is determined fully by its being "*what it is*,"[33] whereas the law of self-identity is not applicable to a Being-for-itself. It "is defined, on the contrary, as being what it is not and not being what it is."[34] This is also why Sartre was so inimical towards all Cartesian leaning conceptions of the ego: The *Cogito* "is indissolubly linked to being-in-itself."[35] It is, in other words, a refusal of freedom as the condition of human reality. "Thus the refusal of freedom can be conceived only as an attempt to apprehend oneself as being-in-itself."[36] Consequently, if we are to ascribe absolute freedom to being-for-itself, we cannot say that it is any one thing or another. In order for being-for-itself to be absolutely free, it must be nothing at all, for to ascribe any attribute to it at all is to put a limitation on its freedom.

The fact that there is no essential quality around which the concept of the self can be permanently fixed does not absolve us of our responsibility for self-creation. Because each of us is radically free, we must also be radically responsible for choosing what we will become. Because we cannot cease choosing so long as we remain living, what we are—that is, the sum of the choices we have made—will never be any one thing. We are and must remain a perpetually unfinished project that not even death will complete. Life is simply a temporary suspension of the nothingness that is death. As Kojève puts it in his exegesis on Hegel's *Phenomenology of Spirit*, "Man is not a Being that *is* in an eternal identity to itself in Space, but a Nothingness that *nihilates* as Time in spatial Being, through the *negation* of this Being."[37] To understand Being as a 'suspended nothingness' does present us with a profound aesthetic license, not only in terms of self-creation but also in terms of the metaphysical capacity for creation in general. It allows us to view metaphysics as an essentially creative act. Because we start from nothing, there is nothing to necessitate one metaphysical construct over another. We simply choose between a veritable plethora of possible metaphysical modes of description without being able to say why it is we have chosen one and not another. Without this choice, without the ability to say, 'This and not that,' there would be no possibility of value whatsoever. The subjective universal judgment, which is the form of value itself, must be predicated on nothingness.

The aesthetic importance of choice was not something that Sartre overlooked. "To choose between this or that is at the same time to affirm the value of that which is chosen for we are unable ever to choose the worse. What we choose is always the better, and nothing can be better for us unless it is better for all."[38] When we assert that something is not only better for one but better for all, we are, of course, passing a subjective universal judgment that calls for, but does not necessitate, the compliance of everyone. They do not enforce any objective standard and, in so doing, leave every possibility open. This is to say that subjective universal judgments do not treat of Being-in-itself, for if they did, there could be no disagreement concerning them. Thus aesthetic judgments and choice, in general, all stem from the same source: Being-for-itself, which, as Jacques Hardré notes, "Is constantly fleeing towards the future. It is fluid and perfectly free. This Self is unceasingly being faced with the necessity of choosing and by its choice, of engaging itself in life."[39] Because the self cannot escape the inevitability of choice, it must continually engage itself in the aesthetic-metaphysical act of self-creation.

From this line of reasoning, a question necessarily arises: Are there aesthetic principles *a priori* that necessitate one mode of self-creation over another? By way of an analogy, Sartre poses some similar questions concerning the creation of works of art. "Does anyone reproach an artist when he paints a picture for not following rules established *a priori*? Does one ever ask what is the picture that he ought to paint?"[40] While one might very well respond that there are plenty of canonical stylistic conventions that could dictate the sort of painting an artist might make, the obvious retort would be to point out that the adherence to any such conventions is as much a matter of choice as is the use of yellow paint instead of blue. There is nothing that *necessitates* that an artist paint in any particular style. "There is no pre-defined picture for him to make," as Sartre puts it.

> The artist applies himself to the composition of a picture, and the picture that ought to be made is precisely that which he will have made. As everyone knows, there are no aesthetic values *a priori*, but there are values which will appear in due course in the coherence of the picture, in the relation between the will to create and the finished work; one cannot judge a painting until it is done.[41]

The work of art—like the constitution of the ego or the axioms of metaphysics—cannot be *a priori* justified. It will become whatever it will become, and whatever it will become will be as a result of the choices involved in its creation and interpretation. The act of choosing is the *a priori* aesthetic function. Without it, there could be no aesthetic values whatsoever, and if there were no aesthetic values, there could be no axioms of metaphysics. In fact, we might go so far as to assert that metaphysics is first and foremost an artistic act that is predicated on the subjective inclination implicit in choice.

188    *Wittgenstein and the Problem of Metaphysics*

This is also why, I would argue, art proves to be such a potent mode of meaning-making: It shows us just how groundless meaning ultimately is, and it does this by first and foremost laying bare the baselessness of choice. It is the exemplar of significance, yet contradictorily it cannot explain how it is that there can be such a thing as meaning in the first place. That meaning should be possible at all is the one question that art leaves untouched, and to reduce it to a finalizable set of axioms that would do away with this conundrum is to be guilty of a kind of Sartrean 'bad faith.' Art, as a Being-in-itself, is not subject to metaphysical valuation *a priori*. We can, of course, as Sartre suggests, valuate a work of art after it is completed, but we must not forget that any such valuation we supply does not negate the possibility of further valuation. Consequently, the work of art is never something that can ultimately be finished. The further one valuates a work of art, the further one alters it, and even if one were to supply every possible valuation of a work of art—be it historical, cultural, ideological, or formal—we would not thereby exhaust its potential. If we were to enumerate every conceivable fact about a work of art, complete with every conceivable interpretation, whether plausible or outlandish, this amassing of valuation would not bring the work of art to a state of eternal and unalterable completion.

What we are denying, in other words, is that there can be such a thing as a metaphysical definition of art that exhaustively fixes the concept in place. The function of a definition is, after all, the delimitation of meaning. To call for a definition of art, therefore, is also to call for its circumscription. To be sure, any interpretation of a work of art attempts the imposition of limits, but it does so only after the fact of its creation and without the benefit of *a priori* necessity. Interpretation, like art-making, more generally speaking, is an activity predicated on the aesthetics of choice, and because of this it is devoid of categorical imperatives. We are free to choose any metaphysical construct we see fit when explaining the meaning of a work of art, and the definitions we select will be the very condition by which the meaning we are attempting to explicate will be possible. What makes meaning possible, in other words, are definitions that themselves cannot be objectively justified by any conceivable standard. A definition is an instance of a judgment of taste that is predicated on the finality of form, which is indicative of subjective universality. There can thus be no justification for any definition because the demarcation of a limitation is predicated on an unfounded aesthetic claim. The finality of form that a definition enjoys is, therefore, nothing until it is manifested in such a choice.

While definitions are the means by which meaning is made possible, they have their limitations when it comes to the explication of art. Even if we were to amass every conceivable definition of art, we would not thereby exhaust its potential. No discourse on art, however far-reaching, can ever have the final say on what art is and what it does. Even a doctrine that advocated the complete merger of art and life would not accomplish this goal. Though it may aim at a more inclusive conception of art, such a doctrine is as much a constrictor of the possibility of art as is any other definition. The statement 'everything is art' does not imply the infinitude of art. Quite to the contrary, a statement of this kind denies that art can be a selectively applicable designation. Not even a claim so broad as 'everything is art' can encompass the totality of art if art is a Being-for-itself that is radically free. That is to say, more to the point, that art is not anything at all. If every predicate is denied art—as a prerequisite of its freedom—then art is necessarily nothing. Nothingness, in other words, is the only conceivable condition of art that is not at the same time a delimitation of art.

The conclusion we seemed force to accept here is that there can be no such thing as a definition or collection of definitions that effectively forecloses on the potential for reevaluation, which is not to say that 'definitions' of art—however necessarily incomplete they might be—are useless. One cannot speak about art without demarcating it in some respect so as to make it suitable for discourse. Even Derrida fully recognized that this "doubling of commentary"—in which a reader inserts an interpretation into a text as though it had always existed there as a pure and direct stand-in for the author's original intent—was a necessary protection against "critical production" authorizing itself "to say almost anything." An important caveat for Derrida, however, was that "this indispensable guardrail has always only protected, it has never opened, a reading."[42] The problem that we face, in other words, is how to prevent the proliferation of meaning into the infinite nebulousness of 'anything goes' while simultaneously avoiding the propagandistic pitfalls of 'sanctioned' interpretations from which we are not permitted to deviate. In the latter case, we encounter the universalizing tendency of aesthetic judgments taken to the extremes of law, whereas in the former, we see the deleterious effects of lawlessness when the creative impulse towards the rejection of commonly agreed-upon standards of judgment is left unchecked. Both ends of this equation must be balanced if we are to have anything useful to say about the work of art.

For Wittgenstein, having something to say about art—whether useful or not—was precisely the problem with which one had to grapple. The difficulty here stems more broadly speaking from the delineation he makes in his early philosophical work between showing and saying. Works of art do not, as far as Wittgenstein was concerned, have a 'sense' in the way a scientific hypothesis might. Rather, whatever meaning they might have is made manifest in the perspective we take towards them. What matters where a work of art is concerned is not an objective quality to which one can point but the way in which one views it. "A work of art forces us – as one might say – to see it in the right perspective but, in the absence of art, the object is just a fragment of nature like any other."[43] What the artwork drives us to do, if we follow this line of reasoning, is to see the world as though it were from a 'meta-perspective,' i.e., as something that can be cognized as belonging to an order of meaning not tied to the logical structure inherent to states of affairs.

This is not to say that art represents the only way of "capturing the world sub specie aeterni." Thought also "has such a way," Wittgenstein says, of "flying above the world" and "observing it from above" as though it were "in flight."[44] In order to see a thing as something other than a mere 'fragment of nature,' in other words, one must be capable of transcending it and seeing it as though it were from a great distance. Not surprisingly, this leads us straightaway into the mystical, and for both the early and the late Wittgenstein, this was due, in no small part, to the inbuilt limitations of language. "The Limit of language is shown by its being impossible to describe the fact which corresponds to (is the translation of) a sentence, without simply repeating the sentence."[45] Strictly speaking, therefore, language says nothing about how it is possible for language to have meaning, and the fact that works of art seem capable of bypassing this limitation helps to explain why they are the exemplar of profundity. "One might say: art *shows* us the miracles of nature. It is based on the *concept* of the miracles of nature. (The blossom, just opening out. What is *marvelous* about it?) We say: 'Just look at it opening out!'"[46]

Seeing a particular thing—a mere fragment of nature—as a work of art, then, is to see it as continuous with the miraculous, and the mystical sense of wonderment which it engenders is made all the more poignant when one realizes that "the work of art does not aim to convey *something else*, just itself."[47] In a manner of speaking, the 'meaning' of art consists in our inability to state what the meaning of art consists in, but saying this, unfortunately, does not get us any closer to a meaningful articulation of the meaning of art. One might conclude—and rightly so—that at its core, art is essentially a contradiction in terms. No wonder, then, that every attempt at providing a definition of art is always doomed before it can even be formulated: Definitions demand the conformity of law, and law does not admit of anything which is not subject to it, that is, to the miraculous. To describe something in law-like terms, therefore, is at the heart of the positivistic desire to strip the mystery from existence, and this desire is, above all else, the very antipathy of art.

*Always an Elsewhere* 191

Perhaps an example from Wittgenstein's early work would help to illustrate the point more clearly. The criterion of meaning that Wittgenstein sets up in the *Tractatus* is based on a strict logical foundation—anything that can be meaningfully said will necessarily be logically coherent. A meaningful statement that abides by this logical syntax has a very circumscribed boundary such that there is nothing ambiguous or mysterious about it. This raises difficulties where questions of ethics and aesthetics are concerned (because they are anything but logically coherent). In his "Lecture on Ethics," Wittgenstein claims that an ethical judgment can never be reduced to a mere statement of fact, nor can a fact be used as the basis for any judgment of value.

> There are no propositions which, in any absolute sense, are sublime. . . . And now I must say that if I contemplate what Ethics really would have to be if there were such a science, this result seems to me quite obvious. It seems to me obvious that nothing we could ever think or say should be the thing. . . . Our words used as we use them in science, are vessels capable only of containing and conveying meaning and sense, natural meaning and sense. Ethics, if it is anything, is supernatural and our words will only express facts.[48]

The supernatural quality that Wittgenstein attributed to ethics was also one that he gave to aesthetics. Strictly speaking, therefore, neither ethics nor aesthetics belong to the world. They do not 'exist' in the same sense as do other mere fragments of nature, such as tables, chairs, lamps, and so on. As a consequence of this, it is not possible to meaningfully speak about ethics or aesthetics because language is only capable of representing possible states of affairs. This is not to say that we cannot, however, treat any given state of affairs from an aesthetic or ethical point of view. Doing so necessitates that we see events and things as embodiments of the "form of purposiveness,"[49] to borrow Kant's phrase, which is precisely the mechanism by which we think of the world as a 'limited whole' that is 'final,' 'complete,' and hence 'intelligible.'

The caveat for Wittgenstein is that such an experience of the world is, strictly speaking, not possible given the metaphysical restrictions under which subjectivity finds itself. "The philosophical I is not the human being, not the human body or the human soul with the psychological properties, but the metaphysical subject, the boundary (not a part) of the world."[50] The limitation of the metaphysical subject presupposes that the subject is incapable of transcending itself. Nevertheless, the subjective limitation of the world also presupposes a responsibility for the world. "What others in the world have told me about the world is a very small and incidental part of my experience of the world. I have to judge the world, to measure things."[51] We see then that the subject is both the limitation of the world (it is the condition of 'sense' *in* the world) and the meaning of the world (it is the condition of the 'sense' *of* the world). The metaphysical subject is thus faced with two diametrically opposed tasks: It must be both the limit and judge of the world. In order to accomplish the latter, it must take a position outside of itself, that is, outside of the limits that it was itself supposed to erect, and in order to accomplish the former, it must stand as the absolute horizon beyond which judgment of any kind is impossible. We therefore cannot take the metaphysical subject as an object of thought because it is the limit of thought. In order to do so, we would have to step outside of this boundary—that is, to step outside the purview of subjectivity so as to understand it as a limited whole rather than the condition that imposes limitations on what is and is not thinkable.

One of the principal difficulties with Wittgenstein's concept of the metaphysical subject comes, in no small part, from his penchant for forbidding "*all being to the impossible*,"[52] as Alain Badiou puts it in *Wittgenstein's Antiphilosophy*. Indeed, the cause of Wittgenstein's mysticism hinges on what Badiou sees as a relatively narrow definition of thought. "Thought, indeed, is the proposition endowed with a sense, and the proposition with sense is the picture, or description, of a state of affairs. The result is a considerable extension of non-thought, which is unacceptable to the philosopher."[53] This extension of non-thought for Wittgenstein included, most notably, philosophy itself. Thus, Wittgenstein's strategic and antiphilosophical goal is "to subtract the real (what is higher, the mystical element) from thought, so as to entrust its care to the act which alone determines whether life is saintly and beautiful."[54] It is this antiphilosophical act which "consists in letting what there is show itself, insofar as 'what there is' is precisely what no true proposition can say."[55] And because no 'true proposition' can say 'what there is', determining its ethical and aesthetic value can likewise not be framed in terms of the propositional truth function.

According to Badiou, one of the key characteristics of Wittgenstein's antiphilosophical act is what he terms its "archiaesthetic" quality, which is not, as Badiou stresses, a matter of simply "substituting art for philosophy."[56] It is rather "a question of firmly establishing the laws of the sayable (of the thinkable), in order for the unsayable (the unthinkable, which is ultimately given only in the form of art) to be *situated* as the 'upper limit' of the sayable itself."[57] Art, taken in this sense—as the form of the unthinkable—is what allows the unthinkable to show itself in the world even though it must, strictly speaking, not be a part of the world. Art is the means by which the limit of the world is exhibited in the world and, as such, does not itself have 'meaning' in the logical sense of the word.

Any meaning that it does have must transcend expression in language, which is functionally the same as saying that it transcends existence.

The conclusion to be drawn from this line of thinking can be summed up as follows: As subjective entities, our perspective on the limits of existence always takes place from within those limits, and thus value—which is precisely what lies beyond the limits of existence—is something that perpetually slips beyond our ability to grasp in any definitive sense. In fact, I would argue, much of what the *Tractatus* has to say hinges on this basic tenet, and it gets what is perhaps its clearest articulation in 6.41.

> The sense of the world must lie outside the world. In the world everything is as it is, and everything happens as it does happen: *in* it no value exists—and if it did exist, it would have no value.
>
> If there is any value that does have value, it must lie outside the whole sphere of what happens and is the case. For all that happens and is the case is accidental.
>
> What makes it non-accidental cannot lie *within* the world, since if it did it would itself be accidental.
>
> It must lie outside the world.

From this passage, we can clearly see that Wittgenstein's conception of value pivots on the difference between what is necessary and what is accidental. Whatever is in the world is accidental but has no value and whatever has value is necessary but outside the world. As Badiou points out, this definition of value is predicated on Wittgenstein's "*two regimes of sense.*"[58] The first of these belongs to that of the proposition. The proposition endowed with a sense is one that shares the same logical structure as a state of affairs, and thus a "proposition has sense from the moment it describes a state of affairs."[59] The regime of propositional sense, however, has no value: "All value detained by a proposition is devoid of any value whatsoever."[60] A proposition with a sense can only describe a state of affairs that happens to be true. This regime of sense, therefore, is completely accidental. Anything that can be true can also be false; it is simply a matter of happenstance that any possible state of affairs is either true or false. When a proposition attempts to express a value as if it were a state of affairs, it ends up expressing nothing, for there is nothing there for it to depict. "If a proposition has no sense," Wittgenstein writes, "Nothing corresponds to it, since it does not designate a thing (a truth-value) which might have properties called 'false' or 'true.'"[61]

The second regime of sense that Badiou points to is the "sense of the world" which is "*entirely separated from the truth* (because it has nothing to do with what is the case)."[62] This regime of sense, unlike the first, has a value. Hence,

Badiou terms it "sense-value" (as opposed to "sense-truth") and "excludes the contingency that marks the eventality of the world. What is in the world is accidental, and its sense is without value, but the sense of the world, which has value, must be 'non-accidental,' which requires that it 'lie outside the world.'"[63] By insisting on the other-worldly quality of value and the intra-worldly quality of truth, Wittgenstein is in effect claiming that truth has no value and value no truth. For Badiou, this divorce of truth and value is one of the most contentious points in Wittgenstein's philosophy. According to Badiou, "The idea that truths, apparently contingent, are enveloped by a necessary sense ... is *the exact theoretical definition of religious faith.* ... And the unprecedented novelty of the antiphilosophical act would in the end only be a return to this ancient belief from which the whole philosophical effort was meant to extirpate us."[64]

Wittgenstein's seeming derision of truth is one that goes against the grain of Badiou's work in general, especially in regards to one of the most central components of his philosophy: generic procedures. There are four such procedures according to Badiou: art, love, politics, and science, each of which is a source of truth. These procedures all crystallize "concepts to such a point that it is almost impossible to give an image of it."[65] The being of truth, Badiou says, is that of a generic multiple, which also makes it unpresentable, although "it can be demonstrated that it may be thought."[66] Thus, truth is not a matter of knowledge; one does not 'know' a truth. Rather, in Badiou's own words, "Truth is always that which makes a hole in a knowledge."[67] Such a concept of truth is, as Badiou readily acknowledges, antithetical to that of modern philosophy, which treats truth as a function of representational accuracy (as it surely is in the *Tractatus*). Contrary to this tradition, Badiou makes a crucial distinction between truth and knowledge. "A truth is, first of all, something new. What transmits, what repeats, we shall call *knowledge*."[68] This presents us with a philosophical difficulty, however: Namely, how do we account for the novelty of truths? How do we explain the "problem of its appearance and its 'becoming'"?[69] Badiou's answer is this: "For a truth to affirm its newness, there must be a *supplement*. This supplement is committed to chance. It is unpredictable, incalculable. It is beyond what is. I call it an event. A truth thus appears in its newness, because an eventual supplement interrupts repetition."[70]

We might point out immediately that a clear symmetry exists here between Badiou's definition of truth and Wittgenstein's: Both are predicated on chance. Despite his apparent dislike of Wittgenstein's two regimes of sense, Badiou's differentiation between truth and knowledge carries an undeniably similar consequence.

*Always an Elsewhere*

> An event is linked to the notion of the *undecidable*. Take the statement: 'This
> event belongs to the situation.' If it is possible to decide, using the rules of
> established knowledge, whether this statement is true or false, then the so-called
> event is not an event. Its occurrence would be calculable within the situation.
> Nothing would permit us to say: here begins a truth.[71]

To explain an event in terms of established knowledge is to deny that it is a truth.
Explanation, in other words, is not a condition under which the occurrence of a
truth can happen. Truths are, and must be, undecidable—their very existence
hangs on this condition. Although Wittgenstein used the term 'truth' as a
designation of fidelity between a state of affairs and the proposition that stands
for it, the fidelity itself is not something that a proposition can picture. There can
be no 'proposition' of truth that pictures the truth of truth. This sense of truth—
the sense of the world as opposed to the sense of the proposition—is the only one
of any value for Wittgenstein. Just as Badiou claims that an event is not an event
if it can be decided according to the rules of established knowledge, Wittgenstein
holds that a value is not a value if it is put in the form of a proposition.

The undecidability of truth is, to be sure, one of the central tenets of Badiou's
philosophical corpus, and it has important aesthetic implications for metaphysics.
"For Badiou," Gabriel Riera points out, "The consequence of undecidability is
that decisions become imperative. Undecidability, therefore, should not be
understood as a barrier, but as a necessary path to encounter the new."[72] This
"encounter with the new" that the novelty of truth precipitates fulcrums on a
seemingly impossible task: deciding the undecidable. "On the basis of the
undecidability of an event's belonging to a situation a *wager* has to be made. This
is why a truth begins with an *axiom of truth*. It begins with a groundless decision
– the decision to *say* that the event has taken place."[73] For all intents and purposes,
however, the wager that Badiou associates with the undecidability of an event is
one that is predicated on a subjective universal judgment. To decide the
undecidability of an event, to say that 'it has occurred,' is a function of aesthetic
predisposition, what Badiou terms "an absolutely pure choice."[74] An axiom of
truth is decided by way of a declaration, 'This and not that.' It cannot, as Badiou
insists, be an object of knowledge because it is the predicate of knowledge. It is
through this act, which really amounts to nothing more than a leap of faith, that
the metaphysical subject is constituted.

> The undecidability of the event includes the appearance of a *subject* of the event.
> Such a subject is constituted by an utterance in the form of a wager. This utterance
> is as follows: 'This event has taken place, it is something which I can neither

evaluate, nor demonstrate, but to which I shall be faithful.' To begin with, a subject is what fixes an undecidable event, because he or she takes the chance of deciding upon it.[75]

The metaphysical subject, by way of its fixing an undecidable event in place, also fixes itself in place. Before this aesthetic judgment occurs, there is no metaphysical subject. "For Badiou the subject is not," Riera writes, "A universal or given category, neither a transcendental nor empirical subject. Subjectivization ... only takes place in the wake of an event."[76] This point is undoubtedly true if what we have in mind is a Kantian transcendental subject that exists prior to an event of truth. There may be, however, a good reason to characterize Badiou's subject as universal and transcendent after such an event has taken place, especially when we consider the fact that the insertion of the subject in the world is the transcendental condition of truth and fidelity to it. As J. D. Dewsbury has remarked, "Fidelity quivers into being, being driven by an intense faith on the part of the subject.... The event only works if this faith, this embrace, is there, and that in being there it persuades others."[77] This persuasion—rhetoric in the broadest sense—is the mechanism that convinces others to make the same leap of faith. It is also, therefore, a subjective judgment of taste because it demands the universal acquiescence of everyone based solely on the aesthetic act involved in deciding an undecidable. Thus the subject may not be universal or transcendental prior to this event, but the decision, once made, makes it so.

I would like to dwell here on the undecidability of the metaphysical subject in terms of its ethical implications, specifically, as we might say, in terms of an 'open-ended commandment,' one that I would characterize as an 'imperative of freedom.' The necessity for this kind of meditation is made all the more pertinent due to the difficulty we encounter when dealing with the problem of disinterest. On the face of it, the very idea of a disinterested, metaphysical subject seems to imply the possibility that the subject is something pre-determined and fixed and place. This characterization of subjectivity we will most vehemently deny because it is an explicit violation of the imperative of freedom, which regards every principle of metaphysics as both subjective and open to revision. It is, in this sense, that the metaphysical subject is a primarily ethico-aesthetic creature because it regards no choice as necessarily self-evident or fundamentally forbidden for all eternity.

The consequence of this, however, is that the metaphysical subject is an entity that is constantly under the duress of revision. As such, we must come to terms with the no privileged access whatsoever to the self—a point that Nietzsche has

Always an Elsewhere 197

already made in the preface of the *Genealogy of Morals*. "The sad truth is that we remain necessarily strangers to ourselves, we don't understand our own substance, we *must* mistake ourselves; the axiom, "Each man is farthest from himself," will hold for us to all eternity. Of ourselves we are not "knowers".[78] The great distance that separates the knowledge of self from the 'actual' self is not one that can be bridged precisely because the metaphysical subject is not constituted prior to the archiaesthetic choice. Even after this choice has been made, however, the self is never something irrevocably fixed in place. It is always open to the revision of future choice, and as such, the only finality of form it may assume is that of freedom. Whatever we may think we may know of the self as it exists in the present moment is always fleeting at best. Any time we manage to get ahold of it as an 'object of cognition,' the thing cognized will have transformed itself into something else altogether. Thus, since there is no facticity from which we may start, no truth in existence save for the truth that we invent, our ethical imperative can thus be expressed as follows: Never treat any metaphysical finality as finalizable in perpetuity.

What we are suggesting, then, is that the metaphysical subject is, and must be, a thing-in-itself. Indeed, it must be a thing outside the world because it is the basis on which the possibility of there being a world is predicated. We can therefore have no knowledge of the self because knowledge itself is grounded on that which is beyond knowledge. "I have therefore," as Kant concludes, "No knowledge of myself as I am, but merely as I appear to myself. The consciousness of self is thus very far from a knowledge of self."[79] While we will not detract from Kant on this point, it does suggest what will be an important line of inquiry for us going forward: Why pursue self-knowledge at all if we can have no hope of attaining it? What possible value can a pursuit doomed to failure have for us? As is usually the case, however, the questions we ask already betray the answers we seek, and it is no different in this instance. For the chief worth of an impossible task is in its impossibility. Its value is in the setting of a goal so absolutely out of reach that there is no prospect of its ever being attained. In this sense, we could characterize the quest for self-knowledge as 'purposive without purpose' since it presupposes no end with which it must comport. It is also in this sense that we are accustomed to speak of the "beauty of life" as exhibiting "the form of purposiveness ... without representation of an end."[80]

This brings us to a point of contention, however. If we regard this quest for self-knowledge as fundamentally process-oriented, that is to say as extending and developing towards no definite end over an indefinite period of time, then we cannot construe time as a universal, *a priori* form of intuition, such as Kant

198  *Wittgenstein and the Problem of Metaphysics*

did. We cannot, in other words, conceive of time as the necessary and unalterable "form of the internal sense, that is, of the intuitions of self and of our internal state."[81] For Kant, the self of which we are conscious, as structured by this form of internal sense, must be a static one. Our experience of the self as existing in time is thus unalterable because the form of our intuition is unalterable. Even though we may not be able to know the self as it truly is apart from the forms of intuition, i.e., as a thing-in-itself, our consciousness of the self is always filtered through time as a universal form of intuition.

It is, then, to Hegel we must turn. For we owe it to his discovery that there could be such a thing as *a priori* forms of intuition that were not universally accessible to the self but were revealed to consciousness according to the progression of time. Even the concept of time itself must be regarded as a form of intuition that alters during the course of history's unfolding. The self, as such, cannot be properly said to 'exist' in universal time, for as Hegel claims, "Only the totality of Spirit is in Time, and the 'shapes', which are 'shapes' of the totality of *Spirit*, display themselves in a temporal succession; for only the whole has true actuality."[82] Consequently, self-consciousness—which was for Kant part and parcel of the transcendental forms of intuition—cannot appear to us except in partial shapes of the totality of Spirit. The 'self-consciousness' of Kant is, in Hegel's terms, only a partial consciousness of self. Actual self-consciousness, that is, absolute consciousness which takes itself as an object, can only occur after Spirit has revealed itself through the due course of time. It is only then that the "shape of self-consciousness" as "*thinking* consciousness *in general*"[83] can reveal itself.

What we are here making allusion to, as should be all too evident, is what Hegel termed the "Philosophy of History," which "means nothing but the *thoughtful consideration of it*."[84] This does not mean, as Hegel is quick to add, that "Thought must be subordinate to what is given, to the realities of fact."[85] To approach the Philosophy of History in such a fashion would be "to force it onto conformity with a tyrannous idea, and to construe it, as the phrase is, '*a priori*.'"[86] It is, therefore, not the proper business of the Philosophy of History to take under examination thought as it is constrained by *a priori* principles of the understanding. To do so would be to repeat Kant's mistake. Rather, "The only Thought which Philosophy brings with it to the contemplation of History, is the simple conception of *Reason*; that Reason is the Sovereign of the World; that the history of the world, therefore, presents us with a rational process."[87] Reason, according to Hegel's usage, refers to "that by which and in which all reality has its being and substance."[88] Summarily speaking, then, we understand the Philosophy of History as the thoughtful consideration of the Reason for History's unfolding and, more importantly, that for the sake of which History unfolds as it does. Without positing such an *end* of History—that is to say, without supposing that History aims towards some ultimate goal—we are incapable of understanding the Reason of History; for to understand the reason for something is also to understand what it is finally for.

This 'what it is finally for,' the "final aim of this progression" is, as Hegel says, "The development of the one universal Spirit, which ... elevates and completes itself to a self-comprehending *totality*."[89] The attainment of the Absolute, in which "everything is the same,"[90] posits the end of History, or more precisely: the end of History as a dialectical becoming. Insofar as it is through difference that History progresses towards the Absolute, to realize the absolute means to actualize non-difference, to negate, once and for all, the possibility of difference. Thus, the end of history can mean nothing other than the end of difference because, in the Absolute, everything is the same. In order to obtain this absolute self-sameness, however, we must presuppose—along with the tautological—the contradictory as well. What we require, in other words, is the antithesis of the absolutely self-same, namely the concept of antithesis itself. "This absolute Notion of the difference must be represented and understood purely as inner difference, a repulsion of the selfsame, as selfsame, from itself.... We have to think pure change, or *think antithesis within the antithesis itself, or contradiction*."[91] Without this ability to think the opposite of the Absolute, we would be incapable of realizing it, and since the Absolute is what is Rational, and the Rational is what is Real, the absolute self-same must presupposes absolute difference as the vehicle of actualizing self-consciousness. Becoming, in other words, is only possible given this fundamental antithesis between tautology and contradiction. This "bifurcation of the simple," as Hegel calls it, is thus "the process of its own becoming, the circle that presupposes its end as its goal, having its end also as its beginning; and only by being worked out to its end, is it actual."[92]

It is from Hegel, then, that we can begin to grasp at the possibility of self-knowledge through the process of becoming what we are—a process that is, as it were, for itself alone and realizes no other end save for that which it presupposes: Absolute self-knowledge. Within this "Hegelian presupposed," we find what Jean-Luc Nancy has called "The reality of sense," which is nothing other than "the subject in which and *as* which the real comes to posit itself as such, comes to be known by a knowing and grasping self."[93] This is, to be sure, a far cry from the supposed universality which Kant afforded his conception of subjectivity, and because of which, we are forever denied entrance into the circle of our own self-becoming. Since we are, according to Kant, rational creatures whose universal, *a priori* faculties of the understanding precludes the possibility of knowing the self in itself, we are barred, by the very transcendental nature of these faculties, from the one path that would allow us to reach this absolute for-itself, i.e., the path of self-becoming, by which we come to know ourselves as free. "It is ultimately with Kant," as Nancy notes, "That freedom as something inconceivable, the inconceivable *as* freedom, originates."[94] This does not imply, however, that freedom can be conceived, for as Nancy hastens to add, freedom "is not conceiving, but receiving: welcoming and upholding an order."[95]

What we therefore mean by the 'undecidability' of the metaphysical subject is roughly equivalent to this 'receptivity of freedom.' It is not, nor can it be, a conception because the very notion of a conception already betrays the exercise of an aesthetic choice, which 'welcomes and upholds' an order. Indeed, such an upholding of order is the germ from which every conception sprouts. Properly speaking, however, freedom does not 'belong' to the metaphysical subject. It is not, as Nancy writes, "Given as a property or as a right. Freedom is nothing given: it is the negation of the given, including this given that would be a 'free subject' defined only by determined rights and liberties."[96] Freedom, here understood as the 'negation of the given,' is the cure for every dogmatism. It is, as it were, the exact antithesis of every self-evident truth of metaphysics. The problem of metaphysics is, in all instances, an expression of the desire, on the part of the metaphysical subject, for 'something given.' Ultimately, however, this desire is never gratified because the metaphysical subject is always faced with an obstacle too difficult to overcome: its own freedom, i.e., the negation of every given.

What Nancy's notion of freedom offers us, then, is another way of expressing the fundamental aesthetic choice of the metaphysical subject. When we say, as we have, that 'everything can be otherwise than it is,' we have simply repeated, in slightly different words, the basic claim that Nancy has already made: Nothing is given. We are therefore thrust headlong into the crisis at the center of the problem of metaphysics. If nothing is given, then there can be no preset principle of metaphysics that does not in some sense already beg the question of its own certainty. The first principle of metaphysics is, therefore, that of metaphysical indeterminacy, which we can state as follows: No principle of metaphysics is given, and thus no principle of metaphysics has any more claim to truth than any other. At this point, the problem of metaphysics, which has always concerned itself with the search for absolute certainty, transforms itself into the problem of aesthetics, which, in the wake of the problem of metaphysics, must concern itself with deciding an undecidable. This decision, which is not made according to any precepts, finds no justification other than the fact that it could have been

*Always an Elsewhere* 201

otherwise. In other words, the basis of every possible decision is always rooted in the negation of the given, namely freedom, which recognizes no decision as either necessary or forbidden. It is through freedom that we come to understand the creative maxim: Every possibility is open. It is through aesthetics, however, that we come to understand how it is possible to select amongst the infinitude of choices. "The greatness of Thought," as Nancy says, "is in the simplicity of the decision that turns itself toward naked manifestation."[97]

The non-determinacy of freedom thus leads us, through the exercise of aesthetic choice, towards the naked manifestation. It provides us, in other words, with the *raison d'être* for why things are the way they are. That which we are willing to make manifest is, in the end, that which we are most inclined to find beautiful, and as such, the ultimate aesthetic criterion is manifestation without substantiation. From here, however, the ethico-aesthetic subject is immediately faced with the question of duty. That is to say, in other words, that the ethical duty of the metaphysical subject subsists in the obligation to posit reasons for aesthetic choices, which are themselves without reason. It is, therefore, an impossible obligation to fulfill because it must seek for the basis of a baseless aesthetic choice that is immanent in the very world itself. Thus, as Nancy writes, "The world that knows itself to be immanent is, at the same time, the world that knows itself to be unconditionally obliged to give sufficient reason for itself."[98]

On this point, however, Nancy identifies a fundamental difference between Kant and Hegel's treatment of the question of duty.

> Kant maintains this necessity within the order of an ought-to-be, in which the reason for the world is infinitely separated from itself ... Hegel, on the other hand, posits that this "duty" itself, the "thought" alone of this duty, of its separation and infinity, has already of itself, in opening time and dividing substance, given rise to the subject.[99]

While it is no doubt true that both Kant and Hegel consider duty an indispensable component of subjectivity, the division between the two, as Nancy makes abundantly clear, is dependent on the trajectory this duty takes. For Kant, subjectivity is a 'being infinitely separated' from the reason for the world. Since we have no hope of ever bridging this infinite separation via the limited faculties of human cognition, our duty towards the 'reason for the world' must take the form of faith. Conversely, for Hegel, subjectivity is a movement out of and back into the infinite. In the mere thought of the infinitely separated reason for the world, we have already discovered the reason for the world: thought thinking itself. Upon reflection, we discover that thought is itself both 'infinitely separated' from the world and immanent in it, and although this thought originates out of itself, it can only become itself by moving towards itself. Duty, in the Hegelian sense, is, therefore, a question of spirituality rather than faith. Whereas faith postulates self-knowledge as situated on an infinitely distant and unreachable horizon, spirituality recognizes that self-knowledge does not consist in attaining the absolute *per se*; it consists in the movement towards it.

This fundamental opposition between Kant and Hegel, which manifests itself in the gap between faith and spirituality, could, in the end, turn out to be irreconcilable. In faith, we find being, and in spirituality, we find becoming, and it is by no means clear how it might be possible to cohesively incorporate the two without doing a disservice to one or the other. It is precisely in this *differend*, however, that the very 'essence' of the ethico-aesthetic subject reveals itself. In faith, we find the aesthetic, and in spirituality we find the ethical, and while each is, in some sense, beholden to the other, the important point is that neither can be reduced to the other. What we discover in the ethico-aesthetic subject, then, is not some unified and undifferentiated whole, but an entity split in two, conjoined by a hyphen which holds together two otherwise insoluble halves. The effect of this hyphenation, we must hasten to add, is not to adjudicate difference. The hyphen, as it were, is a symbolic stand-in for what amounts to an irrevocable alienation. It does not, therefore, denote a thing, but a relation. It is a middle-term only, which signifies the *differend*, and we should not, therefore, treat the intermediation of the hyphen as a resolution that negates the fundamental discord between faith and spirituality, being and becoming, aesthetics and ethics. The naked truth which confronts the subject is, in the last, the recognition that, as Lyotard puts it, "No litigation could neutralize this differend, that would be human, all too human."[100]

Part of the 'solution,' then, is to realize that, strictly speaking, there is no solution that would be, in any appreciable sense of the word, 'human.' In order to litigate the *differend* between faith and spirituality, it would be necessary to decide the matter *sub specie aeternitatis*. To do so, however, we would have to assume the position of the disinterested, metaphysical subject, which is precisely what the injunction of spirituality denies us. Thus, any litigation that gave the appearance of ultimate reconciliation would fail to do so simply by disregarding the mandate of spirituality which categorically denies the possibility of transcendental litigation. Conversely, however, any arbitration which was predicated solely on the dictates of spirituality would only succeed in subsuming the *differend* under its own conditions so as to give the appearance of settlement when in fact, there was only subjugation. It would seem, then, that the only possible way forward out of this conundrum is to maintain the necessity of both faith and spirituality without dissolving the *differend*, which is itself the source of this conundrum. What we will suggest, therefore, is a way of describing the ethico-aesthetic subject that upholds the metaphysics of faith without sacrificing the human, all too human, movement of spirituality.

In order to accomplish this task, we must first postulate a means of incorporating being and becoming that does not seek a fundamental reconciliation between the two but rather seeks to preserve it as a basis for 'religion,' properly understood as the heterogeneous blend of faith and spirituality. Since it denies the possibility of litigating the *differend*, we could call such a religion a hermeneutics of suspicion, insofar as it is antithetical to the dogma of all transcendental litigation. We fall under the spell of such dogma anytime we allow ourselves to be *convinced* of the supremacy of faith over spirituality or spirituality over faith. The irreducibility of one to the other also means that the power of one over the other is checked. Religion, when conceived as the irreconcilable struggle between faith and spirituality for the sole dominion of subjectivity, is, as Nietzsche already warned us, a "dangerous game." For on the one hand, the development of spirituality demands that "whoever allows room in himself again for religious feeling these days must allow it to grow: he cannot do otherwise."[101] On the other hand, it is the growth of spirituality itself that causes one's judgment and feeling to become "befogged, overcast with religious shadows."[102] We must, therefore, be on our guard, for as Nietzsche observed all too keenly, "There is not enough religion in the world even to destroy religions."[103]

It is possible, however, that Nietzsche may have already given us the beginning of an answer, especially when we read him as attempting to incorporate both being and becoming as the two bifurcated halves of one conception of subjectivity. It may seem strange to suggest this at first, especially in light of what Nietzsche called the "Egyptianism" of philosophers, whose

> hatred of the very idea of becoming lead them to think they confer *honour* on a thing when they isolate it from its historical relations, *sub specie æterni*,—when they make a mummy out of it.... For them death, change, and age, just as well as production and growth, are objections,—refutations even. What is, does not *become*; what becomes, *is* not.[104]

Despite Nietzsche's obvious disdain for those philosophers who would denounce becoming outright, there are no good reasons to suppose that this forces us into a wholesale rejection of being. To do so would be to dogmatically adopt what

Nietzsche believed was the fundamentally erroneous belief of metaphysicians: "THE BELIEF IN THE ANTITHESES OF VALUES."[105] Such a belief was, for Nietzsche, one amongst many "provisional perspectives, besides being probably made from some corner, perhaps from below – 'frog perspectives,' as it were."[106] To reject the possibility of being, therefore, simply by maintaining that it is precluded by becoming only perpetuates the unwarranted adherence to the antithesis of values.

Given this dismissal on Nietzsche's part, it should come as no surprise that he allowed himself the possibility of cohabitating two perspectives that are normally treated as polar opposites. After all, the ability to assume a plurality of perspective was, as far as he was concerned, a virtue and not a vice. So, in addition to those instances where we can read Nietzsche as lampooning philosophical Egyptianism, we can also find just as many which advocate a kind of subjective disinterestedness that is much more in keeping with a metaphysics of being. Take, as an example, this excerpt from the preface to *The Anti-Christ*:

> When it comes to spiritual matters, you need to be honest to the point of hardness.... You need to be used to living on mountains – to seeing the miserable, ephemeral little gossip of politics and national self-interest *beneath* you .... You need to become indifferent.[107]

This sort of 'indifference' towards what is 'beneath oneself' is, to be sure, a theme that is often expressed in different ways throughout the corpus of Nietzsche's writings. What is interesting to note, however, is just how frequently the metaphor of 'looking down from a mountain' is repeated by him. For instance, in *Thus Spoke Zarathustra* he writes, "Whoever climbs the highest mountains laughs at all tragic plays and tragic seriousness."[108] Perhaps one reason why Nietzsche was so fond of this metaphor was because it allowed him a way of giving expression to a kind of disinterestedness that was not eternal. It is always possible, and indeed inevitable, to come down from the lofty heights of mountain tops to the lowlands of the valley. Both are but provisional perspectives, and neither can lay claim to truth in any ultimate sense.

Where Nietzsche's view of subjectivity is concerned, then, we cannot give precedence, one way or the other, to being or becoming. To insist that one—and only one—of these is the ultimate feature of subjectivity would be an outright rejection of perspectivism, which does not exclude either as a possibility *a priori*. Whatever subjectivity consists in, it must include, to put it in Zarathustra's words, "Some wandering and mountain climbing: in the end, one experiences only oneself.... What returns, what finally comes home to me, is my own self."[109] In short, a theory of subjectivity that does not include both being and becoming is one that is completely inadequate. It is only as wanderers and mountain climbers that we can tread the path of subjectivity, and it is a path that leads both away from and back into the self. The essential point to bear in mind is that this journey from becoming to being, and being to becoming, is never one that arrives at any ultimate destination. It is always a matter of becoming *towards* being, and being *towards* becoming, and never a matter of settling on one or the other as the ultimate condition of subjectivity.

Perhaps Nietzsche's clearest articulation of the interplay between being and becoming can be found in §270 of *The Gay Science*, in which he appropriates the well-known maxim from Pindar: "*What does your conscience say? –* 'You should become who you are.'"[110] This decree, however, should strike us, and rightly so, as something of an impossible task. Either one is who one is, or one will become who one will become. One cannot 'become what one is' without inviting an apparent contradiction. This, however, is precisely the point. It is only by framing subjectivity in such paradoxical terms that we maintain the *differend* between being and becoming, and hence faith and spirituality. We would also do well to remember that Nietzsche expresses this mandate of subjectivity in blatantly ethical terms. The commandment 'become who you are' is no mere suppositional imperative. It is one that the conscience demands categorical adherence to. A denial of this imperative would be to repudiate one's duty as an ethical subject that is not bound by any presupposition of being.

The observance of this directive is, as it were, the primary way in which we engage in the spiritual movement of becoming, which is nothing other than the development and expression of freedom. However essential this point may be, though, we cannot ignore the fact that it concerns only the first half of the ethico-aesthetic subject. The second component of subjectivity that we must still concern ourselves with is the aesthetics of being. This condition of subjectivity is, unlike the ethics of becoming, not concerned with freedom but rather with law-making. This is a point that Nietzsche seems to hint at in §335 of *The Gay Science*:

> We, however, want to *become who we are* – human beings who are new, unique, incomparable, who give themselves laws, who create themselves! To that end we must become the best students and discoverers of everything lawful and necessary in the world: we must become *physicists* in order to be creators in this sense – while hitherto all valuations and ideals have been built on *ignorance* of physics or in *contradiction* to it. So, long live physics! And even more long live what *compels* us to it – our honesty!

While this passage makes it clear that the ethics of becoming is, for Nietzsche, predicated on the kind of honesty which recognizes that the self is never finalized in perpetuity, it also draws our attention to that task of the physicist that Nietzsche found so admirable: the discovery of everything lawful and necessary in the world. Not, we must hasten to add, in any eternal or inalterable sense that those terms might unfortunately connote. If one thing is abundantly obvious from even a cursory observation of the history of physics, it is that its laws have been, and always will be, subject to revision. This does not mean, however, that they are any less necessary for us as aesthetic subjects. We create ourselves only insofar as we give laws to ourselves.

To be aesthetic in this sense means to give one's self a finality of form. This form is always, without exception, open to the possibility of revision, but this fact in itself does not deny it the status of finality. That is to say, in other words, that every finality of form is alterable through the movement of becoming. Nevertheless, we become what we are only by aiming towards such finality. We cannot become anything unless that becoming is in some sense purposeful. Without the spirituality of becoming, the faith of being is stagnant and lame. Without the faith of being, the spirituality of becoming is purposeless and blind. Thus, 'religion', properly understood in terms of the *differend* between faith and spirituality, is never expressed in any dogmatism that would seek to annul this *differend*. It is for this reason, therefore, that religion finds its perfect expression in the truths of art. For inasmuch as art produces truths, it does so by way of an act—on the part of the metaphysical subject—that fixes the conditions of meaning and knowledge in place. The truths of art, however, must always remain under the jurisdiction of future revision, and as such, they cannot be the timeless foundation of any inter-worldly meaning.

Such truths are the predicates of the possibility of meaning. If art were a matter of knowledge, it would have no value whatsoever. That is not to say that the truths of art do not produce knowledge, but the knowledge itself is not art. Art is an eruption of truth into the world and cannot be justified by a knowledge claim. Such a claim would require an axiom of truth on which to be based, which is what the truths of art were supposed to furnish us with in the first place. A doctrine of art does not treat of art itself—i.e., its truths—it only treats of the knowledge that art produces. The truths of art, however, are not subject to the conditions of knowledge. There is nothing that necessitates their truth save for the willingness of the metaphysical subject to believe in them—to see them as substantiations of the universal in the particular. The truths of art are exhibitions of the transcendent in earthly form. There is, of course, nothing about that earthly form itself that allows us to see art as the emblematic of the mystical. It is through the sheer aesthetic act of belief that the work of art can become possible. Without this, it is nothing but a mere fragment of nature, bereft of any value and devoid of any meaning. If art is to give us a 'sense of the world', it can do so only from outside the world. This, of course, means that inside the world, art does not exist. Thus, there can be no definition of art, for if there were, this would imply the possibility that art could be finalized according to an objective law of nature.

# Notes

1   Wittgenstein, *Notebooks*, 82.
2   Kant, *Critique of Pure Reason*, 1855, 3.
3   Ibid., 498.
4   Wittgenstein, *On Certainty*, sec. 18.
5   Immanuel Kant, *Prolegomena to Any Future Metaphysics That Will Be Able to Come Forward as Science*, 2nd ed. (Indianapolis, IN: Hackett Publishing Company, 2001), 101.
6   Ibid.
7   Kant, *Critique of the Power of Judgment*, 100.
8   Ibid.
9   Kant, *Prolegomena to Any Future Metaphysics*, 56.
10  Ibid.
11  Ibid.
12  Ibid.
13  Karl Jaspers, *Kant*, ed. Hannah Arendt, trans. Ralph Manheim (New York: Harcourt Brace & Company, 1962), 35.
14  Ibid., 87.
15  Ibid.
16  Wittgenstein, *Tractatus Logico-Philosophicus*, 2001, sec. 4.121.
17  Kant, *Critique of the Power of Judgment*, 20: 216.
18  Ibid., 5: 207.
19  Ibid., 5: 211.
20  Jaspers, *Kant*, 78.
21  Ibid.
22  Ibid., 79.
23  Jean-Paul Sartre, "Existentialism and Humanism," in *Art in Theory, 1900–2000: An Anthology of Changing Ideas*, ed. Paul Wood and Charles Harrison (Malden, MA: Blackwell, 2003), 601.
24  Ibid.

25 Ibid.

26 Ibid.

27 Jean-Paul Sartre, *Being and Nothingness: A Phenomenological Essay on Ontology* (New York: Citadel Press, 2001), 290.

28 Jean-Paul Sartre, "The Transcendence of the Ego," in *The Phenomenology Reader,* ed. Dermot Moran and Timothy Mooney (New York: Routledge, 2002), 389.

29 Sartre, *Being and Nothingness,* 50.

30 Sartre, "The Transcendence of the Ego," 404.

31 Sartre, *Being and Nothingness,* 2001, 65.

32 "One does not *find,* one does not *disclose* nothingness in the manner in which one can find, disclose a being. Nothingness is always an *elsewhere.*" Sartre, *Being and Nothingness,* 2001, 65.

33 Ibid., lxv.

34 Ibid.

35 Ibid., 65.

36 Ibid., 416.

37 Kojève, *Introduction to the Reading of Hegel,* 48.

38 Sartre, "Existentialism and Humanism," 602.

39 Jacques Hardré, "Sartre's Existentialism and Humanism," *Studies in Philology* 49, no. 3 (July 1952): 538.

40 Sartre, "Existentialism and Humanism," 602.

41 Ibid.

42 Derrida, *Of Grammatology,* 158.

43 Wittgenstein, *Culture and Value,* 4.

44 Ibid., 5.

45 Ibid., 10.

46 Ibid., 56.

47 Ibid., 58.

48 Wittgenstein, "A Lecture on Ethics," 6–7.

49 It is important to point out that the German words *zweckmäßig* and *Zweckmäßigkeit* were translated into English by James Creed Meredith as "final" and "finality." In subsequent editions of his translation this rendering was replaced throughout with "purposive" and "purposiveness." (See "Note on the Text, Translation, and Revision" in the 2007 printing of Oxford World's Classics edition of *The Critique of Judgment,* xxv). This alternate rendering is also used by Paul Guyer and Eric Matthews in the Cambridge Edition of *The Critique of the Power of Judgment.* In the editor's introduction to that text it is noted that the preference for "purposiveness" as opposed to "finality" is to avoid the connotation of "conclusiveness" that the ordinary English use of the latter word can sometimes imply (xlviii). This is a connotation that we would do well not to forget entirely, however. The "finality of form" which the

object of a judgment of taste exhibits is a function of the disinterested and autonomous subject, whose subjective rationality is itself the "form of finality" in the conclusive sense.

50 Wittgenstein, *Notebooks*, 82.

51 Ibid.

52 Alain Badiou, *Wittgenstein's Antiphilosophy*, trans. Bruno Bosteels (New York: Verso, 2011), 110.

53 Ibid., 107.

54 Ibid.

55 Ibid., 80.

56 Ibid.

57 Ibid.

58 Ibid., 112.

59 Ibid., 113.

60 Ibid.

61 Wittgenstein, *Tractatus Logico-Philosophicus*, 2001, 4.063.

62 Badiou, *Wittgenstein's Antiphilosophy*, 114.

63 Ibid., 113.

64 Ibid., 114–15.

65 Alain Badiou, *Being and Event*, trans. Oliver Feltham (New York: Continuum, 2007), 16.

66 Ibid.

67 Ibid., 327.

68 Alain Badiou, *Infinite Thought: Truth and the Return to Philosophy*, ed. Justin Clemens and Oliver Feltham (New York: Continuum, 2005), 45.

69 Ibid.

70 Ibid., 47.

71 Ibid., 46.

72 Gabriel Riera, "The Ethics of Truth: Ethical Criticism in the Wake of Badiou's Philosophy," *Substance: A Review of Theory & Literary Criticism* 38, no. 3 (2009): 92.

73 Badiou, *Infinite Thought*, 46.

74 Ibid., 47.

75 Ibid., 46–47.

76 Riera, "The Ethics of Truth," 103.

77 J. D. Dewsbury, "Unthinking Subjects: Alain Badiou and the Event of Thought in Thinking Politics," *Transactions of the Institute of British Geographers* 32, no. 4 (October 2007): 453–54.

78 Nietzsche, "The Genealogy of Morals: An Attack," sec. 1.

79 Kant, *Critique of Pure Reason*, 1855, 97.

80 Kant, *Critique of the Power of Judgment*, 5: 236.

81 Kant, *Critique of Pure Reason*, 1855, 30.

82 G. W. F. Hegel, *Phenomenology of Spirit* (Delhi: Motilal Banarsidass Publishing, 1998), 413.

83 Ibid., 120.

84 G. W. F. Hegel, *Philosophy of History* (New York: American Home Library Company, 1902), 51.

85 Ibid., 52.

86 Ibid.

87 Ibid

88 Ibid..

89 Ibid., 133.

90 Hegel, *Phenomenology of Spirit*, 9.

91 Ibid., 99.

92 Ibid., 10.

93 Jean-Luc Nancy, *Hegel: The Restlessness of the Negative* (Minneapolis, MN: University of Minnesota Press, 2002), 10.

94 Jean-Luc Nancy, *The Birth to Presence* (Stanford, CA: Stanford University Press, 1993), 79.

95 Ibid.

96 Nancy, *Hegel*, 67.

97 Ibid., 38.

98 Ibid., 23.

99 Ibid.

100 Lyotard, *The Differend*, 142.

101 Nietzsche, *Human, All Too Human*, sec. 121.

102 Ibid.

103 Ibid., sec. 123.

104 Friedrich Nietzsche, "'Reason' in Philosophy," in *Twilight of the Idols, or, How to Philosophize with a Hammer* (Mineola, NY: Dover Publications, 2019), sec. 1.

105 Nietzsche, *Beyond Good and Evil*, sec. 2.

106 Ibid.

107 Friedrich Nietzsche, "Preface to The Anti-Christ," in *The Anti-Christ, Ecce Homo, Twilight of the Idols, and Other Writings*, ed. Aaron Ridley and Judith Norman, trans. Judith Norman (Cambridge: Cambridge University Press, 2005), 3.

108 Friedrich Nietzsche, "Thus Spoke Zarathustra," in *The Portable Nietzsche*, ed. and trans. Walter Kaufmann (New York: Viking Press, 1968), 153.

109 Ibid., 264.

110 Friedrich Nietzsche, *The Gay Science: With a Prelude in German Rhymes and an Appendix of Songs*, ed. Bernard Williams, trans. Josefine Nauckhoff (Cambridge: Cambridge University Press, 2001), sec. 270.

# Bibliography

Alexander, Hartley Burr. *The Problem of Metaphysics and the Meaning of Metaphysical Explanation: An Essay in Definitions.* New York: AMS Press, 1967.

Allison, Henry E. *Kant's Theory of Taste: A Reading of the Critique of Aesthetic Judgment.* Modern European Philosophy. Cambridge: Cambridge University Press, 2001.

Althusser, Louis. *On Ideology.* New York: Verso, 2008.

Andersen, Hanne. "Kuhn's Account of Family Resemblance: A Solution to the Problem of Wide-Open Texture." *Erkenntnis* 52, no. 3 (2000): 313–37.

Aristotle. *The Politics of Aristotle.* Translated by J. E. C. Welldon. London: Macmillan and Co., 1883.

Ayer, A. J. "Demonstration of the Impossibility of Metaphysics." *Mind* 43, no. 171 (July 1934): 335–45.

Ayer, A. J. *Language, Truth, and Logic.* New York: Dover Publications, 1952.

Badiou, Alain. *Being and Event.* Translated by Oliver Feltham. New York: Continuum, 2007.

Badiou, Alain. *Infinite Thought: Truth and the Return to Philosophy.* Edited by Justin Clemens and Oliver Feltham. New York: Continuum, 2005.

Badiou, Alain. *Wittgenstein's Antiphilosophy.* Translated by Bruno Bosteels. New York: Verso, 2011.

Baker, Gordon. "Wittgenstein on Metaphysical/Everyday Use." *The Philosophical Quarterly* 52, no. 208 (July 2002): 289–302.

Baker, Gordon, and P. M. S. Hacker. "On Misunderstanding Wittgenstein: Kripke's Private Language Argument." *Synthese* 58, no. 3 (March 1984): 407–50.

Baker, Gordon P., and P. M. S. Hacker. *Wittgenstein – Rules, Grammar, and Necessity: Essays and Exegesis of 185–242.* 2nd ed. Chichester, UK: Wiley-Blackwell, 2009.

Baker, Peter, Xiang Chen, and Hanne Anderson. "Kuhn on Concepts and Categorization." In *Thomas Kuhn*, edited by Thomas Nickles. Cambridge: Cambridge University Press, 2003.

Barthes, Roland. *S/Z.* New York: Hill & Wang, 1974.

Bloor, David. *Wittgenstein: A Social Theory of Knowledge.* London: Macmillan, 1983.

Boethius, Ancius. *The Consolation of Philosophy.* Translated by Victor Watts. London: Penguin Classics, 1999.

Bronzo, Silver. "The Resolute Reading and Its Critics: An Introduction to the Literature." *Wittgenstein-Studien* 3, no. 1 (March 2012): 45–80.

Butler, Joseph. *Five Sermons, Preached at the Rolls Chapel and A Dissertation Upon the Nature of Virtue.* Edited by Stephen L. Darwall. Indianapolis, IN: Hackett Publishing, 1983.

Byrne, Alex. "On Misinterpreting Kripke's Wittgenstein." *Philosophy and Phenomenological Research* 56, no. 2 (June 1996): 339–43.

Carlyle, Thomas. *Sartor Resartus: The Life and Opinions of Herr Teufelsdröckh*. London: Chapman & Hall, 1831.

Carnap, Rudolf. "The Elimination of Metaphysics Through Logical Analysis of Language." In *Logical Positivism*, edited by A. J. Ayer. New York: Free Press, 1959.

Carnap, Rudolf. *The Philosophy of Rudolf Carnap*. Edited by Paul Arthur Schilpp. La Salle, IL: Open Court, 1997.

Carruthers, Peter. *The Metaphysics of the Tractatus*. Cambridge: Cambridge University Press, 2009.

Cavell, Stanley. "Excursus on Wittgenstein's Vision of Language." In *The New Wittgenstein*, edited by Alice Crary and Rupert Read. London: Routledge, 2000.

Chisholm, Roderick M. *The Problem of the Criterion*. Milwaukee, WI: Marquette University Press, 1973.

Conant, James. "The Method of the Tractatus." In *From Frege to Wittgenstein: Perspectives on Early Analytic Philosophy*, edited by Erich H. Reck. Oxford: Oxford University Press, 2001.

Conant, James, and Ed Dain. "Throwing the Baby Out: A Reply to Roger White." In *Beyond The Tractatus Wars: The New Wittgenstein Debate*, edited by Rupert Read and Matthew A. Lavery. New York: Routledge, 2011.

Cook, John. *Wittgenstein's Metaphysics*. Cambridge: Cambridge University Press, 1994.

Cook, John W. "Wittgenstein on Privacy." *The Philosophical Review* 74, no. 3 (July 1965): 281–314.

Cornell Way, Eileen. *Knowledge, Representation and Metaphor*. Oxford: Intellect, 1994.

Crary, Alice. "Wittgenstein and Political Thought." In *The New Wittgenstein*, edited by Alice Crary and Rupert Read. London: Routledge, 2000.

Crary, Alice, and Rupert Read, eds. *The New Wittgenstein*. London: Routledge, 2000.

De Vriese, Herbert. "The Myth of the Metaphysical Circle: An Analysis of the Contemporary Crisis of the Critique of Metaphysics." *Inquiry* 51, no. 3 (June 2008): 312–41. https://doi.org/10.1080/00201740802120772.

Derrida, Jacques. *Of Grammatology*. Baltimore, MD: Johns Hopkins University Press, 1997.

Descartes, René. *Meditations on First Philosophy: With Selections from the Objections and Replies*. Translated by John Cottingham. Cambridge: Cambridge University Press, 1996.

Dewey, John. *The Quest for Certainty: A Study of the Relation of Knowledge and Action*. New York: Putnam, 1960.

Dewsbury, J. D. "Unthinking Subjects: Alain Badiou and the Event of Thought in Thinking Politics." *Transactions of the Institute of British Geographers* 32, no. 4 (October 2007): 443–59.

Diamond, Cora. *The Realistic Spirit: Wittgenstein, Philosophy, and the Mind*. Cambridge, MA: MIT Press, 1991.

Diamond, Cora. "Throwing Away the Ladder: How to Read the Tractatus." In *The Realistic Spirit: Wittgenstein, Philosophy, and the Mind*. Cambridge, MA: MIT Press, 1991.

Emmet, Dorothy. "'That's That'; Or Some Uses of Tautology." *Philosophy* 37, no. 139 (January 1962): 15–24.

Engels, Friedrich. "Preface to the 1888 English Edition." In *The Communist Manifesto*. London: Pluto, 2008.

Feibleman, J. K. "The Metaphysics of Logical Positivism." *The Review of Metaphysics* 5, no. 1 (September 1951): 55–82.

Findlay, J. N. "Hegel's Use of Teleology." *The Monist* 48, no. 1 (January 1964): 1–17.

Fine, Arthur. "Fictionalism." *Midwest Studies in Philosophy* 18, no. 1 (1993): 1–18.

Fine, Arthur. "Science Fictions: Comment on Godfrey-Smith." *Philosophical Studies: An International Journal for Philosophy in the Analytic Tradition* 143, no. 1 (March 2009): 117–25.

Finkelstein, David H. "Wittgenstein on Rules and Platonism." In *The New Wittgenstein*, edited by Alice Crary and Rupert Read. London: Routledge, 2000.

Forster, Michael N. *Wittgenstein on the Arbitrariness of Grammar*. Princeton, NJ: Princeton University Press, 2004.

Foucault, Michel. *Madness and Civilization: A History of Insanity in the Age of Reason*. New York: Vintage Books, 1988.

Freud, Sigmund. *Civilization and Its Discontents*. Translated by James Strachey. New York: W. W. Norton & Company, 1962.

Garver, Newton. *This Complicated Form of Life: Essays on Wittgenstein*. Chicago: Open Court, 1994.

Gill, Jerry H. "Saying and Showing: Radical Themes in Wittgenstein's 'On Certainty.'" *Religious Studies* 10, no. 03 (September 1974): 279–90.

Glock, Hans-Johann. *A Wittgenstein Dictionary*. Oxford: Blackwell, 1996.

Goldfarb, Warren. "Das Überwinden: Anti-Metaphysical Readings of the Tractatus." In *Beyond The Tractatus Wars: The New Wittgenstein Debate*, edited by Rupert Read and Matthew A. Lavery. New York: Routledge, 2011.

Goldfarb, Warren. "Kripke on Wittgenstein on Rules." *The Journal of Philosophy* 82, no. 9 (September 1985): 471–88.

Gunnell, John G. *Social Inquiry After Wittgenstein and Kuhn: Leaving Everything as It Is*. New York: Columbia University Press, 2014.

Hacker, P. M. S. "Was He Trying to Whistle It?" In *The New Wittgenstein*, edited by Alice Crary and Rupert Read. London: Routledge, 2000.

Hacker, P. M. S., and Joachim Schulte, eds. "The Text of the Philosopische Untersuchungen." In *Philosophical Investigations*, 4th ed. Oxford: Wiley-Blackwell, 2009.

Haeckel, Ernst. *The Riddle of the Universe*. Translated by Joseph McCabb. London: Watts & Co., 1934.

Hardré, Jacques. "Sartre's Existentialism and Humanism." *Studies in Philology* 49, no. 3 (July 1952): 534–47.

Hartland-Swann, John. "Plato as Poet: A Critical Interpretation." *Philosophy* 26, no. 96 (January 1951): 3–18.

Hegel, G. W. F. *Hegel's Phenomenology of Spirit*. Translated by A. V. Miller. Oxford: Oxford University Press, 1977.

Hegel, G. W. F. *Phenomenology of Spirit*. Delhi: Motilal Banarsidass Publishing, 1998.

Hegel, G. W. F. *Philosophy of History*. New York: American Home Library Company, 1902.

Hegel, G. W. F. *The Encyclopaedia Logic: Part I of the Encyclopaedia of Philosophical Sciences with the Zusätze*. Translated by T. F. Geraets, W. A. Suchting, and H. S. Harris. Indianapolis, IN: Hackett Publishing, 1991.

Heidegger, Martin. *Kant and the Problem of Metaphysics*. Translated by James S. Churchill. Bloomington, IN: Indiana University Press, 1965.

Heidegger, Martin. *Nietzsche*. Translated by David Farrrell Krell. Vol. 1 and 2. San Francisco, CA: HarperCollins, 1991.

Hobbes, Thomas. *Leviathan*. Cambridge: Cambridge University Press, 1904.

Hodges, Michael. *Transcendence and Wittgenstein's Tractatus*. Philadelphia, PA: Temple University Press, 1990.

Hoffman, Paul. "Kripke on Private Language." *Philosophical Studies: An International Journal for Philosophy in the Analytic Tradition* 47, no. 1 (January 1985): 23–28.

Inwagen, Peter van. *Material Beings*. Ithaca, NY: Cornell University Press, 1990.

James, William. *A Pluralistic Universe: Hibbert Lectures at Manchester College on the Present Situation in Philosophy*. Lincoln, NE: University of Nebraska Press, 1996.

James, William. "A World of Pure Experience." In *Essays in Radical Empiricism*. Radford, VA: Wilder Publishing, 2008.

James, William. "Does 'Consciousness' Exist?" *The Journal of Philosophy, Psychology and Scientific Methods* 1, no. 18 (September 1904): 477–91.

James, William. *The Will to Believe and Other Essays in Popular Philosophy*. New York: Longmans, Green, and Co., 1896.

Jaspers, Karl. *Kant*. Edited by Hannah Arendt. Translated by Ralph Manheim. New York: Harcourt Brace & Company, 1962.

Kalderon, Mark Eli, ed. *Fictionalism in Metaphysics*. Oxford: Oxford University Press, 2005.

Kant, Immanuel. *Critique of Pure Reason*. London: Henry G. Bohn, 1855.

Kant, Immanuel. *Critique of Pure Reason*. Translated by Paul Guyer and Allen W. Wood. Cambridge: Cambridge University Press, 1998.

Kant, Immanuel. *Critique of the Power of Judgment*. Edited by Paul Guyer. Translated by Paul Guyer and Eric Matthews. Cambridge: Cambridge University Press, 2000.

Kant, Immanuel. *Groundwork of the Metaphysics of Morals*. Cambridge: Cambridge University Press, 1998.

Kant, Immanuel. *Prolegomena to Any Future Metaphysics That Will Be Able to Come Forward as Science*. 2nd ed. Indianapolis, IN: Hackett Publishing Company, 2001.

Klee, Paul. "On Modern Art." In *Art in Theory, 1900–2000: An Anthology of Changing Ideas*, edited by Paul Wood and Charles Harrison. Malden, MA: Blackwell, 2003.

Klemke, E. D. *A Defense of Realism: Reflections on the Metaphysics of G. E. Moore.* Amherst NY: Humanity Books, 2000.

Kojève, Alexandre. *Introduction to the Reading of Hegel: Lectures on the Phenomenology of Spirit.* Edited by Allan Bloom. Translated by James H. Nichols, Jr. New York: Basic Books, 1969.

Kripke, Saul. *Wittgenstein on Rules and Private Language: An Elementary Exposition.* Cambridge, MA: Harvard University Press, 1984.

Kuhn, Thomas S. *The Structure of Scientific Revolutions.* Chicago: University of Chicago Press, 1996.

Last, Nana. *Wittgenstein's House: Language, Space, and Architecture.* New York: Fordham University Press, 2008.

Leonard, George. *Into the Light of Things: Art of the Commonplace from Wordsworth to John Cage.* Chicago: University of Chicago Press, 1995.

Levinas, Emmanuel. *Entre Nous: On Thinking-of-the-Other.* Translated by Michael B. Smith and Barbara Harshav. New York: Columbia University Press, 1998.

Lucretius. *On the Nature of Things.* Translated by Martin Ferguson Smith. Indianapolis, IN: Hackett Publishing, 2001.

Lyotard, Jean-François. *The Differend: Phrases in Dispute.* Minneapolis, MN: University of Minnesota Press, 1988.

Mackie, Penelope. "Ordinary Language and Metaphysical Commitment." *Analysis* 53, no. 4 (October 1993): 243–51.

McDowell, John. "Wittgenstein on Following a Rule." *Synthese* 58, no. 3 (1984): 325–63.

McGinn, Marie. "Between Metaphysics and Nonsense: Elucidation in Wittgenstein's Tractatus." *The Philosophical Quarterly* 49, no. 197 (October 1999): 491–513.

McGinn, Marie. *Elucidating the Tractatus: Wittgenstein's Early Philosophy of Logic and Language.* Oxford: Oxford University Press, 2006.

McGuinness, Brian. *Wittgenstein: A Life: Young Ludwig 1889–1921.* Berkeley, CA: University of California Press, 1988.

McGuinness, Brian, and Georg Henrik von Wright, eds. *Ludwig Wittgenstein, Cambridge Letters: Correspondence with Russell, Keynes, Moore, Ramsey, and Sraffa.* Oxford: Blackwell, 1997.

Merleau-Ponty, Maurice. "Eye and Mind." In *The Primacy of Perception: And Other Essays on Phenomenological Psychology, the Philosophy of Art, History and Politics.* Evanston, IL: Northwestern University Press, 1964.

Mill, John Stuart. *Utilitarianism.* London: Parker, Son and Bourn, 1863.

Monk, Ray. *Ludwig Wittgenstein: The Duty of Genius.* New York: Penguin Books, 1991.

Moore, G. E. "A Defense of Common Sense." In *Selected Writings*, edited by Thomas Baldwin. New York: Routledge, 1993.

Moore, G. E. *Principia Ethica.* Mineola, NY: Dover Publications, 2004.

Moore, G. E. "Proof of an External World." In *Selected Writings*, edited by Thomas Baldwin. New York: Routledge, 1993.

Moore, G. E. *Some Main Problems of Philosophy.* New York: Collier, 1966.

Nagel, Thomas. *The View From Nowhere*. New York: Oxford University Press, 1989.

Nancy, Jean-Luc. *Hegel: The Restlessness of The Negative*. Minneapolis, MN: University of Minnesota Press, 2002.

Nancy, Jean-Luc. *The Birth to Presence*. Stanford, CA: Stanford University Press, 1993.

Nelson, John O. "How Is Non-Metaphysics Possible?" *International Phenomenological Society* 30, no. 2 (December 1969): 219–37.

Newman, Barnett. "The First Man Was an Artist." In *Barnett Newman: Selected Writings and Interviews*. Berkeley, CA: University of California Press, 1992.

Nietzsche, Friedrich. *Beyond Good and Evil*. Lexington, KY: SoHo Books, 2010.

Nietzsche, Friedrich. *Human, All Too Human: A Book for Free Spirits*. Lincoln, NE: University of Nebraska Press, 1996.

Nietzsche, Friedrich. "Preface to The Anti-Christ." In *The Anti-Christ, Ecce Homo, Twilight of the Idols, and Other Writings*, edited by Aaron Ridley and Judith Norman, translated by Judith Norman. Cambridge: Cambridge University Press, 2005.

Nietzsche, Friedrich. "'Reason' in Philosophy." In *Twilight of the Idols, or, How to Philosophize with a Hammer*. Mineola, NY: Dover Publications, 2019.

Nietzsche, Friedrich. "The Birth of Tragedy from the Spirit of Music." In *The Birth of Tragedy & The Genealogy of Morals*. New York: Anchor Books, 1990.

Nietzsche, Friedrich. *The Gay Science: With a Prelude in German Rhymes and an Appendix of Songs*. Edited by Bernard Williams. Translated by Josefine Nauckhoff. Cambridge: Cambridge University Press, 2001.

Nietzsche, Friedrich. "The Genealogy of Morals: An Attack." In *The Birth of Tragedy & The Genealogy of Morals*. New York: Anchor Books, 1990.

Nietzsche, Friedrich. *The Will to Power*. Vintage Books Edition. New York: Random House, 1968.

Nietzsche, Friedrich. *The Will to Power (Volumes I and II)*. Translated by Anthony Ludovici. Lawrence, KS: Digireads, 2010.

Nietzsche, Friedrich. "Thus Spoke Zarathustra." In *The Portable Nietzsche*, edited and translated by Walter Kaufmann. New York: Viking Press, 1968.

Nietzsche, Friedrich. *Thus Spoke Zarathustra*. Cambridge: Cambridge University Press, 2006.

Nietzsche, Friedrich. "Twilight of the Idols." In *Twilight of the Idols; and, The Anti-Christ*. London: Penguin, 1990.

Novitz, David. "Rules, Creativity and Pictures: Wittgenstein's Lectures on Aesthetics." In *Wittgenstein, Aesthetics, and Philosophy*, edited by Peter Lewis. Burlington, VT: Ashgate Publishing, 2004.

Parmenides. "On Nature." In *Paramenides of Elea: A Verse Translation with Interpretative Essays and Commentary to the Text*, translated by Martin J. Henn. Westport, CT: Praeger, 2003.

Perloff, Marjorie. "From Theory to Grammar: Wittgenstein and the Aesthetic of the Ordinary." *New Literary History* 25, no. 4 (Autumn 1994): 899–923.

Pippin, Robert. *Nietzsche, Psychology, and First Philosophy*. Chicago: University of Chicago Press, 2010.

Plato. *The Republic of Plato*. Translated by Allan Bloom. New York: Basic Books, 1991.

Pollard, Stephen. "'As If' Reasoning in Vaihinger and Pasch." *Erkenntnis* 73, no. 1 (July 2010): 83–95.

Puchner, Martin. "Doing Logic with a Hammer: Wittgenstein's Tractatus and the Polemics of Logical Positivism." *Journal of the History of Ideas* 66, no. 2 (April 2005): 285–300.

Quine, W. V. "Main Trends in Recent Philosophy: Two Dogmas of Empiricism." *The Philosophical Review* 60, no. 1 (1951): 20–43.

Rancière, Jacques. *Disagreement: Politics and Philosophy*. Translated by Julie Rose. Minneapolis, MN: University of Minnesota Press, 2004.

Read, Rupert, and Matthew A. Lavery, eds. *Beyond The Tractatus Wars: The New Wittgenstein Debate*. New York: Routledge, 2011.

Reichenbach, Hans. "The Philosophical Significance of the Theory of Relativity." In *Albert Einstein: Philosopher-Scientist*, edited by Paul Arthur Schilpp, 4th printing. New York: Tudor Publishing Company, 1957.

Rhees, Rush. *Wittgenstein's "On Certainty": There – Like Our Life*. Oxford: Blackwell, 2006.

Riera, Gabriel. "The Ethics of Truth: Ethical Criticism in the Wake of Badiou's Philosophy." *Substance: A Review of Theory & Literary Criticism* 38, no. 3 (2009): 92–112.

Rorty, Richard. *The Linguistic Turn: Essays in Philosophical Method*. Chicago: University of Chicago Press, 1992.

Rousseau, Jean-Jacques. *Discourse on the Origin of Inequality*. New York: Classic Books America, 2009.

Rousseau, Jean-Jacques. *The Social Contract*. Translated by Maurice Cranston. London: Penguin, 2003.

Russell, Bertrand. *A History of Western Philosophy*. New York: Simon & Schuster, 1972.

Russell, Bertrand. *Introduction to Mathematical Philosophy*. 2nd ed. London: G. Allen & Unwin, 1920.

Sainsbury, R. M. *Fiction and Fictionalism*. London: Routledge, 2010.

Sartre, Jean-Paul. *Being and Nothingness*. Translated by Hazel Barnes. New York: Washington Square Press, 1992.

Sartre, Jean-Paul. *Being and Nothingness: A Phenomenological Essay on Ontology*. New York: Citadel Press, 2001.

Sartre, Jean-Paul. "Existentialism and Humanism." In *Art in Theory, 1900–2000: An Anthology of Changing Ideas*, edited by Paul Wood and Charles Harrison. Malden, MA: Blackwell, 2003.

Sartre, Jean-Paul. *Existentialism Is a Humanism*. New Haven, CT: Yale University Press, 2007.

Sartre, Jean-Paul. "The Transcendence of the Ego." In *The Phenomenology Reader*, edited by Dermot Moran and Timothy Mooney. New York: Routledge, 2002.

Steinberger, Peter J. "Hobbes, Rousseau and the Modern Conception of the State." *The Journal of Politics* 70, no. 3 (July 2008): 595–611.

Stengel, Kathrin. "Ethics as Style: Wittgenstein's Aesthetic Ethics and Ethical Aesthetics." *Poetics Today* 25, no. 4 (Winter 2004).

Stroll, Avrum. *Moore and Wittgenstein on Certainty*. New York: Oxford University Press, 1994.

Summerfield, Donna M. "Philosophical Investigations 201: A Wittgensteinian Reply to Kripke." *Journal of the History of Philosophy* 28, no. 3 (July 1990): 417–38.

Tilghman, Benjamin. *Wittgenstein, Ethics, and Aesthetics: The View from Eternity*. Albany, NY: State University of New York Press, 1991.

Vaihinger, Hans. *The Philosophy of 'As If': A System of the Theoretical, Practical and Religious Fictions of Mankind*. Translated by C. K. Ogden. Mansfield Center, CT: Martino Publishing, 2009.

Waismann, Friedrich. *Ludwig Wittgenstein and the Vienna Circle: Conversations Recorded by Friedrich Waisman*. Edited by B. F. McGuinness. Malden, MA: Blackwell, 1979.

Weinberg, Julius R. "Are There Ultimate Simples?" *Philosophy of Science* 2, no. 4 (October 1935): 387–99.

Wenzl, Aloys. "Einstein's Theory of Relativity, Viewed from the Standpoint of Critical Realism, and Its Significance for Philosophy." In *Albert Einstein: Philosopher-Scientist*, edited by Paul Arthur Schilpp, 4th printing. New York: Tudor Publishing Company, 1957.

Werhane, Patricia H. "Some Paradoxes in Kripke's Interpretation of Wittgenstein." *Synthese* 73, no. 2 (November 1987): 253–73.

Weston, Jessie L. *From Ritual to Romance*. Mineola, NY: Dover Publications, Inc., 1997.

Whitehead, Alfred North. *Process and Reality*. 2nd edition. New York: Free Press, 1979.

Williams, Linda L. *Nietzsche's Mirror: The World as Will to Power*. Lanham, MD: Rowman & Littlefield, 2001.

Wilson, George. "Semantic Realism and Kripke's Wittgenstein." *Philosophy and Phenomenological Research* 58, no. 1 (March 1998): 99–122.

Wittgenstein, Ludwig. "A Lecture on Ethics." *The Philosophical Review* 74, no. 1 (January 1965): 3–12.

Wittgenstein, Ludwig. *Culture and Value*. Chicago: University of Chicago Press, 1984.

Wittgenstein, Ludwig. *Lectures and Conversations on Aesthetics, Psychology, and Religious Belief*. Edited by Cyril Barrett. Berkeley, CA: University of California Press, 2007.

Wittgenstein, Ludwig. *Notebooks 1914–1916*. Chicago: University of Chicago Press, 1984.

Wittgenstein, Ludwig. *On Certainty*. Oxford: Blackwell, 1977.

Wittgenstein, Ludwig. *Philosophical Grammar*. Berkeley, CA: University of California Press, 2005.

Wittgenstein, Ludwig. *Philosophical Investigations*. 4th ed. Oxford: Wiley-Blackwell, 2009.

Wittgenstein, Ludwig. *Philosophical Occasions, 1912–1951*. Edited by James Klagge and Alfred Nordmann. Indianapolis, IN: Hackett Publishing, 1993.

Wittgenstein, Ludwig. *Philosophical Remarks*. Chicago: University of Chicago Press, 1980.

Wittgenstein, Ludwig. *Preliminary Studies for the "Philosophical Investigations":*
*Generally Known As the Blue and Brown Books*. New York: Harper Torchbooks, 1960.

Wittgenstein, Ludwig. *Remarks on the Foundations of Mathematics*. Edited by G. H. von
Wright, R. Rhees, and G. E. M. Anscombe. Cambridge, MA: The MIT Press, 1983.

Wittgenstein, Ludwig. *Tractatus Logico-Philosophicus*. Translated by D. F. Pears and
B. F. McGuinness. London: Routledge, 2001.

Wittgenstein, Ludwig. *Tractatus Logico-Philosophicus*. Translated by C. K. Ogden. New
York: Barnes & Noble, 2004.

Wittgenstein, Ludwig. *Zettel*. Berkeley, CA: University of California Press, 2007.

Wright, Crispin. "Kripke's Account of the Argument Against Private Language." *The*
*Journal of Philosophy* 81, no. 12 (December 1984): 759–78.

Young, Julian. *Friedrich Nietzsche: A Philosophical Biography*. Cambridge: Cambridge
University Press, 2010.

Žižek, Slavoj. *Less Than Nothing: Hegel and the Shadow of Dialectical Materialism*.
London: Verso, 2013.

# Index

*A Defense of Realism* 146
*a priori* 23, 26, 58, 60, 65, 78, 90, 108, 127,
    143, 159, 179–80, 184, 187–8, 197–8,
    200, 204
A World of Pure Experience 75, 82
Abrams, M. H. 87
aesthetics
    of choice 24
    importance of 12
    larger system of 12
    meaning of 22
    problems 2
Alexander, Hartley Burr 22
Allison, Henry 94
analytic
    interpretations 150
    propositions 66
    psycho 16
    tradition 30, 39
Andersen, Hanne 134, 146
Arendt, Hannah 207
Aristotle 21, 100, 105, 117
Art, meaning of 190
Ayer, A. J. 9, 44, 51, 80, 120, 144

Badiou, Alain 14, 192–6, 209
Baker, Gordon 85–6, 91–3, 107–8, 113–15,
    118, 133, 146
Baker, Peter 146
*Being and Nothingness* 115, 184–5, 208
*Beyond Good and Evil* 15, 44, 47, 105, 118,
    147, 210
*Birth to Presence, The* 210
*Blue and Brown Books, The* 116, 160
Boethius 2, 15
Bronzo, Silver 16
Butler, Joseph 81

Cage, John 114
Carlyle, Thomas 87
Carnap, Rudolf 28, 44, 57, 81
Carruthers, Peter 71, 82, 150

Cartesian 8, 21, 40, 72, 140, 178, 186
Cavell, Stanley 98, 116, 133
Chen, Xiang 146
Chisholm, Roderick M. 172
Churchill, James S. 43
Conant, James 4, 16
*Consolation of Philosophy* 15
Continental tradition 9
Cook, John W. 72–3, 75, 82, 117
Cornell, Eileen 134, 146
Crary, Alice 4, 16, 97, 116
*Critique of Pure Reason* 118, 124, 159, 173,
    207, 209–10
*Critique of the Power of Judgment* 43–4,
    115, 173, 207–9

Dain, Ed 16
Das Überwinden: Anti-Metaphysical
    Readings of the Tractatus 16
Descartes, René 27, 44, 74, 125, 129,
    145, 185
Dewey, John 143, 147
Dewsbury, J. D. 196, 209
Diamond, Cora 5, 16
*Die Philosophie des Als Ob* 34
*Differend, The* 168–70, 175, 202–6, 210
dogmatism 24, 31, 48, 54, 95, 200, 203,
    206
doubt 3, 11, 27, 58, 67, 92, 98, 122, 127,
    133, 136, 141–2, 149, 151, 154, 161,
    170, 201

Egyptianism 203–4
elementary propositions 71, 75, 79
Emmet, Dorothy 67, 81
empiricism 24, 29, 31, 33, 48, 54, 65, 72–3,
    75, 82, 86, 101, 120–1, 125, 134, 138,
    140, 158, 179, 196
Engels, Friedrich 47
epistemology 9, 21–2, 50, 86, 90, 105, 127,
    132, 139, 141–3, 149, 159, 164
ethico-aesthetic 37, 178, 196, 201–3

ethics 9, 11, 58, 74, 151, 153, 155–6, 158, 160, 162, 169, 173, 202, 208–9
ethics as style 173
*Existentialism and Humanism* 184, 207–8
Eye and Mind 15–16

Family resemblance 92, 97–9, 102, 105, 134, 146, 162
Feibleman, J. K. 29, 31, 40, 44–5
Findlay, J. N. 33, 45
Fine, Arthur 45–6
First Man Was an Artist, The 15
fly-bottle 10, 109
form of life 8, 37, 92, 99–102, 105, 109, 112, 117, 140–4, 166, 173
Forster, Michael 107, 118
Frege, Gottlob 9, 27, 71, 77
Freud, Sigmund 47

Garver, Newton 100–2, 117, 159, 173
*Genealogy of Morals, The* 15, 104, 118, 197, 209
Gill, Jerry H. 141–2, 147
Glock, Hans-Johann 116
Goldfarb, Warren 5, 16, 114
grammar 43–4, 103, 105–11, 113, 116–18, 127, 130, 163
Gunnell, John 133

Hacker, P.M.S. 6, 16–17, 48, 91–3, 107–8, 114–15, 118
Hardré, Jacques 187, 208
Hartland-Swann, John 6, 17
Hegel, Georg Wilhelm Friedrich 32–5, 45–7, 186, 198–202, 208, 210
*Hegel: The Restlessness of The Negative* 210
Hegelian dialectic 32–3
Heidegger, Martin 17
Hobbes, Thomas 46
Hodges, Michael 69, 81, 155
Hoffman, Paul 114
Human, All Too Human 147, 202–3, 210
Hume, David 3

idealism 72, 87, 98–9, 132
*Into the Light of Things* 86, 114
*Introduction to Mathematical Philosophy* 62, 81

James, William 24, 31, 44, 72, 75, 82, 169
Jaspers, Karl 181, 207
judgment
    aesthetic 94–5
    empirical 140
    Kantian 12
    unjustifiable 95
judgments of taste 21, 23, 88, 94–6, 127, 158–9, 177, 180–3

Kant, Immanuel 12, 22, 43, 105, 108, 118, 157, 159, 162, 177–8, 180, 184, 191, 197, 201–2, 207, 209–10
Klee, Paul 41, 48
Klemke, E. D. 132, 146
*Knowledge, Representation and Metaphor* 146
Kripke, Saul 89, 91–3, 114–15
Kuhn, Thomas S. 133–9, 146–7

language-games 8, 39, 93, 97, 99, 101, 103, 108, 110, 117, 125, 127, 139–40, 164, 168
Lavery, Matthew A. 16
laws of
    experience 181
    logic 181
    nature 181
    thought 41
Lebensform 100, 117
Leonard, George 86, 114
Lewis, Peter 174
limit of
    cognition 182
    language 190
logic 8, 30, 45, 49, 60–1, 64, 70, 74, 90, 96, 132, 137, 151, 157, 159, 161, 163, 170, 181–2, 191–3
Logical Positivists 3, 27–30, 44–5, 65
Lucretius 7, 32, 45

McDowell, John 89, 114
McGinn, Marie 4, 16, 19, 43
*Madness and Civilization: A History of Insanity in the Age of Reason* 15
*Material Beings* 85, 113
mathematics 9, 62, 81, 171, 175
Merleau-Ponty 3, 15–16

# Index

metaphysical propositions 26, 51–2, 58, 70, 179

*Metaphysics of Tractatus, The* 71, 73, 82, 172

monism 25, 72–3, 75

Monk, Ray 11, 17, 44, 66

Moore, G. E. 64–7, 81, 123–32, 145–6, 160–1, 173–4

*Moore and Wittgenstein on Certainty* 129, 145

mysticism 3, 6, 37, 72–3, 138, 153–4, 171–2, 177, 179, 190, 192, 207

*Nachlass* 2, 41, 152

Nagel, Thomas 157, 173

Nancy, Jean-Luc 199, 210

Natural Supernaturalism 87, 114

negation 33, 125, 186, 200–1

Nelson, John O. 31, 45

neo-Hegelianism 131

neutral monism 72–3, 75

Newman, Barnett 2, 15

Nickles, Thomas 146

Nietzsche, Friedrich 3, 15, 21, 37, 47, 99, 104–5, 117, 122, 143, 147, 151, 196, 204, 206, 210

nominalism 29

normative 28, 94, 127, 138–9

Novitz, David 166–7, 174

Ogden, C. K. 46, 155, 173

*On Certainty* 8, 20, 115, 120, 124, 128, 133, 139, 141, 145, 161, 168, 172, 175, 180, 207

open texture 134, 146

ordinary language 39, 85–6, 103, 105, 110–11, 113, 130

Perloff, Marjorie 86, 113

*Phenomenology of Spirit* 45, 47, 186, 210

picture Ttheory 8, 11, 38–9, 50, 57, 61, 69–70, 72, 76, 96

Pippin, Robert 105, 118

Platonism 6–7, 17, 28–9, 43, 75, 97, 116, 150

pluralism 76

poetry 2, 6, 15, 17, 56, 65, 150, 152, 166, 173

*Principia Ethica* 64, 66, 81, 160–1, 173–4

Private Language Argument 89–93, 95, 102, 104, 114–15, 127

Problem of Criterion, The 22, 149, 172, 180

*Proof of an External World* 123–4, 127, 145

proofs 12, 31, 41, 55, 59, 65, 70, 77–8, 92, 108, 116, 122–3, 132–3, 171, 177

proposition
  *a priori*,58
  elementary 71, 75, 79
  epistemological 90
  of logic, 158
  logical 70, 77–8
  metaphysical 3, 26, 51, 179
  Moore's 130
  of natural science, 19, 49
  ontological, 71, 85
  philosophical, 19, 27
  pseudo, 52
  self-referential, 170
  of TLP, 19
  true, 124, 192

psychoanalysis, 49

psychology, 9, 15, 74, 82, 105, 117–18, 122, 134, 143, 165, 167–8, 174, 180, 191

radical empiricism 24, 72–3, 75, 82

Read, Rupert 16, 116

realism 70, 80, 114, 131–2, 146

Reichenbach, Hans 55, 80

relativity 54–5, 80

representational 3, 14, 48, 61–2, 69–70, 90–1, 106–8, 146, 158, 194, 197

Rhees, Rush 131

Riera, Gabriel 195, 209

Rorty, Richard 30, 45

Rousseau, Jean-Jacques 46

rule-following paradox 87–9, 91–3, 95, 102, 134

rules, 7, 23, 71, 87, 92, 94, 98, 107, 111, 114, 116, 125, 158, 166, 170, 174, 187, 195

Russell, Bertrand 9, 12, 17, 27–8, 57, 62–3, 72, 76–7, 81–2, 111, 160, 171

Sartre, Jean-Paul 13, 95, 115, 177, 184–8, 207–8

saying vs. showing 19, 42, 51, 61, 77, 83, 141, 147, 189, 213

Schlick, Moritz 65
Schopenhauer, Arthur 9, 118, 156
science 13, 19, 30, 46, 65, 75, 90, 105, 121,
 136, 138–9, 149, 165, 178, 191, 194,
 205, 207, 210
sense vs. nonsense 8, 121
senseless 38, 44, 91, 121, 152, 156
signs 49, 67–9, 78–9, 96–7, 101
silence 2, 41, 51, 53, 57, 59, 63, 65, 67, 73,
 75–7, 79, 81, 163
simples 2, 7, 58–9, 64–5, 67–8, 72, 76, 81,
 103, 111, 120–1, 161, 168, 185,
 198–9
skepticism 31, 54, 89, 91, 127, 129, 146,
 178, 181
solipsism 69–70, 129
*Some Main Problems of Philosophy* 131,
 146
Stengel, Kathrin 154–5, 173
Stroll, Avrum 129, 145
*Structure of Scientific Revolutions, The*
 133, 147
*sub specie aeternitatis* 153–4, 202
surveyability 106
syntax 29, 79, 107–8, 191
Søren Kierkegaard 9, 150

tautology 48, 62–3, 66–8, 78–81, 90, 120–1,
 127, 162–3, 199
therapeutic 4, 20
*Throwing Away the Ladder: How to Read
 the Tractatus* 16
Tilghman, B. R. 163, 174
Tolstoy, Leo 9, 118
transcendence 14, 36, 40, 50, 74, 81, 87,
 132, 156, 173, 181, 193, 196, 198,
 200, 202–3, 208
*Transcendence and Wittgenstein's Tractatus*
 69, 81–2, 173

truth
 axiomatic 177
 beauty 183
 conditions 25, 29
 eternal 38
 irrefutable 28
 metaphysical 25
 radiant 183
 truthfulness 32
 unalterable 38
 unassailable 28, 79

universal 12, 23, 27–8, 42, 94, 98, 103, 108,
 129, 181–5, 196, 199–200, 206

Vaihinger, Hans 34, 46
value 4, 10, 14, 17, 28, 42, 73, 123, 130,
 154, 156–7, 160, 162, 173, 204,
 206–8
visual field 63, 70, 154
von Gersdorff, Carl 123
Vriese, Herbert De 52, 80

Waismann, Friedrich 27, 44
Was He Trying to Whistle It? 16–17
Way, Cornell 134, 146
Weinberg, Julius 65, 81
Wells, H. G. 111
Wenzl, Aloys 80
Weston, Jessie 1
will to power, the 17, 103, 117, 144
Williams, Linda L. 118
*Wittgenstein's Metaphysics* 49, 56, 69, 71–2,
 82
*Wittgenstein: A Social Theory of Knowledge*
 146
world-riddle 36–7, 47, 149, 151–75

Žižek, Slavoj 34

Printed in the USA
CPSIA information can be obtained
at www.ICGtesting.com
LVHW011648091223
766046LV00004B/141